P9-CDL-969

Dennis Deninger's book is a must-read for anyone interested in the history and evolution of sports broadcasting, as well as the various aspects that make it one of the most interesting and complex of topics. You will be hard-pressed to find a more comprehensive and insightful treatment. The author is a real pro, one of the sports television production pioneers whose thoughtful essays in this book take the reader inside an industry at the center of American life and one which has undergone profound change. Dennis is a good friend with whom I was honored to work at ESPN in the network's formative years. His wide-ranging experience allows him to give the reader a unique and broad perspective on the live sports landscape. Anyone interested in sports broadcasting will devour and enjoy this book.

Mike Aresco, *Commissioner, The American Athletic Conference*

Live Sports Media is superbly researched and organized. It's a comprehensive, invaluable resource, highly recommended for anyone seeking to understand how sports broadcasting has grown, and where it is headed next. It's also a very entertaining read, rich in stories from many broadcasting insiders. I've been in the industry for 35 years and still learned plenty from the book. Dennis Deninger's status as a longtime producer of major live events and studio programming gives him a unique insight and perspective on the many facets of this complex industry.

Chris Fowler, *ESPN/ABC Host and Commentator*

Dennis Deninger's combination of extensive production experience in sports television and decades as a professor at Syracuse University's prestigious Newhouse School make this comprehensive look at broadcast sports especially credible.

Bob Costas, *MLB Network Host and Play-by-play Announcer*
Former NBC Sports Host and Commentator

Dennis Deninger has skillfully provided the reader a practical 360-degree look at sports media, which is the epicenter of sports business. Dennis' experience as a sports broadcast executive, his connections in sport and sports media, and his aptitude for teaching make this book a compelling and educational read. This is sure to be beneficial to all who are in or want to enter the sports industry.

Todd Martin, *CEO, International Tennis Hall of Fame*

Dennis Deninger does a detailed dive into the history, impact, and grip TV sports has on the American public. Good soldiers know their history. By reading this book those entering the business will have a great understanding of where it has been and where it is potentially going. I highly recommend this book to anyone thinking about entering the business.

Fred Gaudelli, *Executive Producer, NBC Sunday Night Football, Sports Broadcasting Hall of Fame Class of 2020*

Dennis Deninger really knows his stuff and has unique insight into every aspect of sports broadcasting. From soup to nuts, he has a keen understanding of all the ingredients that go into a successful production and an appreciation for the impact sports broadcasting has had in society. His passion for sports media permeates through this book and he loves nothing more than to share that enthusiasm with others.

Ian Eagle, *CBS Sports/YES Network/Turner Sports Host and Commentator*

Wondering how sports on TV changed America? Read this book and enter the network broadcast booths and stadiums that altered America's viewing and spending habits. A fascinating look behind the scenes at one of the most important US business sectors.

Rick Burton, *David B. Falk Professor of Sport Management, Syracuse University*
Former Commissioner, National Basketball League, Australia

Week in and week out, and more than ever before, live sports is the engine that powers the big business of broadcasting. As one of the industry's leading innovators who kept that engine running at peak performance over an accomplished Emmy Award-winning career, Dennis Deninger provides unique insider perspectives on the fascinating evolution of sports broadcasting, and on its profound impact on American culture. In *Live Sports Media: The What, How and Why of Sports Broadcasting,* you'll learn about an industry that permeates every corner of society from the very best.

Frank Supovitz, *CEO, Fast Traffic Events and*
Former NFL Senior Vice President

"How did broadcasting become such a foundational aspect of professional sports? Dennis Deninger takes you behind the scenes to answer that question and reveal the ins and outs of live sports media. Dennis is a multiple Emmy Award-winning ESPN veteran who has also been honored for excellence in teaching at Syracuse University. He has an impressive command of the sports media industry, and I have seen first-hand how passionately he shares his insights with students. This book is a must for all young, aspiring sports broadcasters."

David Falk, *Founder and CEO, FAME Benefactor, Falk College*
of Sport and Human Dynamics at Syracuse University

Where was this book when I was fighting to learn about and break into sports broadcasting? Deninger's energy, enthusiasm, and industry intelligence shine through. This is master's level reading on the ever-changing world of sports, its broadcast connections, and inner workings.

Rob Stone, *Fox Sports Host and Commentator*

Live Sports Media

In *Live Sports Media: The What, How and Why of Sports Broadcasting,* Dennis Deninger provides an all-encompassing view of the sports television industry from his own perspective as an Emmy Award-winning producer at ESPN, at a time of seismic shifts in the industry. Technological advances and the proliferation of sports content across multiple media platforms have increased accessibility to sports events of all kinds across the world. Shifts in viewing habits and audience preferences are changing the dynamic of sports media and the sports industry as a whole. The result: more power for some sectors and diminished power for many others, to which professionals in the field need to rapidly adapt.

This second edition has been substantially updated to explore the impact of COVID-19 disruptions on sports and the growth of women's sports broadcasting and evolving sports, as well as political statements made in sports: Black Lives Matter and "taking a knee." It illustrates the origins, impact, reach, economics, production, and presentation of sports on video media – including, but not limited to, television. It takes the reader behind the scenes to describe the forces and processes that have shaped and continue to change sports content, its delivery, and how it connects with fans. Dennis Deninger draws from his experiences as an expert in the industry to expose how the choices and decisions that are now being made affect the programming, content, storytelling, production, advertising, and delivery of the sports broadcasting that we will see in the next season and how it will evolve in the years to come.

This practical, entertaining book provides insights into sports broadcasting that sports management, media, and journalism students and learning practitioners will not find anywhere else.

Dennis Deninger is a multiple Emmy Award-winning television production executive and innovative educator who has produced live sports television from six continents and across the United States. He spent 25 years at ESPN leading production teams for studio programming, live remote events, and digital video platforms. He is a professor of practice at Falk College of Sport and Human Dynamics at Syracuse University, USA, where he has been recognized for Faculty Excellence in Teaching. He was the founding director of the Sports Communications graduate program at Syracuse University's Newhouse School of Public Communications, his alma mater.

Live Sports Media

The What, How and Why of Sports Broadcasting

Second Edition

Dennis Deninger

Routledge
Taylor & Francis Group

NEW YORK AND LONDON

Second edition published 2022
by Routledge
605 Third Avenue, New York, NY 10158

and by Routledge
4 Park Square, Milton Park, Abingdon, Oxon, OX14 4RN

Routledge is an imprint of the Taylor & Francis Group, an informa business

© 2022 Dennis Deninger

The right of Dennis Deninger to be identified as author of this work has
been asserted in accordance with sections 77 and 78 of the Copyright,
Designs and Patents Act 1988.

All rights reserved. No part of this book may be reprinted or reproduced or
utilised in any form or by any electronic, mechanical, or other means, now
known or hereafter invented, including photocopying and recording, or in
any information storage or retrieval system, without permission in writing
from the publishers.

Trademark notice: Product or corporate names may be trademarks or
registered trademarks, and are used only for identification and explanation
without intent to infringe.

First edition published by Routledge 2012

Library of Congress Cataloging-in-Publication Data
Names: Deninger, Dennis, author.
Title: Live sports media : the what, how and why of sports broadcasting /
Dennis Deninger.
Other titles: Sports on television.
Description: Second edition. | Abingdon, Oxon ; New York, NY :
Routledge, 2022. | Includes bibliographical references and index.
Identifiers: LCCN 2021032298 | ISBN 9780367761202 (hardback) |
ISBN 9780367761219 (paperback) | ISBN 9781003165590 (ebook)
Subjects: LCSH: Television and sports. | Television broadcasting of sports. |
Mass media and sports.
Classification: LCC GV742.3 .D44 2022 | DDC 791.45/6579--dc23
LC record available at https://lccn.loc.gov/2021032298

ISBN: 978-0-367-76120-2 (hbk)
ISBN: 978-0-367-76121-9 (pbk)
ISBN: 978-1-003-16559-0 (ebk)

DOI: 10.4324/9781003165590

Typeset in Times New Roman
by Deanta Global Publishing Services, Chennai, India

To Gail

Contents

Contents

List of Figures

Acknowledgments

I want to thank all the accomplished professionals who have so generously shared their time, insights, and expertise over the course of my career and in the preparation of this book. I have been inspired by the singular sports and media innovators Bill Rasmussen, David Falk, and Bill Fitts, the man who gave me the opportunity of a lifetime when he brought me on board at a fledgling network called ESPN.

I am grateful for the contributions of so many friends and colleagues from "The Worldwide Leader" including Bill Bonnell, Phil Dean, Chris Fowler, Sam Gore, Luke Jensen, Chris LaPlaca, Burke Magnus, Jimmy Pitaro, Kent Samul, and Brian Williams. Thanks to Mike Tirico, Fred Gaudelli, and Drew Esocoff at NBC Sports, to Ian Eagle, Jodi Logsdon, and Bryan Kosowski at CBS Sports, Doug White at Turner Sports, and Rob Stone at Fox Sports.

Steve Mayer at the NHL, Mark Quenzel and Onnie Bose at the NFL, Micah Tannenbaum at the NBA, Dave Coletti at Disney, and Sandy Montag of the Montag Group all shed fresh light on the ever-changing dynamic of live sports media. Michael Veley and Michael Schoonmaker have been my champions at Syracuse University, and my research assistant Brad Trust has been invaluable.

My family, my dear friends, and my students have been my most dedicated supporters. They smile and understand when I go off on a tangent about how what we see on television is brilliant or could be much better. I cannot begin to describe how much all these wonderful people mean to me.

DD

Preface

Athletic competitions have affected how people perceive life and their roles within social groups since the ancient Olympic Games began in Greece in 776 BC, and most certainly back even farther before recorded history. On the North American continent for more than 1,000 years, the game of lacrosse has affected the social relations among groups of native people, their tribes, and their families. Before a game, people would meet for ceremonial feasts and agree upon the stakes and rules. These meetings helped develop relations between nations, families, and competitors. In some cases, tribes would play a game of lacrosse to settle disputes instead of taking up arms against each other in battle.

Sport continues to be a powerful social force, disseminating and reinforcing the values that regulate how people behave, setting examples for how to go about attaining goals and determining acceptable solutions for problems. And it presents individuals and groups with a means to escape from the reality of their daily lives, if only for a few hours, into a world of entertainment and celebration populated by talented, charismatic stars capable of remarkable performances, powerful leaders, and teams, all with their legions of adoring followers. The word "sport" itself came into English in the late 14th century as "disport," meaning a diversion that carried one away from work or serious matters, a recreation or amusement. Its origin is in the Latin verb "portare," to carry. When you imagine how difficult daily life would have been in the 1300s, any recreation or amusement must have been a relief and a welcome escape.

For centuries, games of sport were strictly local events in cities and villages. Advances in transportation and communications broadened people's awareness of what games their fellow citizens were playing on the other side of the county or hundreds of miles away, and that led to organized competitions. Local newspapers stimulated public interest in the 19th century when they started telling the stories of these competitions: horse races, walking races, bicycle races, and the newly invented sports of baseball, basketball, gridiron football, soccer and volleyball. The audience expanded geometrically beginning in 1920 when radio started broadcasting live sports directly into people's homes. National networks that linked hundreds of radio stations together gave nations their first common media experience, instantly engaging listeners from far-flung communities in live boxing matches, baseball, or college football games, and turning star athletes into household names.

The introduction of television in the late 1930s was a breakthrough. This book will start there and focus on how sports television developed domestically and internationally and how sport became important content watched by billions and, with its massive reach, affected the media, our economy, culture, society, and politics. We will examine how changes in viewer behavior are affecting the balance of power in sports and the media and go behind the scenes to explain how programming executives make decisions about what the public will see across their multiple platforms. We will describe the intricate process of producing live events and talk with sports commentators who have years of experience about what it takes to be a successful communicator.

The professionals covering any game or match deliver human narratives of hardships endured, commitments made, dedication to family and mentors, and goals achieved or yet to be attained. These stories are laced with lessons about the value of courage, hard work, dedication, self-discipline, leadership, cooperation, loyalty, and honesty. The characteristics represented by sports teams, athletes, and the sports themselves are part of what defines us as people, groups, and nations.

Watching these events on television and digital media gives people from different places and different backgrounds and across every generation some common ground and topics that start conversations. Sports reflect our times and our history, helping us connect with each other, with the past and the future. In this book, we will look at the challenges now being faced by the live sports media and the entire sports industry. Based on my experience leading studio, remote, and digital production teams at ESPN for more than 25 years, my conversations with industry leaders, and my research from the past decade teaching at Syracuse University, I will make projections as to what lies ahead, what will remain the same, and where change will take us in the seasons to come.

The Sports and Media Partnership

Live sport in the 21st century is part of the ever-broadening spectrum of entertainment available via the electronic media, sharing bandwidth alongside dramas and comedies, news and information, reality and game shows, musical performances, and every new iteration of documentary, commentary, cooking, home improvement, or automotive programming. Think of sports events as the original reality television: unscripted entertainment playing out live before your eyes with unexpected plot turns, spontaneous moments of elation and disappointment, and often surprise endings. Television shines a powerful spotlight on star performers and successful teams, enhancing the magnitude of their rivalries, milestones, and the importance of their stories during a game, a season, or a career.

Sports organizations and the electronic media are partners in delivering events to the public. The organizers stage the competitions, and the media promote and present the content with all its messaging to the public. Together they share the advertising, sponsorship, and subscription revenue, which amounts to billions of dollars, euros, and various currencies every year. It is a symbiotic relationship with both parties benefiting from their joint efforts. Rights payments by the media fuel the economic engine of sports.

The electronic and digital media benefit from sports because the games and events attract a proven, loyal audience of millions who will buy subscriptions to sports television and digital services. These fans are the target for sponsors and advertisers who pay the media dearly for the opportunity to communicate their sales messages to so many potential customers on such popular platforms. The media convergence of the 21st century has made it possible for a content producer to distribute video, information, stories, and promotion via every medium and channel, including streaming and social media, direct to consumers. The greater the cross-platform, cross-promotional power of these media producers, the greater the benefit derived by their sports team, league, and organizer partners. Big money and massive audiences create power for the sports industry and the media: economic, social, cultural, and political power.

DOI: 10.4324/9781003165590-1

THE SPORTS AUDIENCE

In the first two decades of the 21st century, the top 20 most-watched television programs in the United States were all Super Bowls. The Nielsen Company reported that the most-watched single program in the history of American television was Super Bowl XLIX on February 1, 2015. An average of 114,440,000 viewers per minute watched the New England Patriots defeat the Seattle Seahawks on CBS, with an additional 973,000 streaming the live game and another 368,000 watching the Spanish language feed. The game was also transmitted live with commentary in more than 30 languages to over 170 countries and territories, adding several million more international viewers to the total audience. By comparison, the most-watched American entertainment program during that 20-year period was *The Oscars* telecast on March 2, 2014, which averaged 43.63 million viewers per minute in the United States, less than half the audience of any Super Bowl from 2001 to 2020. In the years since 2015, the number of television viewers for Super Bowls has declined slightly, but the number of viewers streaming the game has grown geometrically. The US television audience has dropped below 100 million for a few Super Bowls, but when the streaming numbers are combined with the total "out of home" viewers and those watching on Spanish language channels, the "Total Audience Delivery" (TAD) for the Super Bowl is still the largest draw in the entire video entertainment spectrum with an audience each year of around 90–100 million viewers per minute.

If the only people who watched Super Bowls were the fans of the two teams playing in that game, the total audience would be much smaller. Clearly, the game's power to bring family and friends together for Super Bowl parties helps build the audience as does the attraction that Americans have for big events like the Olympics, *The Oscars*, and championship games. As a result, Super Bowl Sunday has become the most important advertising day of the year in the United States. An audience of millions for every minute of a live program means there will be plenty of commercials sold to advertisers keen on increasing awareness and sales for their products and services. The audience is so large, and demand is so high that the asking price for a single 30-second spot in the Fox telecast of Super Bowl LIV in February of 2020 was $5.6 million. Kantar Media estimated that Fox collected $435 million for the advertising it sold during Super Bowl LIV. Fox also sold commercials during their five hours of pre-game programming and the post-game celebration, which brought the network's revenue total to almost half a billion dollars for that one day.

The network televising the Super Bowl in any one year is by no means the only network covering the event or using it to generate revenue. For example, ESPN originates several days of "surround" programming for its television networks as well as ESPN.com, ESPN+, and ESPN Radio each year from the site of the Super Bowl. The NFL Network loads up its schedule the week before the Super Bowl with up to 100 hours of content related to the game. NBC has hosted *The Today Show* and other regular series from the Super Bowl site, plus a variety of networks create and produce programs that connect with fans and/or the host city. Sport and general interest websites, apps, and publications cover all the Super Bowl week activities as do radio networks and local stations.

All these platforms sell advertising, and all those dollars piled together represent a major economic impact from this one televised NFL football game. The economic impact of live sports is even more impressive when you add the billions of dollars spent on media rights and advertising for every regular season professional and collegiate football, NBA, Major League Baseball, National Hockey League, and international soccer game, plus every tennis, golf, auto racing, skiing, figure skating, and other sports event staged worldwide.

SHARING THE WEALTH

Sports is big business in the United States and around the world, providing a livelihood for millions of people far beyond the few thousand celebrity athletes who have multimillion-dollar contracts and endorsement deals. Research by PwC showed that in 2019, before the coronavirus pandemic, the total spent on sports media rights, gate receipts, sponsorship, and merchandising in North America alone exceeded $73 billion. If you add the $95.9 billion in sales of sports apparel and footwear, sports equipment purchases totaling $25 billion, and the billions more paid by Americans to buy bicycles, snowmobiles, motorcycles, pleasure boats, and RVs, the importance of sports in the creation of jobs and income is abundantly clear.

It would be impossible to extrapolate what percentage of that money is attributable to the fact that live sports are available across a variety of media every day of the year reaching millions of consumers who buy the shoes, hats, jerseys, and equipment that they see their favorite athletes wear. They consume the sports drinks and foods that athletes consume. They pay the monthly fees charged by the subscription video, cable, digital, or satellite providers who deliver the live programs to their homes and mobile devices, and they buy tickets and travel packages for future games to be played by the teams they follow.

The promotional value of dramatic sports events and the inspiring, amazing sports stories shown live on television and digital services cannot be underestimated. In the early years of television, many leagues and teams feared that live television coverage would result in fewer people attending games in person because they could choose to sit home and watch, never having to open their wallets. That did happen in the early 1950s when television was in its infancy. But since television and sports have become so universal, the reverse has proven to be true: a lack of television exposure can consign a league or team to anonymity and red ink.

The economics, advertising, and power of sports in the media are major topics that will be covered in depth later in this text. When the stakes are measured in the billions, the pressure on everyone involved in the production, programming, promotion, and sponsorship of live sports media events is multiplied. We will examine each of these functions in detail and identify the sets of skills and attributes required of these professionals in the coming chapters.

A MATTER OF IDENTITY

Each year I have assigned my students to write a short "self-portrait" to reflect upon how televised sport has influenced who they are, their perceptions of races other than their own, how they spend their time, what they wear, even the expressions they use in everyday speech. Their "self-portraits" have been most revealing both to me and to the students who take the time to think about what defines them as individuals. Live sports available on every screen accessible to these young people are far more pervasive and compelling than ever before, which has shaped them differently from their parents or grandparents.

"My life would be considerably different if I didn't have televised sport in my life," wrote one 21-year-old male. "Actually, I can't even imagine what my life would be like. I ask my dad from time to time what it was like when he was growing up when there was far less sports on television." The young man said his father responded by saying that he "didn't really know," but that it must be like remembering how we all existed before there were cell phones.

Young men and women from small towns in New Hampshire, Delaware, and upstate New York have all described how live sports on television provided their first opportunity to learn about African Americans, Hispanic Americans, and athletes from foreign countries and witness their remarkable accomplishments. They said it helped broaden their understanding of humanity and prepared them for the diversity on campus and in the world outside their hometowns.

Kate from outside New York City explained that "the sports media has been crucial in shaping my social beliefs and values, especially in today's society." She said that "because athletes have the ability to use social media to spark social change, it has encouraged me to become a stronger ally with those in support of racial equality."

Aidan was born in England, but his family moved to the United States when he was a child. He explained how access to live coverage of English Premier League games has created a powerful bond for his family. "Every single member of my immediate family follows a different football club," he said.

> As you can imagine, game days are pretty heated in my household, everyone constantly watching games in different rooms with their reactions to a goal or a mistake being heard throughout the house. There have even been a couple [of] arguments because of something that has happened during a rivalry game. But this dynamic is not something that I would change for the world. Without the beauty of sports media and broadcasting, we wouldn't even be able to have this family dynamic.

A senior from Seattle echoed the observations of many when he wrote that, "televised sport has provided me with the ability to connect and share experiences with others, even absolute strangers." He said, "I truly believe sport in any form, but especially at the collegiate and professional levels, is a form of social currency."

These first-person accounts clearly demonstrate the multilayer effects that the partnership of sports and the live sports media have had and continue to have on the social and cultural development of young people. Similar self-portraits from students in any nation within the reach of the sports media would no doubt speak of many if not all the same results.

FACING CHALLENGES TOGETHER

The live sports media provide a stage upon which Americans and people around the world have dealt with the most important social issues of the day. Over the years, sports have both reproduced and challenged stereotypes, myths, and prejudices about ethnic groups, nationalities, age groups, gender, and orientation. That was never more evident than in the year 2020 following the deaths of George Floyd, Breonna Taylor, and many other Black Americans at the hands of police. Representing the diversity of their players and the cities and nations they call home, professional leagues established social justice committees, coalitions with their players' associations, and initiatives that they supported with millions of dollars. The NBA, NFL, and many other leagues in the United States and abroad are working with their media partners to develop additional programming and funding sources to promote racial equality and social justice. The ability of sports organizations around the world to connect with people via the media is a powerful tool to denounce racism and spread messages of equality and justice for all.

No world crisis or event has had a greater impact on organized sports than the COVID-19 pandemic that swept the globe in the year 2020. The effects are perhaps most comparable to World War II, which forced the cancellation of the Olympic Games in 1940 and 1944. The 1940 games had been scheduled to take place in Tokyo, and the host city that had been selected for 1944 was London. The pandemic forced the postponement of the 2020 Summer Olympics along with its hundreds of hours of live media coverage until 2021. Ironically, Tokyo again was the host city affected.

However, during World War II, even after the United States entered the hostilities at the end of 1941, the Major League Baseball, National Football League, and National Hockey League seasons were all played as scheduled each year. So were all three Triple Crown horse races, the US Open tennis tournament, and collegiate basketball and football games including the annual New Year's Day bowls. The sports organizers took their lead from President Franklin D. Roosevelt's "Green Light" letter to Baseball Commissioner Kenesaw Mountain Landis in January of 1942, a month after the attack on Pearl Harbor. In response to a letter from Landis asking if baseball should continue while the nation was at war, Roosevelt wrote, "I honestly feel that it would be best for the country to keep baseball going." He made the point that the millions of people who were working longer hours and harder than ever "ought to have a chance for recreation and for taking their minds off their work even more than before."

These sports continued as scheduled in the United States during World War II, but they were disrupted by the COVID-19 pandemic. Seasons and events were time-shifted, abbreviated, or canceled, played in "bubbles" to reduce the risk of spreading the virus, and/or contested in stadiums or arenas with no fans allowed in the stands. It also forced the cancellation of entire seasons for millions of high school athletes across America who had hoped to play a variety of scholastic sports.

The impact of World War II on the televised coverage of sports was minimal because the medium was still in its infancy. Scheduled television service had begun in 1939 with only a handful of transmitting stations in East Coast cities, and very few homes equipped with TV sets. By comparison, 75 years later, the effects of COVID-19 on the live sports media were unprecedented. The sheer volume of sports content that had normally been available year after year, and for which the media conglomerates had committed massive sums of money for live broadcasting rights, was dramatically reduced. When the Major League Baseball season was cut from its regular 162 games to a 60-game schedule in 2020, that meant that only 37 percent of the normal live event content would be provided for the league's media partners. Pushing the opening day of the season from March 26, 2020, forward to July 24, 2020, left a four-month void that television programmers scrambled to fill with alternate shows and events. Most of this "plan-B" programming would not attract anywhere near the size of the expected live baseball audience and would therefore create a serious shortfall in advertising revenue for each of MLB's broadcast partners. This pattern of lost hours of attractive live sports coverage and lost income was replicated across virtually every sport. When the NCAA canceled "March Madness," the men's college basketball championship for 2020 that would have included 67 televised games in an 18-day period, the loss in broadcast advertising revenue alone was estimated at close to $1 billion.

Now the sports industry and the media together are facing the challenges of a post-pandemic world which can never completely return to the normalcy last experienced in 2019. The most important and long-lasting impact of the pandemic on the live sports media may well be how people's behavior has been altered. The orderly linear nature of lives around the globe has been eroded. A considerable percentage of the people who started working from home or lost their jobs during the pandemic will never return to the schedule of commuting to and from the office Monday through Friday, with evening and weekend hours reserved for the enjoyment of live sports.

Random, non-linear patterns that now integrate work and non-work activities into what used to be the block of hours spent in an office or on the job site have displaced more predictable, linear personal schedules for millions of people. In the pre-pandemic era, when people were living more on daily schedules, watching a game in the evening was part of that schedule for millions. With more people adopting wide open, flexible schedules due to working at home, unemployment, or early retirement, regular viewing patterns changed. One by-product was the dramatic growth during the pandemic of non-linear, subscription-on-demand options for video entertainment such as Netflix, Disney+, ESPN+, Prime Video, Hulu, Peacock, Paramount Plus, Discovery+, HBO Max, and many more. Flexibility and freedom are what define these non-linear, "watch what you want when you want it" streaming services. Sports, with their scheduled games, are rigidly timed and therefore much more linear than non-linear.

During the pandemic, the life-and-death reality of the virus and the fear of contracting it changed perspectives and made other parts of our lives, like the sports we had followed on television, seem less important for many people. Their importance was diminished further by the fact that the games were being played without avid, cheering fans whose emotions, loyalties, and in many cases, wagers had hung in the suspense of the outcome. One of the great attributes of sport is that it serves as a social facilitator, bringing people together to experience the excitement and the fun of a live event as a community. The pandemic temporarily stole away many of the fundamental elements that have always made sports so engaging and so much fun. The shared anticipation of a matchup, the social gathering at games or in front of televisions, spirited post-game conversations at work or school, and for millions of young people, even the basic opportunity to play were all diminished in the era of social distancing. The suspension or cancellation of hundreds of games and events made appointment viewing more confusing and less predictable, which led to a dramatic drop in sports audience ratings. Empty seats in stadiums and arenas were a grim reminder of the pandemic and may have contributed to the retreat many individuals made into the scripted stories of fiction that fill the menus of subscription video services, most of which offer little or no sports content.

Another factor that presents a challenge for sports organizers and their media partners is the decline in sports participation among Generation Z, which was already noticeable before the pandemic hit. The number of American high school students participating in organized scholastic sports during the 2018–19 school year fell for the first time after 32 consecutive years of steady growth. The mass cancellation of high school sports that accompanied the crisis could push many young people farther away from playing fields and deeper into their digital worlds. Millions of youngsters did not get the chance to play high school basketball, soccer, football, or any sport when their teams disbanded. With the resumption of regular schedules of practices and games, there may be less interest among many students who found other pursuits and social media options to occupy their time while sports activities were suspended.

Regaining the pre-pandemic heights of popularity and profitability is a difficult task for the sports industry and the live sports media. During the pandemic, people around the globe became aware of the new, varied entertainment choices that were available and they got used to having on-demand access to this content at any hour of the day or night. People's habits and behaviors once altered tend to be very resistant to change. Even as large percentages of the population were vaccinated and sports resumed play on regular schedules, there was a discernible leveling-off of ratings for live sports programming, falling short of their pre-pandemic levels of viewership.

All is not lost however, and the setbacks should not be irreversible. Sports leagues and organizers in partnership with the media that provide their lifeblood of revenue must reassert themselves as part of the daily social narrative. It will take some creativity. They must together send the message that they are valuable and beneficial: that engaging with live sports provides entertainment, inspiration, community benefits, and social connectivity which can serve as the perfect antidote for social distancing. The value is in how live sports are viewed simultaneously by thousands and millions of diverse people of all ages and every demographic, and how those sports help connect people across the divides that separate us. The communication, the sense of belonging, and the community identification that sport generates must be presented as an important part of life and popular entertainment in the post-pandemic world.

BIBLIOGRAPHY

Brown, Maury, "Record 114.4 Million Watch Super Bowl XLIX, Making It Most-Watched TV Program in U.S. History." *Forbes*, 2015. https://www .forbes.com/sites/maurybrown/2015/02/02/record-114-4-million-watched

-patriots-seahawks-in-super-bowl-xlix-smash-last-years-by-2-2-million/ ?sh=4771104365e6

National Federation of State High School Associations. "Participation in High School Sports Registers First Decline in 30 Years." National Federation of State High School Associations, 2019. https://www.nfhs.org/articles/ participation-in-high-school-sports-registers-first-decline-in-30-years/

Nielsen, "Tops of 2015: TV and Social Media." *Nielsen*, 2015. https://nielsen .com/us/en/insights/article/2015/tops-of-2015-tv-and-social-media/

Nielsen, "Super Bowl LV Draws Nearly 92 Million TV Viewers." *Nielsen*, 2021. https://www.nielsen.com/us/en/press-releases/2021/super-bowl-lv -draws-nearly-92-million-tv-viewers/

Pepitone, Greg, Peter Schwartz, and Priyanka York, "At the gate and beyond: PwC Outlook for the sports market in North America through 2023." *Price-Waterhouse Cooper*, 2, 2019. https://www.pwc.com/us/en/industries /tmt/assets/pwc-sports-outlook-2019.pdf

Roosevelt, Franklin D. "Letter from Franklin Roosevelt to Kenesaw Mountain Landis, 1942 January 15." National Baseball Hall of Fame and Museum, 1942. https://collection.baseballhall.org/PASTIME/letter-franklin-roosevelt -kenesaw-mountain-landis-1942-january-15-0

Swallen, Jon. "Super Bowl LIV: The Numbers." *Kantar Media*, 2020. https:// www.kantarmedia.com/us/thinking-and-resources/blog/super-bowl-liv -the-numbers

The Beginnings of Televised Sport

RCA President David Sarnoff used these words to introduce television to the American public in 1939.

> "It is with a feeling of humbleness that I come to this moment of announcing the birth in this country of a new art so important in its implications that it is bound to affect all society. It is an art which shines like a torch of hope in a troubled world. It is a creative force which we must learn to utilize for the benefit of mankind."

The occasion was the opening of the RCA exhibit at the New York World's Fair on April 30, 1939. RCA's station W2XBS (XBS for "experimental broadcast station") began the first regular schedule of television broadcasting in the United States on that date with President Franklin D. Roosevelt's speech opening the World's Fair.

"Now we add sight to sound," said Sarnoff, whose Radio Corporation of America owned the NBC Red and Blue radio networks. Millions of people each day tuned in for the entertainment and news programs on radio sets that were manufactured and sold by RCA. The more appealing the product that NBC created and broadcast, the more demand they created for their radios. RCA's development of its television station and regularly scheduled broadcasts followed the same formula: give people reasons to buy one of the new RCA television receivers that the company introduced at the World's Fair.

It is estimated that there were fewer than 400 operating television sets in New York City that could receive the inaugural transmission. But television as a technological innovation was introduced to thousands of visitors to the RCA Pavilion over the course of the World's Fair that summer. They could walk in front of a large, bulky television camera and watch in wonderment as they appeared live on a tiny black and white screen.

THE FIRST TELEVISED SPORTS

The first sports event to receive television coverage anywhere in the world was the 1936 Olympic Games in Berlin, although it was not a broadcast. The video was not transmitted to any home TV sets but was instead fed via

DOI: 10.4324/9781003165590-2

coaxial cable to 25 "public television offices" set up around the city by the German government. Over the course of the Olympics, a total of 162,000 people reportedly watched the video from three television cameras that were in place at the Olympiastadion augmented by a film of competitions shot by 24 photographers, then processed and edited. Adolf Hitler's government was intent on using the Olympics to show the world the superiority of "The Fatherland" in all fields, athletic, cultural, and technological.

Three years later and less than three weeks after the World's Fair opened, live sports coverage made its debut on American television. On May 17, 1939, W2XBS took one camera from the RCA Pavilion to Columbia University's Baker Field and placed it on top of a 12-foot-high platform erected for the occasion on the third base side of home plate (Figure 2.1). The event was the second game of an afternoon college baseball doubleheader between Princeton and Columbia Universities. Scheduling on W2XBS was obviously very flexible in those days of television's infancy: there was no way to know exactly how long the first game of the doubleheader would last, so the broadcast simply started when the players took the field for game two.

Bill Stern became America's first television sportscaster when he opened the show saying, "Good afternoon ladies and gentlemen. Welcome to the first telecast of a sporting event. I'm not sure what it is we're doing here, but I certainly hope it turns out well for you people who are watching." Bill Stern was the host of NBC Radio's *Bill Stern's Sports Reel*, a show that began in 1937 and ran until 1956.

Stern knew radio, but his uncertainty with doing live television was warranted: no one had ever done live TV sports in the United States, and he had no way of seeing what was going out on the telecast to the small number of television sets in use in the New York City area. He had no monitor, just the microphone in front of him into which he gave his commentary

■ **Figure 2.1** The first televised American sporting event was a college baseball game between Columbia and Princeton on May 17, 1939, in New York. (Photo by Mark Rucker/Transcendental Graphics, Getty Images)

of the game. Princeton won 2-1 in 10 innings to sweep the doubleheader. They had won the first game 8-6.

NBC's director in the TV truck, Burke Crotty, may have cringed when he heard Bill Stern say that they were not sure "what it is we're doing here," but it was new ground they were breaking that afternoon in May 1939. Crotty's budget for the broadcast was reportedly $3,000, which at the time was more than the average American family earned in one year. (The US Bureau of the Census reported that in 1939 the median income for a family was $2,700.) Three years later, Burke Crotty would leave the comfort of his TV truck and serve in World War II, which began in Europe in September 1939. When he returned from his military service, Crotty became the first director of NBC TV's *Baseball Game of the Week* series.

The shortstop on the field for Columbia in the first televised game was Sid Luckman, who went on to be inducted into the Pro Football Hall of Fame. Luckman played tailback on Columbia's football team and was the Chicago Bears' first draft pick in 1939. He was the National Football League's first great T-formation quarterback and was selected "All-NFL" five times. Luckman threw seven touchdown passes in one game on November 14, 1943, against the New York Giants at the Polo Grounds. He was named the NFL's Most Valuable Player for 1943 after he threw for five touchdowns in that year's NFL Championship Game.

The morning after this historic telecast, Louis Effrat wrote his account of the game in *The New York Times*. "This encounter, listed for seven innings, was televised by the National Broadcasting Company, the first regularly-scheduled sporting event to be pictured over the air waves." Considering how small television screens were in 1939, barely larger than a playing card, and that there was only one camera covering the entire game, it is unlikely that any action beyond the infield was visible in this grainy black and white inaugural sports telecast.

THE DECADE OF EXPERIMENTATION

NBC and its owners at RCA were encouraged by the results of this first sports telecast and saw the potential of live sports as programming content for their television station. In the ensuing months, NBC's one remote truck with two cameras set up at a variety of events in the New York City area. They had to stay within range of their transmitting tower atop the Empire State Building, a radius of 20 miles. And the only television receivers that could pick up their live broadcasts were in New York area homes or at the World's Fair site in Flushing Meadows, Queens.

Televising any sport for the first time is always a grand experiment. NBC had to be anxious to determine which sports would work well on television and attract an audience that could help generate sales of RCA sets. The first boxing match ever televised in the United States was former world heavyweight champion Max Baer vs. Lou Nova at Yankee Stadium on June 1, 1939, two weeks after the college baseball game broadcast. It was immediately apparent that boxing would be perfect for television. All the action took place in a confined space, the venue would have its own lighting above the ring, and boxers like Baer and Joe Louis, the reigning world heavyweight champion, were among the limited number of national sports celebrities who could attract a large television audience. Louis had achieved "hero" status in June of 1938 with his crushing first-round defeat of Germany's Max Schmeling at Yankee Stadium.

Baseball had the largest fan base of any sport in the United States in the 1930s and 1940s, standing out as "America's pastime" during that era. Making baseball work on television was understandably a priority for any network that wanted to attract sports fans and the advertisers trying to sell them products. Second to baseball at the time was college football, well ahead of the NFL, which would not emerge as a national powerhouse until after the 1958 NFL Championship Game that was decided in sudden death before a television audience estimated to be over 40 million.

Major League Baseball debuted on W2XBS on August 26, 1939, with the Cincinnati Reds visiting the Brooklyn Dodgers at Ebbets Field. Legendary sportscaster Red Barber was at the microphone, and the only television director in the country with live baseball experience, Burke Crotty, was back in the truck. Barber was 31 and in his first year as the voice of the Brooklyn Dodgers having moved to New York from Cincinnati where he had called Reds games on the radio since 1934. There could not have been a more qualified commentator to call this historic Reds vs. Dodgers game. But just like Bill Stern at the Columbia-Princeton game, Barber did not have a monitor to watch what pictures were being broadcast. The only way he could tell which camera was shooting the action was to take note of when the red "tally" lights on top of each camera lit up. More people saw the game in the stands at Ebbets Field than on television. Eight years later, the World Series made its television debut when the New York Yankees played the Brooklyn Dodgers with their rookie first baseman Jackie Robinson in 1947.

NBC produced its first tennis telecast in August 1939, and then in September premiered college football with a game from Triboro Stadium on Randall's Island in New York City between Waynesburg State and Fordham University. The National Football League made its inauspicious television debut on October 22, 1939, when the Philadelphia Eagles played the NFL's Brooklyn Dodgers at Ebbets Field also on W2XBS. The Dodgers were renamed the Tigers for the 1944 season and then folded, but they made history by recording the first-ever NFL victory on television, 23–14 over the Eagles.

A HISTORICAL PERSPECTIVE

The United States that in 1940 was first getting a glimpse of this new technological wonder called "television" was a very different country than the digitally connected nation of more than 325 million people that we know today. The US Census of 1940 reported a population of 132 million with New York by far the most populous state with 13,479,149. California, which in the 21st century is home to more than 12 percent of the total US population, only had 6,907,387 residents in 1940, placing it behind New York, Pennsylvania, Illinois, and Ohio.

Even though Europe was at war in 1940, there was peace in the United States and a distinct isolationist spirit sought to keep America out of foreign conflicts. Prosperity was returning after the Great Depression, and a majority of voters were happy enough with the job being done by President Roosevelt that in November of 1940 they awarded him an unprecedented third term in the White House. There was at least one radio in 86.6 percent of all American homes in 1940. In the Northeast, radio penetration had reached 96.2 percent. There were 1,878 daily newspapers with a total circulation of 41,132,000 every day. Americans got their news from the newspaper or on the radio, which was also their primary mass entertainment medium.

In Major League Baseball, there were eight teams in the American League and eight in the National League. They played a 154-game regular season and the two teams at the top of their respective leagues met in the World Series. There were no playoffs and no teams west of St. Louis. The National Football League had only 10 teams with the Green Bay Packers the western-most franchise. Chicago was home to two of those 10 NFL teams, the Bears and the Cardinals. The National Hockey League had only seven teams, none west of Chicago or south of New York. (The Brooklyn Americans would fold after the 1941–42 season, reducing the NHL to its famed "Original Six" until expansion came in 1967.) The National Basketball League was playing professional games in Midwestern cities, but the NBA did not exist.

In 1940, when television was very much in the experimental stage, RCA's W2XBS in New York was leading the way in sports. W2XBS became WNBT TV on July 1, 1941, the nation's first commercial TV station, and then changed its call letters to WNBC in 1948, when it merged operations with WNBC AM radio. NBC's only challenger in the early days of television was Allen B. Dumont's W2XVT, which he founded in Passaic, New Jersey, in 1938. It later became WNEW TV Channel 5 and is still on the air as WNYW TV. Before he founded Allen B. Dumont Laboratories Inc., in 1931, Dumont had worked as an engineer with Lee De Forest, the inventor of the Audion and triode tubes and more than 300 other patented electronic innovations. Dumont's was the first company to make cathode ray tubes for television screens in the United States. Starting with W2XVT, and with the goal of selling Dumont television sets, he built what would become the Dumont Network, a major competitor of NBC and CBS until the mid-1950s.

The *Broadcasting Yearbook* of 1941 listed a total of 25 experimental television stations operating in 1940, and 18 others that had construction permits. Every one of them had an "X" in its call letters to indicate "experimental." Among the stations on the air in addition to W2XBS and W2XVT were:

- W2XAB, licensed to the Columbia Broadcasting System, the predecessor of WCBS TV.
- Two stations licensed by the Philco Radio and Television Corporation in Philadelphia.
- Five General Electric Co. stations of which two were in Schenectady, New York, at GE headquarters, two in nearby New Scotland, New York, and one in Boston.
- There was a station in San Francisco and one in Los Angeles licensed by the Don Lee Broadcasting System, a company founded by a Cadillac dealer who had radio stations in both cities.
- Two stations were licensed to RCA Manufacturing Co. in Camden, New Jersey.
- One station owned by the Zenith Radio Corporation in Chicago.
- Two stations licensed to universities: Kansas State in Manhattan, Kansas, and Purdue in Lafayette, Indiana.
- One station operated by the *Milwaukee Journal* newspaper in Wisconsin.

Among those with construction permits as the decade of the 1940s began was Howard Hughes, the celebrity business magnate, aviator, and motion picture producer. His Hughes Tool Company productions division was preparing to build stations in Los Angeles and San Francisco.

SPORTS DOMINATED THE TV SCHEDULE

When World War II came to an end in 1945, television was still a very young medium that very few people had seen. That fall NBC began airing regular Saturday afternoon college football games, but they were limited to a small number of East Coast universities that would allow coverage. There was virtually no "primetime" television schedule other than sports in 1945. The genre was easy to produce using only a few cameras, it didn't require any scripts or paid actors, writers, or producers, and any rights payments by stations or networks were either small or non-existent.

NBC debuted the *Gillette Cavalcade of Sports* in November 1944 and used it to anchor the network's programming on Monday and Friday nights. For 16 years until 1960, the series was a television primetime fixture with boxing matches that featured top fighters from every weight class. The first heavyweight championship bout ever televised was part of the "caval-cade": Joe Louis vs. Billy Conn on June 19, 1946, from Yankee Stadium. Louis knocked Conn out in the eighth round to retain his title.

The Major League Baseball World Series made its debut on television on September 30, 1947, as the Yankees represented the American League against the National League champion Brooklyn Dodgers with their rookie first baseman Jackie Robinson, who that year became the first Black man ever to play in a World Series game. Robinson's groundbreaking season increased interest in professional baseball that summer, but far more fans listened on their radios than saw the games on television.

In 1948, during the prime viewing hours of 7–11 pm Eastern Time the four networks combined had 27.5 hours of sports programming, most of it boxing or wrestling matches from New York area venues. ABC added two nights of *Roller Derby* to its primetime lineup in 1949, but as more televi-sion stations went on the air and more sets were sold, the nightly menu of sports was gradually replaced by more entertainment, scripted comedy, and drama programs that appealed to a broader audience. By comparison, just 10 years later, the 1958 primetime schedule for all networks combined had only 2.5 hours of sports: the *Wednesday Night Fights* on ABC and the *Gillette Cavalcade of Sports*, which still anchored Friday nights for NBC.

THE DECADE OF FULFILLMENT

The great promise for television as a "creative force" in the United States that David Sarnoff foresaw in 1939 was fulfilled in the decade of the 1950s, perhaps not quite to the "benefit to mankind" that he had envisioned, but certainly as a means of informing, entertaining, and connecting mil-lions of people simultaneously. By the time Americans were hanging 1950 calendars on their kitchen or office walls, the number of television stations in the country had grown to 117, a dramatic increase from only two in 1940. There were TV stations in 34 of the 48 states (Alaska and Hawaii did not join the union until 1959), which meant that there was no local television available in Arkansas, Colorado, Idaho, Kansas, Maine, Mississippi, Montana, Nevada, New Hampshire, North Dakota, South Carolina, South Dakota, Vermont, or Wyoming.

The number of commercial television stations would not have grown geo-metrically if the new medium had not shown great potential as a money-maker. In 1950, fewer than one in 10 American homes had a television, but several factors and forces were coming together that would launch the TV boom of the 1950s. The post-war era saw millions of new marriages usher in the baby boom, housing starts were at record levels, and the average work week began to shrink giving more people more leisure time to enjoy in their new homes with their new families. TV signals from all the new broadcasting stations brought more programming to more regions of the country, which put a television at the top of a typical family's list of "most-wanted household items."

In 1950, the United States had a population of 150 million people, but the number of TV households was only 3,880,000, a penetration rate of just under 9 percent. By 1955, in the span of just five years, that figure had grown to 30.7 million, which represented 64.5 percent of American households. If you were a sports fan who had not yet bought a television, the events of the 1950s would have given you every reason you needed to make a withdrawal from your savings account and dash out to the local appliance store.

TV GOES COAST TO COAST

Before September 4, 1951, less than half the small number of American homes that did have televisions could watch the same broadcasts at the same time. Television networks fed their programs to affiliated stations across the continent via a system of microwave relays that were 30 miles or less apart. Any station that was outside the range of those microwave relay stations had to produce its own local shows and fill out the broadcast day with films and kinescopes (film recordings of television shows) that were shipped to them from their affiliated network in New York.

AT&T had been working on a transcontinental system of microwave repeaters augmented by some coaxial cable connections in the late 1940s. Each relay station was on a small plot of land and consisted of a building and a steel tower for an antenna that could be as tall as 125 feet if there was no convenient hill nearby. The initial line for this transmission system that AT&T nicknamed "TD2," connected New York and Chicago. At the same time, a line was being built to link Chicago to San Francisco and a third line would connect San Francisco to Los Angeles on the west coast.

On that September date in 1951, President Harry S. Truman addressed the opening session of the Japanese Peace Treaty Conference in San Francisco, and it was seen live nationwide. Coast-to-coast radio had been providing Americans in every state a common communications experience since the 1920s, but the ability that we have long taken for granted for people across the country to simultaneously watch the same news or sports events and the same entertainment programs as a nationwide audience was not a reality until the day of that speech in 1951.

DUMONT PIONEERS REGULAR SEASON NFL AND NBA

It is no coincidence that the first-ever live coast-to-coast telecast of an NFL football game came just a few months later. On December 23, 1951, the Dumont Network aired the NFL Championship game from the Los Angeles Memorial Coliseum, and viewers across the country saw the Los Angeles Rams defeat the Cleveland Browns 24–17. Dumont paid the NFL a rights fee of $75,000 for the event, which was made more interesting by the fact that the Cleveland Rams had won the NFL Championship in 1946 then immediately abandoned Ohio and headed west to make Los Angeles their home. The Browns were founded that same year and quickly filled the void in Ohio by attracting the majority of former Rams fans with their success under legendary coach Paul Brown.

Dumont had televised Sunday NFL games during the fall of 1951, but they were not shown coast to coast, and most were New York Giants games. Dumont owned television stations in New York, Washington, D.C., and Pittsburgh, so virtually all the NFL games they broadcast from 1952 to 1954 were home games for the teams in those three cities. The network contracted directly with each of the teams and became the first to air an NFL game in the prime evening viewing hours. Dumont's series of Saturday night NFL games in the 1953 and 1954 seasons launched prime-time professional football 17 years before the celebrated debut of *ABC's Monday Night Football* in 1970.

Dumont also pioneered National Basketball Association coverage on television with 13 games in the 1953–54 season for which it paid the NBA a rights fee of $39,000. The league had been created in 1949 by the merger of the National Basketball League (NBL), which had started as the Midwest Basketball Conference in 1935, and the Basketball Association of America (BAA), which was founded in 1946. The NBL had teams in Minneapolis, Denver, Sheboygan, Wisconsin, Waterloo, Iowa, two franchises in New York: the Rochester Royals and the Syracuse Nationals, Ft. Wayne, Indiana, and the Tri-cities of Rock Island and Moline, Illinois, and Davenport, Iowa, shared a team. Many had started as semi-professional factory teams like the Ft. Wayne Zollner Pistons, named for Fred Zollner whose company manufactured pistons for the automotive industry. The team moved to Detroit in 1957.

The BAA had more big city teams and was primarily an East Coast league with the Boston Celtics, Chicago Stags, Cleveland Rebels, Detroit Falcons, New York Knickerbockers, Philadelphia Warriors, Pittsburgh Ironmen, Providence Steamrollers, St Louis Bombers, Toronto Huskies, and Washington Capitols. By the time the NBA hit national television in the 1953–54 season, it had consolidated to just nine teams: Boston, New York, Philadelphia, Baltimore, Syracuse, Rochester, Ft. Wayne, Milwaukee, and the Minneapolis Lakers, who won the league championship that year and would move to Los Angeles in 1960.

Several team owners in professional sports and university programs were still unsure whether television would help or hurt their profits and their prospects for future growth. Many feared that if fans could sit home and watch games free of charge on their TV sets that attendance at the arenas or ballparks would slip. Beginning in 1952, the National Collegiate Athletic Association (NCAA) limited television exposure of college football to only one national broadcast game per week. There were a few professional team owners who experimented with prohibiting television coverage for part of a season then comparing their attendance figures to when the games were televised. What they found was that television exposure broadened their fan base and made more people interested in their product and their stars. More fans meant increased profits and higher rights fees from television networks, and it also signaled the end of small-town teams in the big leagues. If you could draw from hundreds of thousands of potential fans in a major metropolitan area like Detroit, it didn't make economic sense to keep your team in Ft. Wayne, Indiana.

MAKING SPORTS HISTORY LIVE ON TV

Two historic events in the 1950s solidified television as the preeminent vehicle for the distribution of sports in America, and they both took place at Yankee Stadium in New York. The first was on October 8, 1956, as the Yankees played the Brooklyn Dodgers in Game 5 of the World Series. Don Larsen, the Yankees pitcher, threw the one and only perfect game in World Series history. No one had done it before, and to this date, no one has done it since. The final score was Yankees 2 Dodgers 0. The Dodgers' starting pitcher Sal Maglie won Game 1 of the Series, and he had pitched a no-hitter against the Phillies in the final week of the regular season. Maglie was on the mound for Brooklyn for the entire nine innings of Game 5 and gave up only five hits, but Larsen won the day and a place in history by allowing no hits, no runs, no walks, and the Yankees made no fielding errors.

The historic game was televised by NBC with Mel Allen, the voice of the Yankees, and Vin Scully, the Dodgers play-by-play announcer, sharing duties at the microphone. A crowd of 64,519 had gathered that late Monday afternoon with the Yankees and Dodgers tied at two games apiece. Brooklyn was the defending champion, having beaten the Bronx Bombers in 1955 for their only World Series championship.

The 27-year-old Larsen had never come close to a no-hitter before, but with the series tied two games apiece, Larsen pitched the greatest game of his life, recording 27 Dodger outs in a row. *The New York Times* quoted home plate umpire Babe Pinelli as having told Larsen after his historic performance: "You were wonderful, just wonderful. [Larsen had] the greatest pin-point control I've ever seen. Even if the Dodgers had not swung at some of those slow curves they would have been strikes." The Yankees went on to win the 1956 World Series four games to three.

If you were a baseball fan in America and did not own a television set on Monday, October 8, 1956, you undoubtedly felt as if you had been left out as history was being made. The following weekend and in the months to come thousands headed for their local hardware and appliance stores to join the ranks of TV owners so as not to be left behind in the dwindling ranks of the "unconnected."

"THE GREATEST GAME EVER PLAYED"

By 1958, television was well on its way to transforming America in the same way that it was transforming most countries in the developed world. Television was becoming a national connective tissue in a process that radio, newspapers, newsreels, and the movies had begun but that was unprecedented in the history of mass media. Millions of people from border to border laughed, cried, rejoiced, and reacted in unison as they witnessed history together on television. Americans all came to know the same characters such as comedian Milton Berle, the "Beav" on *Leave it to Beaver*, Lucille Ball on *I Love Lucy*, or Marshall Dillon on *Gunsmoke*. On Sunday, December 28, 1958, Johnny Unitas added his name to the national lexicon. Unitas was the quarterback for the Baltimore Colts who faced the New York Giants in the 1958 NFL Championship Game at Yankee Stadium. This game was the Super Bowl of its day because the American Football League had not yet been founded. There was only one professional football league, the NFL, and its most important contest of the year was the Championship Game live on NBC.

Professional football still lagged behind college football in nationwide popularity, but it was on the rise in the 1950s, and its increased television exposure during the decade was a major contributing factor. A viewing audience that grew to an estimated 40 million watched Unitas march the Colts 86 yards in the final two minutes to tie the game in regulation at 17–17, sending it to overtime. Tie games during the regular season ended as a draw, so there was no precedent for deciding a game in overtime. No season-ending Championship Game in the history of the NFL had ever ended with a tie score, so most of the players on the field weren't sure what would happen.

A coin was tossed to decide who would get possession of the ball as the overtime period began. The Giants won the toss, but they failed to make a first down and were forced to punt. Unitas, the Colts' 25-year-old steely-eyed, crew-cut quarterback engineered an 80-yard drive in 13 plays that ended when running back Alan Ameche crossed the goal line from one yard out for the winning touchdown. The Colts won 23–17, and America was watching.

However, television viewers almost missed the winning touchdown. In the overtime period, with the Colts on the Giants' eight-yard line, NBC lost its feed from Yankee Stadium. Apparently in the feverish crowd activity during the exciting final drive, one of the main transmission cables at field level was accidentally disconnected. An NBC business manager who was assisting with statistics on the sidelines took matters into his own hands in hopes of delaying the game long enough for the network's technicians to fix the problem. Stan Rotkiewicz darted onto the field, wrestled the game ball away from the referee, and ran off in the opposite direction. The radio announcers thought they were seeing the antics of a "drunken fan," but Stan Rotkiewicz saved the day for NBC's viewers. The disconnected cable was fixed, and the television signal was restored in time for millions to see Ameche's one-yard plunge.

This dramatic winner-take-all title game attracted attention and captured the imagination of the American public. It took its place alongside Don Larsen's perfect game on a short list of truly memorable communal events that millions witnessed simultaneously and were then replayed in conversation and stories during the days, weeks, and years to follow.

When the decade came to a close in 1960, the promise that television represented at its introduction 21 years earlier was being fulfilled. A remarkable 42 million sets had been manufactured and sold in the United States since 1950, increasing the penetration rate to 87.1 percent of American homes compared with only 8.9 percent just 10 years earlier. This rapid and nearly universal spread of audio and visual communication gave the public access to sources of information and entertainment that transformed the nation. In the span of 10 years, the United States had become a connected community brought together by shared experiences and instantly reachable by broadcasters and advertisers as well as social, cultural, and political leaders. Many of the most memorable and enjoyable shared experiences for the people living in those 45,750,000 television households were live sporting events.

BIBLIOGRAPHY

Broadcasting Publications Inc. "1941 Yearbook." In *The Weekly Newsmagazine of Radio Broadcast Advertising*, 388. Washington, DC, 1941. https://worldradiohistory.com/Archive-BC-YB/1941/1941-BC-YB.pdf

Broadcasting Publications Inc. "1950 Yearbook." In *The Newsweekly of Radio and Television Telecasting*, edited by Sol Taishoff, 506, Washington, DC, 1950. https://worldradiohistory.com/Archive-BC-YB/1950/1950-BC-YB.pdf

Castleman, Harry and Podrazik, Walter J. *Watching Television: Six Decades of American Television*. Syracuse, NY: Syracuse University Press, 2003.

Cornell University. "The History of Television." Cornell University. https://www.cs.cornell.edu/~pjs54/Teaching/AutomaticLifestyle-S02/Projects/Vlku/history.html#:~:text=During%20the%201939%20World's%20Fair,president%20to%20ever%20be%20televised

Drebinger, John. "Larsen's Well-Timed Masterpiece." *The New York Times*, 1956. http://archive.nytimes.com/www.nytimes.com/packages/html/sports/year_in_sports/10.08.html

Effrat, Louis. "Columbia Loses Twice; Fordham, C.C.N.Y. Win." *The New York Times*. 1939. https://timesmachine.nytimes.com/timesmachine/1939/05/18/issue.html

Koppet, Leonard. "Baker Field: Birthplace of Sports Television." Columbia University. http://www.college.columbia.edu/cct_archive/spr99/34a.html

Misc. Baseball. "Some Notes on Don Larsen's Perfect Game in the 1956 World Series." *Misc. Baseball*, 2010. https://miscbaseball.wordpress.com/2010/06/04/some-notes-on-don-larsens-perfect-game-in-the-1956-world-series/

Schools, Tom. "Broadcasting The Olympic Games, The Media and The Olympic Games–Television Broadcasting." The Olympic Museum, 2016.

Truesdell, Leon E. "United States Summary." In *Sixteenth Census of The United States: 1940– Population*, edited by Leon E. Trusdell, PhD of the Bureau of the Census, 6 & 14. Washington DC, February 1942.

TV History. "Number of TV Households in America 1950–1978." *The American Century*, 2014. https://americancentury.omeka.wlu.edu/files/original/60e94905a0e02050a5b78f10b1b02b07.jpg

The Modern Era Creates a New Sports TV Reality

Sports television was transformed in the decade of the 1960s. It began to more closely resemble the product that millions of fans have taken for granted in the seasons and years that have followed. In the United States, sports broadcasting started the decade as an overwhelmingly local commodity and became a national force thanks primarily to the enactment of one law passed by Congress in 1961. The Olympic Games, which are now one of the most-anticipated, most-watched sporting events around the world, first came to American television in 1960. A vast assortment of other sports and competitions that had never been seen by the masses came to television in the 1960s beginning with the debut of *ABC's Wide World of Sports* in 1961.

Every sports viewer today expects to see instant replays of all the critical plays, all the goals, home runs, touchdowns, spectacular shots, and catches in every game, but before 1963, there were no replays in any games, ever. If it happened and you missed it, there was no second, third, or fourth replay from multiple angles. Aerial coverage of sports events began in earnest at the 1960 Orange Bowl game. NBC did use the Goodyear blimp for shots from the sky at the Rose Bowl in Pasadena, California in 1955, but it did not become a sports staple until the 1960s. And as the decade began, virtually all sports viewing was done in black and white. In 1960, less than 10 percent of American homes had a color television. One of the first major live sports events broadcast in color was the 1962 Rose Bowl in Pasadena, California, on NBC, which undoubtedly helped stimulate sales of color sets. However, no network committed to full-time color broadcast transmissions until November of 1966 when NBC set that precedent, introducing each of its programs "in living color" with a brief animation of the network's peacock logo that had multicolored paintbrushes for tail feathers. By the end of the decade, 75 percent of American homes had at least one color television set, a trend that had also taken hold in most developed nations around the world.

DOI: 10.4324/9781003165590-3

A NEW FOOTBALL LEAGUE

A process that would dramatically change the sports industry and how Americans watched televised sports was set in motion on December 28, 1958, in a hotel room in Houston, Texas. It would include a band of wealthy investors who called themselves "The Foolish Club," a clandestine meeting in an airport parking lot, political horse-trading on Capitol Hill, and a TV producer covered in bird poop. It would culminate in the creation of the most-watched single-day sporting event in the history of the world, the Super Bowl.

In that Houston hotel room, a 26-year-old man who a few years earlier had been a backup receiver for the Southern Methodist University football team sat watching the Baltimore Colts defeat the New York Giants in overtime for the NFL Championship. Lamar Hunt had traveled to Houston from his native Dallas to attend the Southwest Conference Holiday Basketball Tournament. Hunt, the son of oil billionaire H.L. Hunt, had spent a good deal of his time in 1958 exploring how he could establish the first professional baseball or football team in Texas.

After watching "The Greatest Game Ever Played" on that black and white hotel room TV, Hunt realized that his mind was made up. "My interest emotionally was always more in football," he said, "but clearly the '58 Colts vs. Giants game, sort of in my mind made me say, 'Well that's it. This sport has everything, and it televises well.'" Lamar Hunt had a good sense of how important "televising well" would be for any sport in the years to come.

In the spring of 1958, Hunt had contacted National Football League Commissioner Bert Bell and told him that he was interested in bringing an NFL franchise to Dallas. The NFL was a 12-team league with no teams in either the American Southeast or Southwest. Bell explained to Hunt that his owners were not interested in expanding beyond that number until they could sort out the situation in Chicago where the league had two teams, the Bears and the Cardinals. The problem was that the Cardinals were perennial losers on the field (they averaged eight losses per 12-game season for the decade of the 1950s) and at the gate they lagged far behind the crosstown Chicago Bears. Bell suggested that Hunt contact the Cardinals' owners, Walter Wolfner and his wife, Violet Bidwill Wolfner, to see if they might be interested in selling the team to Hunt who would then be granted league approval to move it to Dallas.

Violet Bidwill had inherited the Cardinals in 1947 upon the death of her father, Charles Bidwill. She married Wolfner, a St. Louis businessman, in 1949. Hunt talked with the Wolfners several times in 1958, but nothing substantive ever developed. The Wolfners did eventually give up their battle with George Halas and his Chicago Bears for the hearts and wallets of

Chicagoans, but not until two years after Hunt had made his offer to buy the team. The Cardinals moved to Walter Wolfner's hometown of St. Louis in 1960 and subsequently left St. Louis in 1988 to play in Arizona. Team ownership remained in the Bidwill family throughout.

Hunt set up one last meeting with Walter Wolfner in February 1959, hoping against hope that he could convince him to sell the Cardinals. The meeting was in Florida where the Wolfners had a winter home. The surroundings may have been sunnier than Chicago, but for Hunt, the result was the same: Walter Wolfner said he would not sell the team. In fact, he boasted to Hunt that several other wealthy investors including Kenneth "Bud" Adams from Houston had approached him about selling the Cardinals, but that he had refused them all. Hunt said that he thanked Wolfner for his time and headed for the Miami airport.

On his flight back to Dallas Hunt said, "A light bulb came on!" If there were all these investors who wanted to buy an NFL team for their home cities but who had been turned down, why not contact each of them and together start a new football league with all new teams? Hunt said that he asked a flight attendant for some paper, and before the plane landed in Dallas, he had sketched out a document on three pages of American Airlines stationery that he called "Original 6 and First Year's Operations." It is the plan that would launch the American Football League. Hunt, the son of a billionaire with millions to spend on a professional football team, was not in the first-class cabin. He was flying in coach.

Hunt took his time to polish the plans, then started calling the list of investors that he referred to as his "Original 6." He told them that if they could not get NFL franchises, they should consider forming a new league with him. He convinced Bud Adams and four others to join him in what Hunt called "The Foolish Club," foolish for going up against the long-established NFL which had new momentum following the success of its 1958 championship game. The six original cities for Hunt's new league would be Dallas, where Hunt would finally get his professional team, Houston, Denver, Los Angeles, New York, and Minneapolis. Only two of these cities had NFL franchises at the time, Los Angeles and New York. The owner of the new Los Angeles team would be Barron Hilton of the Hilton Hotel chain who named his team the "Chargers" in part because Hilton also owned the Carte Blanche charge card company. The Chargers played just one season in Los Angeles before moving to San Diego in 1961. (They returned to Los Angeles at the beginning of the 2017 season.)

A week after the Chicago meeting, the "Original 6" christened their new venture the American Football League. Ralph Wilson of Detroit was granted the league's seventh franchise on October 28, 1959, for the Buffalo Bills. (Wilson had hoped to set up his team in Miami, but he was unable to negotiate a deal to play at the Orange Bowl.) William Sullivan of Boston became the league's eighth owner on November 22, 1958, the date of the

AFL's first player draft. The draft went 33 rounds and was held in secret. Each of the eight teams got one territorial pick for a top college player from their region who could be used as a draw to help sell tickets, plus 32 other selections who they would attempt to sign.

When the NFL saw how serious Hunt was about his plans for a rival league, they did offer him an expansion franchise for Dallas in late 1959. However, by that time Hunt said he had "sunk too much money into this," and had made too many commitments to his fellow "Foolish Club" owners to consider accepting an NFL offer. The NFL responded by granting their Dallas franchise to Clint Murchison and Bedford Wynne, who founded the Cowboys' franchise that would begin play in the fall of 1960 and compete directly against Lamar Hunt's Dallas Texans.

The NFL couldn't derail Hunt from moving ahead with the American Football League, but the league did entice the AFL ownership group from Minneapolis to take an NFL franchise instead. On January 27, 1960, they backed out of the AFL and one day later at the NFL owners' meeting in Miami were granted their charter as the Minnesota Vikings. It didn't take the AFL long to find a replacement to keep the league at eight teams: on January 30, 1959, a group from Oakland, California, headed by local businessman Y. Charles "Chet" Soda signed up. The team would be called the "Oakland Señors," which had been the number one choice in a local newspaper readers' poll. The name lasted three weeks and was dropped in favor of "Raiders," which had come in third in the poll.

Perhaps the single most important factor in making the AFL's inaugural season in 1960 a reality was the agreement the new league signed with the ABC television network on June 9, 1960. The contract was for five years of weekly live games beginning that September, plus the AFL Championship Game and an AFL All-Star game. ABC agreed to pay a total of $8.5 million over five years to the AFL, which divided the revenue equally among its eight clubs in accordance with a revenue sharing concept that Hunt began considering after a meeting in 1958 with former Dodgers' president and general manager Branch Rickey. At the meeting, which was to begin planning for the launch of a third professional baseball league, former Cleveland Indians owner Bill Veeck had recommended that any new league should pool all its earnings, including all television rights payments, and divide the revenue equally among its clubs to keep them all profitable.

The five-year contract would pay the AFL $1.7 million per year. Divided eight ways each team got $212,500 per season, enough when combined with ticket sales and other revenue to put the AFL on a course toward solvency in its first year. Hunt and the AFL owners had retained attorney Jay Michaels from the MCA talent agency to negotiate with ABC on their behalf. (Decades later Jay Michaels' son, Al Michaels would become one of the foremost play-by-play television voices on NFL games with a career spanning more than 40 years.)

The AFL contract with ABC was historic in that it was the first between an American television network and a professional football league for a full season or more of games. Until then, each NFL team had negotiated its own regular season local and regional television packages, some in concert with one or two other teams. The National Football League was born in the 1920s when radio was just getting started and television did not exist. As local TV stations sprang up in the 1940s, they negotiated contracts with teams in their area and based the price of television rights on the number of viewers each station could reach with commercial messages on behalf of their paid advertisers. As a result, there was a huge disparity in total earnings between the large-market teams and those in smaller cities. The New York Giants could charge $350,000 per year for their television broadcast rights, 10 times the $35,000 that the Green Bay Packers were collecting in the league's smallest market.

Alvin "Pete" Rozelle had been hired as commissioner by the NFL owners in January of 1960, three months after Bert Bell's death. Rozelle was the Los Angeles Rams' 33-year-old general manager when he was selected to lead the league. One of his first and most important tasks was to convince his new bosses that they should follow the example of the upstart AFL and share their television revenues. "He said that for the strength of the league, they had to share the money equally or the league would go to hell," remembered Jim Kensil, who was one of Rozelle's aides in 1961. Rozelle succeeded in convincing the NFL owners, but it was a hard pill to swallow for those who were making the most money in the biggest cities.

One year after the American Football League's groundbreaking agreement with ABC, Rozelle signed a two-year, $9.3 million contract with CBS that would share television revenues equally among the 14 NFL franchises. (The league had grown from 12 to 14 teams with the addition of the Dallas Cowboys in 1960 and the Minnesota Vikings in 1961.) However, that contract, which would have taken effect for the 1962 season, was nullified by United States District Court Judge Allan K. Grim who found it in violation of the Sherman Antitrust Act. The league had sought Judge Grim's opinion based on his experience as the presiding judge in the 1953 *United States v. National Football League* case that dealt with television blackout policies, which the federal government contended were illegal under the Sherman Antitrust Act. In his decision dated July 20, 1961, Judge Grim ruled that the same was true for the contract between the NFL and CBS. He found that the contract was the product of an agreement among the NFL clubs to eliminate economic competition among themselves for the sale of television rights to home games. Since the contract gave CBS the sole right and discretion to determine which games would be telecast and where, the rights the individual clubs had to decide which of their games could be aired were abridged. Judge Grim concluded, "I am therefore obliged to construe the Final Judgment as prohibiting the execution and performance of [this] contract." He told the NFL that for a contract with

CBS to be acceptable in the courts, the league would need Congress to approve an exemption from the Sherman Antitrust Act to cover all television rights agreements. Pete Rozelle quickly mounted a concerted effort to lobby Congress for that exemption.

The Sports Broadcasting Act of 1961

Backed by the considerable political clout of his powerful team owners and with some advice from his old University of San Francisco college friend Pierre Salinger, who was working in The White House as President John F. Kennedy's press secretary, Rozelle's mission in Washington proved successful. Less than three months after he started his lobbying efforts, both the House and Senate had approved Public Law 87-331 and sent it to President Kennedy for his signature in September of 1961. The Sports Broadcasting Act of 1961, as it came to be known, exempted any professional football, baseball, basketball, or hockey league in the United States from antitrust regulation in any contracts made for the "sponsored telecasting" of their games.

This broad exemption covering multiple sports made possible the nationwide broadcasting of sports that has been the norm for more than half a century. Professional sports teams and leagues in America have the Sports Broadcasting Act to thank for helping them become national brands with fan bases in the millions. Viewers across the country have become accustomed to tuning in games played at venues hundreds or thousands of miles away between distant teams with nationally known reputations and stars. Had Congress not acted to in effect change sports from a regional television product into a national one, the leagues, teams, and players all would be earning a fraction of the incomes they now receive. And teams in smaller cities that could never have made enough money to compete with big city franchises for top players and coaches, instead survived without being forced to move or fold. The legendary coach Vince Lombardi said that the Sports Broadcasting Act "probably saved football in Green Bay."

Additional sections of and amendments to the Sports Broadcasting Act of 1961 allowed professional leagues to "black out" television broadcasts in the home markets of their teams, addressing the fears of team owners who thought people would choose to sit home and watch games on television instead of buying tickets. The Act also states that any professional football league choosing to televise its games on Friday nights or Saturdays in competition with high school or college football during those seasons would lose the antitrust exemption.

After the new law was enacted, the NFL and CBS renegotiated the two-year rights contract that had been nullified, making it a three-year agreement. CBS paid the NFL just over $5 million for the rights to nationally televise games in the 1962 season. That figure swelled to more than $15 million for the 1964 season, which was the third year of the deal. In 1966, the Sports Broadcasting Act was amended to also cover the mergers of two or more professional football leagues provided that the combination of their operations would increase and not decrease the total number of clubs operating. That amendment helped pave the way for the merger of the NFL and AFL which made the Super Bowl possible. In a *New York Times* article following Rozelle's death in 1996, former Cleveland Browns owner Art Modell said, "Congress sanctioning the single network deal is the most significant thing Pete ever did."

THE AFL ON ABC

The American Football League proved to be an innovator in more ways than simply how they structured their television contracts. "We were selling excitement and entertainment," said league founder Lamar Hunt, "we had to be different. We couldn't afford to be dull." From its very first game September 9, 1960, the league set out to differentiate itself from the NFL. The Denver Broncos defeated the Boston Patriots 13-10 that Friday night before an announced crowd of 27,597 at Boston University's Nickerson Field. The game was not televised. ABC would begin its innovative coverage of the AFL two days later, on Sunday, September 11, 1960.

Beginning with its first season, the AFL incorporated the two-point conversion as an option after touchdowns. (The NFL did not add this element of drama to its games until 1994.) The AFL teams also put players' names on the backs of jerseys to help fans identify who was carrying the ball or who had just made a tackle without having to consult a printed program. And perhaps more important than any innovation or rules change, the AFL opened its arms to talented African American players in far greater numbers than the NFL teams of the era had done up to that point. This helped create what sportswriters of the day described as a "wide open" style of play that favored speed and athleticism, which, in turn, made for a more exciting television product.

Beginning with its first telecast, ABC, in concert with the league, developed its own style of "AFL coverage" that emphasized excitement and entertainment. The network pioneered new camera locations to show viewers at home angles they had never seen before, and new audio configurations with shotgun microphones that brought the audience closer to the action. To deal with poor attendance in the early years, AFL teams would group their fans around the 50-yard line to give the appearance of a reasonably full house to viewers at home who would not see too many empty seats. Nothing makes a sporting event on television look less important than empty seats and meager attendance, which unfortunately was the case for virtually every televised event during the COVID-19 pandemic.

ABC's "AFL coverage" helped avoid this problem by eliminating as many wide shots of the stadium from their telecasts as possible. Watch a recording of any early AFL telecast and you will see that the cameras focused on the field and the players, and little else. On a kickoff, ABC would show the kicker, then once the ball was kicked out of frame, the shot would cut to the kick returner and wait for the ball to come back into view as he caught it and began to run. In that way, ABC avoided panning with the flight of the ball across what would have been a background of sparsely occupied seats on the far side of the field.

Roone Arledge was a producer at ABC Sports and the chief architect of the "AFL coverage." In his autobiography *Roone* he said, "we also set out to make our stars familiar to our viewers. When for example wide receiver Don Maynard of the New York Titans caught a pass, his name, position and stats would appear immediately on the screen." For decades since, television sports viewers have grown accustomed to these "hero graphics" providing statistical or personal information about players who have just stepped into the spotlight.

When Lamar Hunt had first approached the television networks about a rights deal for his brand-new league, NBC and CBS both declined. In 1960, ABC was a distant third in every category from ratings to profits, so the opportunity to televise live professional football was more attractive to their leadership than it may have been to the other two national television networks. The efforts and innovations that Roone Arledge and his fellow producers and directors poured into the telecasts, and those that Lamar Hunt and the league developed to create an entertaining product on the field, combined to turn the AFL into a valuable broadcast product in just a few short years.

It did not take long for NBC, which had no live professional football programming at the time, to recognize that value. In January of 1964, NBC negotiated a new five-year $36 million contract with the American Football League which would quadruple the AFL's television revenue when it was scheduled to take effect in the fall of 1965. The $36 million divided eight ways would yield $4.5 million per team over the life of the contract, just under a million dollars each per year. If ABC had fulfilled the final year of its AFL deal and televised the 1964–65 season, the network would have been in a "lame duck" position, its telecasts promoting and building the AFL's teams and stars to the increased benefit of NBC. ABC executives saw no reason to add value and audience to what would become a competitor's programming property the following season, so they ceded their AFL rights for the 1964–65 season to NBC and saved paying $1.7 million for the final year of their original five-year, $8.5 million contract.

After NBC, with its stronger local affiliate stations and higher-rated programming lineup, started airing AFL games on Sundays in 1964 the audience grew. The NFL on CBS was still the leader by far in ratings and sponsorship, but Lamar Hunt's upstart league was making an impact, especially as it built star power with the signing of big-name college stars like Joe Namath. Namath was the highly successful quarterback from the University of Alabama who was the overall number one pick in the 1965 AFL draft. He was nicknamed "the $400,000 quarterback" after the New York Jets signed him to what at the time was the richest rookie contract ever in pro football history. In the NFL Draft that year, Namath was selected 12th by Walter Wolfner's St. Louis Cardinals. The size of the Jets' three-year contract offer, which included a $100,000 signing bonus and the opportunity to play in the nation's media capital, made Namath's choice of team a foregone conclusion. In New York, "Broadway Joe" became an important pillar of the AFL's success in the 1960s and 1970s.

THE OLYMPICS COME TO AMERICAN TELEVISION

The Olympics have become such an overwhelming and powerful television presence in the past several decades that it may seem hard to believe that the Games were not televised in the United States until 1960. The Winter Olympics were staged in Squaw Valley, California, that year, and ABC signed a contract with the organizers to purchase the US television rights for $50,000. But ABC backed out of the deal choosing not to spend the additional money it would cost to produce coverage from a remote ski resort and transport the programs from there to San Francisco where they would be broadcast onto the network. (The ski resort was renamed "Palisades Tahoe" in 2021).

CBS chairman William S. Paley stepped in to replace ABC as the American broadcaster at the request of an old friend, Walt Disney. The Squaw Valley Olympic organizers had hired Disney to produce the opening ceremony and provide entertainment for the event. They also sought his company's help with ticketing, parking, and security, based on the expertise that Disney had gained operating Disneyland since 1955.

CBS made history when it agreed to present 13 hours of coverage from Thursday, February 18 through Sunday, February 28, 1960, the first Olympic coverage ever on American television. The first show was a half-hour recording of the Disney-produced opening ceremonies, and each weeknight at 11:15 pm Eastern time CBS broadcast 15 minutes of edited highlights from that day's competitions. CBS was live for only one to three hours per weekend day and for the women's figure skating finals on Tuesday evening February 23. All the shows were hosted by Walter Cronkite, the CBS News reporter who was still two years away from being named anchorman of the *CBS Evening News with Walter Cronkite*, a position he held until 1981, becoming known during his tenure as "the most trusted man in America." One of the reporters CBS assigned to join Cronkite was Jim McKay, who would join ABC the following year and become the face of Olympics telecasts in the United States for a generation. They were joined at Squaw Valley by Harry Reasoner, who was one of the original hosts of *60 Minutes* when it debuted on CBS in 1968, and Olympic figure skating champion Dick Button, the winner of gold medals in the 1948 and 1952 games. Button served as an Olympic television commentator until age 80, when he did NBC's analysis of figure skating at the 2010 Winter Games in Vancouver, British Columbia.

The 14 shows that CBS broadcast from Squaw Valley in February of 1960 were enough to whet the appetite of American viewers for Olympic coverage and to open the network's eyes to the Olympics as a new source for compelling programming. The great potential for the success of the Olympics on television was hinted at by *The New York Times*, which wrote on February 21, 1960, that spectators at Squaw Valley had a "more dramatic over-all view of the ski jumping" than anyone watching on television but that "the slalom provided more effective close-ups on the screen than were available to the crowds lining the slopes." "More effective close-ups" of American and international athletes in action spoke to the ability of television to tell stories and bring pictures into your home that would be otherwise inaccessible.

Encouraged by how well their shows from Squaw Valley had been received, CBS paid $394,000 for the rights to televise the Summer Olympics from Rome later that year in August and September. That was nearly eight times the $50,000 price paid for the 1960 Winter Olympic rights, but CBS was rewarded with plenty of remarkable stories to tell that attracted American audiences. Wilma Rudolph, a polio victim at an early age and the 20th child in a family of 22 from Tennessee, won three gold medals in the 100 meters, 200 meters, and 4×100 meters relay; Cassius Clay, who would go on to win the world heavyweight boxing championship as Muhammad Ali, was 18 years old when he won the gold medal in Rome in the light-heavyweight division; American Rafer Johnson won the Olympic decathlon in the 1960 Games, and the American men's basketball team led by Oscar Robertson, Jerry West, and Jerry Lucas crushed the competition and won gold.

CBS programmed 20 hours of Olympic coverage from Rome, all of it hosted by Jim McKay from New York, not from the Italian capital. A CBS crew of approximately 40 was in Rome producing the events and recording them onto videotapes that were flown out every night to Idlewild Airport (now JFK International), where a messenger would pick them up and deliver them still cold from the plane's cargo hold to Grand Central Station. In a CBS studio set up there at the train station, McKay wrote his leads and recorded the show opens, bridges, and closes needed to assemble each evening's telecast. No shows from the Rome Olympics were live because there were no commercial communications satellites orbiting the Earth in 1960.

One sports fan who was enthralled watching the Olympic programs in 1960 was 28-year-old Roone Arledge. Arledge, who went on to become president of ABC Sports and then ABC News, had not yet been hired for his first job at ABC. Watching the CBS shows from Squaw Valley, Arledge said in his autobiography *Roone* that there was "a magic in seeing the divided world come together in sport." He said he took particular note of the figure skating competition with its "spotlight on single performers, the limited time spans, and the suspense of waiting for the judge's decisions," which convinced him that figure skating was a "made-for-television event."

Roone Arledge was producing the Shari Lewis puppet show on the local New York NBC station when he was hired by Ed Scherick at Sports Programs, Inc. to work on the new NCAA football package that Scherick was producing for ABC in 1960. One year later, Scherick sold his company to ABC, bringing Arledge with him along with Chester R. "Chet" Simmons, a colleague since the founding of the company in 1957. When the small Sports Programs Inc. group became ABC Sports, Scherick was rewarded with an appointment as ABC's vice president of sales and Simmons became the first executive producer of the new ABC Sports. Later in his career, Chet Simmons became president of ESPN for the network's first three years, then was the first commissioner of the short-lived United States Football League (the USFL).

Arledge was convinced that ABC had to get into the Olympics business to secure the future of its fledgling sports division. In 1962, he and Simmons convinced ABC's vice president of programming, Tom Moore, that they should bid for the 1964 Winter Olympics in Innsbruck, Austria. Together, Arledge and Simmons boarded a plane for Austria and returned with a broadcast rights contract for $500,000, which the Austrians insisted had to be secured with a bank guarantee because ABC had backed out of its 1960 Winter Olympic agreement. When ABC's board of directors approved the deal, they opened the doors that would make ABC the "network of the Olympics" from 1964 until 1988. During that stretch, ABC Sports televised six Winter Games and four Summer Olympics, concluding with 94.5 hours of coverage from the 1988 Winter Olympics at Calgary for which the network paid $309 million in broadcast rights.

Beginning with the 1988 Summer Games in Seoul, South Korea, NBC assumed the Olympic mantel and has since guaranteed its exclusivity by paying a total of $12 billion for the television, online, and mobile rights to each of the Winter and Summer Games from the year 2014 through 2032. That is an average of more than $1 billion per Olympiad. Compare that with the $444,000 that CBS paid for both the Winter and Summer Games in 1960, and the overwhelming growth in the power and value of the Olympics as television programming is self-evident.

The 1964 Olympic Summer Games in Tokyo marked a major turning point for all of sports television. It was the first major sporting event carried live via satellite around the world. Less than two months before the Tokyo

Games' opening ceremony on October 10, 1964, NASA had launched the SYNCOM 3 communications satellite that was built by Hughes Aircraft. It was the first ever to be placed into a geosynchronous orbit, which meant that it would orbit the Earth at a position 22,300 miles above the Equator once per day, keeping pace with the Earth rotating below. As a fixed point in the sky, the satellite could relay television signals continuously from Japan or from any uplink in Asia to receiving stations on the West Coast of the United States for re-transmission and broadcast. The transmission process worked the same in the reverse direction from North America to Asia. One year later in 1965, Intelsat 1, nicknamed Early Bird, was placed in geosynchronous orbit over the Atlantic Ocean, making live television and telephone communications possible between North America and Europe. Also built by Hughes Aircraft technology, Early Bird was used to transmit ABC's live coverage of the 1968 Olympic Winter Games from Grenoble, France.

Once television audiences in the United States and around the world could watch the Olympics all together at the same time, the nature and magnitude of the event changed. It became an international spectacle of competition, sportsmanship, entertainment, and politics with a vast revenue stream from world television and sponsorship rights. Because of the billions of viewers it reached, the Olympics became a platform from which messages, official and unofficial, could be delivered instantaneously to people in every corner of the world. It would never again be a simple gathering of athletes from a relatively small number of nations whose sole purpose was athletic competition.

ABC'S WIDE WORLD OF SPORTS

International sports events would become the backbone of a new series that ABC launched in 1961 as a 20-week summer fill-in show. Over the next four decades, *ABC's Wide World of Sports* would introduce Americans to the World Cup soccer final, the Indianapolis 500, the Daytona 500, British Open golf, the 24 Hours of Le Mans, and the Iditarod Sled Dog Race in Alaska, as well as international figure skating championships, gymnastics, track and field, and world championship boxing events. In its run, which ended in 1998, the series did 4,967 events in over 100 different sports from 53 countries and 46 American states.

Ed Scherick, who launched ABC Sports, had the idea to do a series with a unique flavor that would feature a myriad of events from around the world, lesser-known and unfamiliar athletic competitions far beyond the realm of football, baseball, basketball, and hockey. ABC needed programming to help fill its 1961 summer schedule. In the fall the NCAA football package filled Saturday afternoons on ABC, and the new AFL games were the anchor on Sundays in the fall, but the only sports that the network had after football season were *Saturday Night Fights*, a bowling series called *Make*

That Spare, and a Dodgers and Giants baseball package. Scherick put his concept for a global sports variety series into Roone Arledge's hands, and he ran with it.

When Arledge was producing the puppet show for the local NBC television station he had learned that NBC's corporate library had an archive of *The New York Times* on microfilm. His idea was to go through the archive to find all the obscure sporting events for which the *Times* had reported results but that were not being televised in the United States. Arledge was then a full-time ABC producer, so he feared that he might be recognized if he visited his former employers to paw through the archives. Instead, he sent his young production assistant Chuck Howard over to NBC's 30 Rockefeller Plaza headquarters to scan through the microfilm. Within 48 hours he had Howard's list, a "compendium of worldwide sporting events" with their dates and locales.

With the mantra "if something is visually exciting, let's try it," Arledge set off on a quest for the television rights to everything from baton twirling to Irish hurling. One of his first stops near the end of 1960 was just a few blocks away in Manhattan at the New York Athletic Club, where the Amateur Athletic Union (AAU) was holding its annual meeting. For a small upfront fee and a guarantee of $50,000 after the new series debuted, Arledge bought the exclusive US rights to televise every AAU competition to be held in 1961, including the United States vs. the Soviet Union track and field meet scheduled for July in Moscow.

The premiere of *ABC's Wide World of Sports* on Saturday afternoon April 29, 1961, combined live coverage of two AAU track and field events: the Penn Relays in Philadelphia and the Drake Relays from Des Moines, Iowa. Making his ABC debut as the host at the Penn Relays was Jim McKay, whom Arledge had hired away from CBS for a $1,000 fee per episode. The show was going to be called *ABC's World of Sports*, but six days before its premiere, "Wide" was added to the title. "Wide" certainly did not describe its audience in the first several weeks on the air in May and June of 1961. The show did not attract very many viewers and was in jeopardy of being canceled. But the event that helped the series turn the corner was that United States-Soviet track and field competition from Moscow in late July that was part of the AAU package Roone Arledge had negotiated several months earlier.

In 1961, the Cold War between the United States and the Soviet Union was at its height. An American U2 high-altitude spy plane had been shot down in Russian air space in May of 1960, and its pilot Francis Gary Powers was being held prisoner in the USSR. At the United Nations General Assembly in New York in October of 1960, Soviet Premier Nikita Krushchev had taken off his shoe and pounded it on the lectern shouting, "we will bury you!" The Berlin Wall was completed in 1961 making it the starkest example of the "Iron Curtain," the heavily guarded border that separated eastern European countries under Soviet military control from the republics and democracies of western Europe. The very fact that American athletes could go "behind the Iron Curtain" to compete in Moscow was international news, and the ability to see them in the Soviet capital, to get a rare glimpse into what clearly was considered "enemy territory" attracted attention in the United States among sports fans and average citizens to the coverage on *ABC's Wide World of Sports*.

When ABC's team of 25 producers and technicians arrived in Moscow with their 20 tons of television equipment, however, they found that the AAU had apparently not properly informed the Soviet organizers that an American network would be televising the event back to the states. Arledge credits the political and sports connections of their Russian guide Roman Kislev for working out the agreement that allowed the broadcast to proceed.

The critical and ratings success of this United States vs. Soviet event convinced ABC to renew *Wide World* for a full 52-week season in 1962. When the new season debuted, the show came on the air with an introduction that captured its essential mission and has been remembered by generations of viewers: "Spanning the globe to bring you the constant variety of sport. The thrill of victory and the agony of defeat. This is *ABC's Wide World of Sports*." Roone Arledge said he wrote the script on a flight back to New York from an assignment in London in late 1961. It replaced the original show open which wasn't nearly as poetic or gender-neutral: "Sports, in its unending variety, unfolds on *ABC's Wide World of Sports*. Capturing the sight and sound, the emotion, the beauty and history-making achievements, wherever men gather to compete in this great wide world of athletics."

Over the course of its 38 years on the air, the "constant variety" of *Wide World* included sumo wrestling, figure-eight stock car racing, demolition derbies, the Cheyenne Frontier Days Rodeo, barrel-jumping ice skaters, and a favorite that became a hallmark of the series, the Acapulco Cliff Diving competition. Roone Arledge said that he first heard about this event when he and Jim McKay were in Mexico in 1961 to cover a tennis event. Arledge met with the promoter of the cliff diving who said he would sell the US television rights to ABC for $100,000. That figure was double what had been paid in 1960 for the rights to the entire Winter Olympics, so Arledge flew home to New York.

McKay stayed behind to complete the tennis show, and a few days later he called Arledge to say, "We got the cliff diving." McKay explained that he had gone directly to the divers themselves, and they had agreed to appear on TV for $10 per dive. There were countless other milestones along the way in the 38 years of *ABC's Wide World of Sports* including:

- The first underwater camera in the pool for a swimming event at the 1961 National AAU Swimming and Diving Championships.

- The first European sports event ever televised live via satellite to the United States, the 24-Hour Grand Prix of Endurance from Le Mans, France in 1965.
- The first live boxing championship from Europe, which featured Muhammad Ali defending his world heavyweight title against Britain's Henry Cooper from London in 1966.
- The first sports coverage from Cuba since Fidel Castro's takeover 12 years earlier, the United States vs. Cuba volleyball matches from Havana in 1971.
- The "ping pong diplomacy" table tennis matches from Beijing, China in 1971 that became a hallmark of then-President Richard Nixon's efforts to open avenues of communication and trade between the United States and China.

The impact that *ABC's Wide World of Sports* made on American television cannot be underestimated. For millions who only knew the major sports, it broadened horizons, interests, and appetites. It helped increase awareness and awaken curiosity about what people in different states and different countries did for competition and entertainment. One of the universal truths that have made sport popular across the generations is that people care about other people. And *Wide World* emphasized the personalities of the individual athletes in each event. The personal stories and interviews that Roone Arledge developed for *Wide World* came to be known as "Up Close and Personal," which has been an important thread in the coverage of the Olympics and many other sports telecasts ever since.

THE FIRST INSTANT REPLAY

The defining technology of sports on television today is arguably "instant replay." We count on replays from multiple angles to immediately tell us if a receiver was in or out of bounds, if an outfielder made the catch or trapped the ball, which sprinter crossed the finish line first, or what caused a massive wreck in an auto race. Replays settle arguments and start new ones. They are an inextricable fixture in every broadcast of every sport. But not one event that aired on American television from 1939 until the end of 1963 ever included a single instant replay. Zero replays in 24 years of sports broadcasts.

Videotape machines that recorded moving pictures and sound onto magnetic tape made replays possible, but the first machines introduced by the Ampex Corporation in 1956 had serious limitations. For example, you could play a tape back only on the machine that had recorded it. At first, videotapes were not interchangeable because different machines had incompatible speeds and their recording and playback apparatus were not perfectly matched. To play any video back on the two-inch-wide tapes, these massive machines required a 10-second "pre-roll" for the pictures and audio to synchronize. Made up of two huge pieces the size of a large freezer and weighing 1,200 pounds, the machines were anything but portable, making their use anywhere other than in a studio control room all but impossible.

The first time a taped replay was used in an American sports telecast was on November 25, 1961, during halftime of the Syracuse vs. Boston College football game, which was part of ABC's new live NCAA football package. A highlight from the first half was played back during the halftime studio report from an ABC control room in New York. Roone Arledge said that when he saw that video excerpt, even though it was primitive, "you could see the future."

Credit for the first instant replay during a live event goes to Tony Verna who was the director of the Army-Navy football game on CBS December 7, 1963. Verna had been a freelancer on the CBS crew that produced the 1960 Summer Olympics from Rome, and it was there that the seed of his idea was first sown. In his book *Instant Replay: The Day that Changed Sports Forever*, Verna explained how he learned how to use the second audio track on the tapes being recorded in Rome to leave cues for the technicians and producers in New York who would be receiving each day's coverage by airplane overnight. Only one track of audio was played back for broadcasts, so no one at home would hear Verna's audio cues on track two. His goal was to make it easier for the New York crew to find the right scenes and edit the shows for air. Today that would be accomplished using digital time-code readers, but the early videotape machines only had mechanical tape counters that would not match the recording machines in Rome.

Just three years later at age 29, Verna was directing college football for CBS and was searching for a way to make the games more interesting for the viewer at home during the 30–60 seconds of inaction between plays. He convinced his bosses to let him put one of the 14 videotape machines that CBS had in its New York control room onto a train to Philadelphia for the game at Franklin Field. His idea was to have the tape operator in his truck put one audio tone on the second audio channel (which could be heard only in the TV truck), when the team with the ball went into its huddle, and two quick tones on the tape when they broke the huddle. Verna figured that when he heard the two tones on playback there would be approximately 10 seconds before the ball was snapped. To replay a touchdown or pass completion in the broadcast he would need those 10 seconds of pre-roll for the videotape to synchronize.

Tony Verna told producer Bill Creasy about his plan on the train ride to Philadelphia. The Army-Navy game had increased significance that season: a special tribute to President John F. Kennedy was being produced as part of the day's coverage. The president had planned to attend the traditional rivalry game between the service academies, but he was assassinated in Dallas on November 22, 1963. The Army-Navy rivalry game had been postponed until the first week of December out of respect for the fallen president.

The play-by-play commentator assigned to the game, Lindsey Nelson, said that he didn't hear about Verna's replay idea until they were in a cab together on the way to the stadium. Verna says Nelson's first reaction upon hearing the plan was, "What? You're going to do what?" It would be Nelson's job to explain what the audience was seeing for the very first time, helping them comprehend that the same team had not scored again on the very next play.

Verna was not surprised that the CBS technicians in New York had shipped him the least reliable of their 14 videotape machines, but he was troubled by the quality of the only reel of two-inch magnetic tape they sent. It had 5-4-3-2-1 film style "leaders" physically spliced into it for *I Love Lucy* shows and lots of Duz detergent commercials. Apparently at $300 per reel, CBS was unwilling to give their young college football director a new tape.

During the game, Verna had cameras keyed on the Navy quarterback, Roger Staubach, who was an All-America and destined for a hall of fame career in the NFL. But Staubach didn't have a very good game, and the technicians in the CBS truck were having so many problems with the tape machine and the used tape that it was impossible to get a replay cued up to play back in the live telecast. Finally, in the fourth quarter, Army's quarterback Rollie Stichweh ran off tackle for a touchdown, and Verna told his play-by-play commentator, "Lindsey we've got it. Go!" The truck cut to the black and white replay in real time, not slow motion, and Nelson said, "This is not live, ladies and gentlemen, Army did not score again!"

That was the only replay they could manage in the entire game, but Verna and his team had changed sports television. A month later he was directing the 1964 Cotton Bowl from Dallas, Texas, and his lead commentator was Pat Summerall, the former New York Giants placekicker who was on his first play-by-play assignment. During that Cotton Bowl telecast on CBS Summerall coined the term, "instant replay." No sports telecast has been the same since.

BIBLIOGRAPHY

Arledge, Roone. *Roone: A Memoir*. New York, NY: HarperCollins Publishers, 2003.

Associated Press. "Big Dollars and a Big Dream." *The New York Times*, 2009. https://www.nytimes.com/2009/08/30/sports/football/30afl.html

Becker, John. "Why Oakland Team Changed from Señors to Raiders." *The Mercury News*, 2020. https://www.mercurynews.com/2020/04/14/on-this -date-april-14-when-oakland-had-to-change-it-was-adios-senors-hello -raiders/

ESPN Press Room. "50th Anniversary of Wide World of Sports Celebrated." 2011. https://espnpressroom.com/us/press-releases/2011/04/50th-anniversary-of -wide-world-of-sports-celebrated/

Garcia, Ahiza. "NBC's $12 billion invest in the Olympics is looking riskier." *CNN Business*, 2018. https://money.cnn.com/2018/02/24/media/nbc -olympics-ratings-12-billion-rights/index.html

MacCambridge, Michael. *America's Game: The Epic Story of How Pro Football Captured a Nation*. New York: Anchor Books, 2005.

Sandomir, Richard. "Rozelle's N.F.L. Legacy: Television, Marketing and Money." *The New York Times*, 1996. https://www.nytimes.com/1996/12/08 /sports/rozelle-s-nfl-legacy-television-marketing-and-money.html

Spence, Jim and Diles, Dave. *Up Close and Personal: The Inside Story of Network Television Sports*. New York, NY: Scribner, 1988.

Verna, Tony. *Instant Replay: The Day That Changed Sports Forever*. Beverly Hills, CA: Creative Book Publishers International, 2008.

Pro Football Was Made for Television

American gridiron football was made for television, even though the game was being played decades before anyone imagined that the transmission of pictures and sound to a box in your house would ever be possible. Football's pattern of intermittent short bursts of action allows time between each play for television commentators to discuss what just happened, and point out who excelled or failed, how a play worked or did not work, what adjustments need to be made, and why the next play is now more or less important. The introduction of instant replays in 1963 was a natural enhancement to fill the gaps between plays with more precise explanations and discussion.

Sports like soccer and hockey provide fans in the stands with a much more continuous flow of action, but they do not provide opportunities for all the replays, analysis, and resets that make football a superior television product. Individual sports such as tennis and golf have pauses between shots, but their ability to draw a large television audience relies to a great degree on the popularity of the players competing in any given match. The team sports on the other hand have built up regional and national followings that start with loyal fans in their home cities and regions then spread across nations and borders with the assistance of the media to dramatize stories of team success and turn standout players into celebrity stars.

Time Magazine called professional football "the sport of the '60s" in a December 1962 article that featured Green Bay Packers' head coach Vince Lombardi on the cover. This proclamation came at the end of the first season of the National Football League's new contract with CBS and after the American Football League had been televised by ABC every weekend in the autumn for three consecutive seasons.

The article was effusive in its praise of professional football.

> Football, as the pros go at it, is a game of special brilliance, played by brilliant specialists. So precise is the teamwork that a single mistake by one man can destroy the handiwork of ten. Action piles upon action, thrill upon guaranteed thrill, and all with such a bewildering speed that

at the end the fans are literally limp. No other sport offers so much to so many. Boxing's heroes are papier-mâché champions, hockey is gang warfare, basketball is for gamblers and Australia is too far to travel to see a decent tennis match. Even baseball, the sportswriters' "national pastime," can be a slow-motion bore.

Professional football was being embraced by millions who watched every Sunday to see teams of "brilliant specialists" meeting in high-stakes struggles filled with drama, intensity, good guys vs. bad guys rivalries, and personal stories of achievement, disappointment, and redemption. The other American sports referred to in the *Time Magazine* article were not at their strongest in the 1960s and did not have the regular national television exposure on two networks that put the NFL and AFL in the spotlight. Boxing would have to wait until 1964 for Muhammad Ali, its most charismatic, vocal, and controversial champion, to spark new interest when he won the world heavyweight championship at age 22. In the years that followed, Ali, Joe Frazier, and George Foreman would prove to be far more than "papier-mâché champions." Bobby Orr and Wayne Gretzky made hockey much more than "gang warfare," but Orr did not play his first NHL game until 1966, and Gretzky debuted 12 years later.

Basketball in the early 1960s was emerging from the college game-fixing scandals of the 1950s, and the NBA had teams in only eight cities, none in the South. New young stars like Wilt Chamberlain, Bill Russell, and Oscar Robertson coupled with the Boston Celtics' string of eight consecutive NBA titles that began in 1959 were helping basketball turn the page. In tennis, Australian men did dominate the late 1950s and 1960s. After Tony Trabert won the US Open in 1955, there was a 13-year stretch before another American man would win that title. That man was Arthur Ashe, and his historic victory in 1968 helped open tennis to a more diverse set of fans and participants. Althea Gibson was the first African American grand slam champion, winning the women's singles at Roland Garros and Wimbledon in both 1957 and 1958 and reaching number one in the world. But those tournaments were not televised live back to the United States, limiting their impact on the public. The first American woman tennis star of the television era was Billie Jean King who won the first of her 12 grand slam singles titles at Wimbledon in 1966, the year that she reached the number one ranking.

Baseball had the biggest names in all of American sport during the 1960s. The 1961 race between New York Yankee teammates Roger Maris and Mickey Mantle to eclipse Babe Ruth's record of 60 home runs in a season had captured the nation's imagination. Willie Mays, Henry Aaron, Duke Snider, Stan Musial, and Sandy Koufax were just a few of the stars who were household names in the 1960s. But NBC's *Game of the Week* was the only national live baseball coverage on television, and it was a single game every Saturday that rotated among all the teams. That meant that you might see one of the big stars one weekend, then not again for several weeks. And on television, the pace and visual impact of baseball could not compare to professional football.

In October 1965, the Harris Poll asked a sampling of Americans "what is your favorite sport?" The most popular answer came back "pro football," knocking baseball from its perennial perch at the top for the first time. Professional football has remained the fans' favorite in every poll since, extending its margin over all other sports. The 1965 Harris Poll signaled a sea change in the passions and preferences of American sports fans which was clearly fueled by two national television networks providing weekly live coverage of "action piling upon action," the "thrill upon guaranteed thrill," and the "bewildering speed" of the NFL and AFL.

CREATING THE BIGGEST MEDIA EVENT IN ALL OF SPORTS

The NFL and the AFL had a tenuous sometimes bitterly contested co-existence during the early 1960s, each league with its own television contract, its own separate draft of collegiate players, and its own growing legion of fans. The AFL antagonized the NFL with a 1960 lawsuit in US District Court that charged the NFL and its team owners with "monopolization, attempted monopolization and conspiracy to monopolize major league professional football." The court found in favor of the NFL in 1962 and dismissed all claims of monopoly or conspiracy. The lawsuit was a costly provocation that angered NFL leaders and left scars that would not heal for years.

The NFL had no intention of helping the AFL succeed, but its TV blackout policy may have inadvertently resulted in AFL games attracting larger audiences. The NFL never televised any games in a metropolitan area on Sundays when the team based there was playing a home game at its stadium. For example, if the Bears were playing at Soldier Field, television viewers in the Chicago area could not watch an Eagles or Rams or any alternate NFL game on that Sunday. The NFL would go dark in Chicago, but if viewers changed the channel, they would find ABC's AFL game of the week. New viewers every week helped the AFL build a national fan base.

The competition between the AFL and the NFL was perhaps most spirited in the two metropolitan areas where each league had a team: New York had the NFL Giants and AFL Jets, and in the San Francisco Bay area, the NFL's 49ers competed for fans and television ratings with the Oakland Raiders of the AFL. The other teams in each league enjoyed pro football exclusivity in their home markets. When the proposal to merge the two leagues was first raised, the issue of in-market competition immediately came to the forefront. One of the preconditions demanded by NFL owners was that the AFL should be forced to move the Jets and Raiders to other cities so that the Giants and 49ers could regain their cherished market exclusivity.

Any hopes that the NFL owners had of forcing AFL franchises to move were dashed by the growing popularity of the Jets and Raiders in their home regions, and in the case of New York, by two other important factors. The Jets moved into the brand-new Shea Stadium in September of 1964, and Jets' owner Sonny Werblin, a noted impresario who had been a talent agent with MCA, signed Joe Namath in 1965. Shea Stadium had five tiers that sat nearly 60,000 fans for football, and at the time was the most modern football stadium in the United States. Namath became such a media sensation in New York that the Giants' ownership admitted that any attempt by them to force the Jets to move would have been met with public outcry and derision.

Namath's three-year $427,000 contract made it clear to owners in both the AFL and NFL that only the richest teams would be able to sign the best players, and that the weaker small-market teams may face the prospect of moving or going out of business. To avoid that fate, secret negotiations began in 1965 between Carroll Rosenbloom, owner of the NFL Baltimore Colts, and Ralph Wilson, the owner of the AFL Buffalo Bills. These talks did not reach a merger agreement because the AFL balked at the NFL's insistence upon market exclusivity and at the price tag the NFL had placed on membership for the eight AFL clubs: a reported $50 million.

Dallas Cowboys' General Manager Tex Schramm knew each team's financial success, if not survival, required that the two professional football leagues merge, although he said years later that he would have liked nothing better at the time than to kill the AFL. He contacted NFL Commissioner Pete Rozelle in the spring of 1966 and said he wanted to work on a merger. Rozelle gave Schramm the green light as long as he kept all meetings secret and that he dealt with only one representative of the rival league.

On April 4, 1966, Schramm called Lamar Hunt, owner of the team that Schramm's Cowboys had driven out of Dallas to Kansas City, and asked if Hunt "might be able to come to Dallas to discuss a matter of mutual importance." Two days later, Hunt got off a plane at Dallas' Love Field and met Schramm at the 12-foot-tall bronze Texas Ranger statue that was a centerpiece in the terminal until its removal in 2020. They walked out to the parking lot and climbed into Schramm's Oldsmobile so they wouldn't be seen together. The two men sat in the car talking for 45 minutes. Hunt recalled Schramm saying, "I think the time has come to talk about a merger if you'd be interested in that." Hunt replied, "Fine, I'm interested." The conditions Schramm laid out that day included admitting all the existing AFL franchises into the NFL with Pete Rozelle as commissioner. The two men agreed to talk again in a few weeks about a more detailed framework for the merger.

On May 3, Schramm got back to Hunt after having discussed the NFL's bargaining position with Rozelle. He told Hunt that the NFL would admit each of the original eight AFL franchises for a fee of $2 million each, plus another $2 million from the expansion Miami Dolphins who were scheduled to begin play in the 1966 season. That came to a total of $18 million. A week later, Hunt responded by telling Schramm that an agreement could be reached.

The friction between the two leagues increased that same week however, when the New York Giants appeared to have violated the unwritten agreement not to poach players from the rival league. The Giants signed Pete Gogolak, the AFL Buffalo Bills' kicker, to a three-year contract. Gogolak had played out his option year with the Bills and was a free agent, which made him fair game in the eyes of the Giants' ownership. News of the trade came out at the NFL owners' meeting on May 16 in Washington, D.C., where many feared a bidding war for players would ensue, costing them each thousands if not millions of dollars. In response, Al Davis, the newly elected AFL Commissioner, immediately drew up a plan to target the NFL's top 10 players. He was sure that the threat of soaring player salaries would now make a merger of the two leagues inevitable.

Schramm called Hunt from the NFL meetings to assure him that despite the outcry over the signing of Gogolak, the merger plans they had discussed were still on track. The NFL owners would be called to a meeting in New York in a few weeks and there the details of the merger proposal would be revealed. At that meeting, only two NFL owners opposed the merger plan: the San Francisco 49ers and the New York Giants, the two teams that were dealing with home market competition from AFL franchises. But they changed their "nays" to "yeas" when the other NFL owners voted to take the $18 million the league would receive in AFL entry fees and give $10 million to the Giants and the remaining $8 million to the 49ers as compensation for the crosstown competition that only they faced.

When Lamar Hunt finally pitched the merger plan to his fellow AFL owners on June 1, 1966, the loudest objections he heard were to the $2 million payment each team would have to make as a condition for joining the NFL. These complaints evaporated when Hunt explained that he had worked out a deal allowing each AFL owner to settle his team's $2 million entry fee by stretching the payments out over 20 years in installments of only $100,000 per year (Figure 4.1).

On June 8, 1966, the following joint statement from the two leagues was released to the public: "The NFL and AFL today announced plans to join in an expanded major professional football league. It will consist of 26 teams in 25 cities – with expectations of additional teams in the near future." The main points of the agreement were listed:

- Pete Rozelle would be the commissioner.
- A world championship game would be played at the end of the 1966 season.

■ **Figure 4.1** From left to right are Tex Schramm, General Manager of the Dallas Cowboys; NFL Commissioner Pete Rozelle; and Lamar Hunt, founder of the American Football League, after announcing in June of 1966 that the NFL and AFL would merge. (Photo credit Getty Images/Bettman Archive)

- All existing franchises would be retained.
- No franchises would transfer to other cities.
- Two new franchises would be added no later than 1968, with two more teams as soon thereafter as practical.
- Inter-league pre-season games would begin in 1967, and there would be a single league schedule starting in 1970.
- A common draft was to be held in January 1967.
- Two-network TV coverage would continue.

Neither CBS nor NBC had been party to the merger discussions. The first they heard about the combination of the two properties was the day the joint statement was made, and neither network was happy. Each had paid for exclusive rights to a league championship game, and those two games would now become virtual semi-finals, less important than the new "world championship game" announced by the two leagues. This new final game was to be played following the regular season that would kick off in September of 1966, only three months hence. It is further testament to Pete Rozelle's skills as commissioner that he managed to get CBS and NBC to pay the NFL an additional $1 million each for the rights to jointly televise the game that would become the first Super Bowl.

HORSE TRADING ON CAPITOL HILL

The only hurdle left for the AFL-NFL merger would be approval from the US Congress. The Sports Broadcasting Act of 1961,which granted an antitrust exemption to professional sports leagues for the negotiation of their broadcast rights, would have to be amended to extend that exemption to also cover the combination of two previously competing leagues. The proposed legislation went to the House Judiciary Committee, and that is where it could have died.

The committee chairman was Representative Emmanuel Celler, a Democrat from New York who at age 78 was in his 43rd year in Congress. Celler was a strong proponent of antitrust laws, and he had no intention of expanding any exemptions because he saw a single professional league as a monopoly. Commissioner Rozelle feared that without an antitrust exemption, the league could be vulnerable to costly antitrust lawsuits, the sum of which he said, "could easily be larger than the total value and net assets of all the existing franchises." He also said that if Congress did not approve the exemption before the following January, plans for any new expansion teams would also probably die. That would get the attention of representatives from states who hoped new franchises would boost their local economies and elevate the stature of their major cities.

With the 1966 football season more than a month old and his hopes for Congressional action hung up in the House Judiciary Committee, Rozelle sought lobbying help. He called David Dixon, a friend whose fraternity brother at Tulane had been House Majority Whip Hale Boggs of Louisiana.

Through Dixon, the NFL made it clear that a new team in Louisiana would have no problem getting league approval if Boggs could assist in getting the extended antitrust exemption passed. New Orleans was already under consideration by the league as a possible site for an expansion team. Boggs saw the value this could have for the state of Louisiana and for his political future. He had won re-election in his deep South district as an opponent of civil rights legislation in every campaign since 1946. He voted against the Civil Rights Act of 1964. But in July of 1965, Boggs made an impassioned speech on the floor of the House in favor of the Voting Rights Act, a stand that did not sit well with many of his more conservative constituents. If he could take credit for bringing an NFL team to New Orleans, he knew it would help him politically. He promptly attached the antitrust exemption for a combined league to an Investment Tax Credit bill that had already been approved by the House. With the help of Senator Russell Long of Louisiana, a fellow Democrat, and Republican Senate Minority Leader Everett Dirksen of Illinois, he was assured of final legislative approval and a signature from President Lyndon Johnson.

In his book *America's Game*, Michael MacCambridge set the scene on October 21, 1966, when final approval would be put to a vote. On his way up the steps to the Capitol rotunda, Rozelle said, "Congressman Boggs, I don't know how I can ever thank you enough for this. This is a terrific thing you've done."

Boggs replied, "What do you mean you don't know how to thank me? New Orleans gets an immediate franchise in the NFL." Rozelle's reported response was, "I'm going to do everything I can to make that happen." Boggs turned around as if heading back to the committee room and said, "Well, we can always call off the vote while you...." At that, the NFL Commissioner said, "It's a deal Congressman. You'll get your franchise." Less than a year later, the New Orleans Saints made their NFL debut. The NFL won approval for the amendment to the Sports Broadcasting Act granting permission for all the teams of the combined league to negotiate as a single entity for future television rights. And Hale Boggs did win re-election in 1966, albeit by a smaller margin than in previous years.

THE FIRST SUPER BOWL

Lamar Hunt's three young children each had a "Super Ball," a toy from Wham-O Inc. that was all the rage in the 1960s. Seeing them cheerfully bouncing the ball, Hunt got the idea for a short nickname he could use when discussing the new world championship game that the merger would create. In a note to Pete Rozelle, Hunt said, "I've been calling it the Super Bowl, which obviously can be improved upon." Rozelle didn't like the term "super" which he equated with other empty superlatives like "neat," "cool," or "fantastic." He wanted a title with sophistication like "The Championship."

When the NFL champion Green Bay Packers met the AFL champion Kansas City Chiefs on January 15, 1967, at the Los Angeles Memorial Coliseum, the official title was the "AFL vs. NFL World Championship Game." But almost everyone including the media was calling it the "Super Bowl," and in 1969 it became the game's official title for Super Bowl III. The NFL chose to use Roman numerals to give the new creation a sense of tradition and permanence, and to avoid the confusion of using years as identifiers since the Super Bowl played early in one year would determine the champion from the previous year's regular season.

This first championship game between the two professional leagues was also the first time either league had played its title game at a neutral site, which more than likely explains why the game was not a sell-out even though tickets sold for just \$6–\$12. All previous NFL and AFL league championships had been played at one of the two teams' home stadiums. The attendance at "Super Bowl I" was 61,946, far short of the Los Angeles Coliseum's 93,000 capacity, which left more than 30,000 seats embarrassingly empty if they were to be seen on national television. Rozelle's pregame solution was to have the public address announcer urge the scattered fans to move down closer to the field and toward the 50-yard line. He knew the appearance of a larger crowd would make the game look more important on television.

CBS had the responsibility of producing the game telecast and providing a feed to NBC, which would add its own commentary, graphics, replays, and commercials in a separate TV truck. The CBS production plan for this championship game was very similar to the network's regular season complement of seven primary coverage cameras, but it was upgraded to include an extra hand-held camera in the tunnel to get shots of the teams coming onto the field, and they hard-wired cameras into each of the two locker rooms for post-game interviews and celebration shots. The coverage was minimal compared with the 60+ camera productions at Super Bowls in the 21st century.

Accommodating NBC and sharing facilities was the most difficult part of Super Bowl I for CBS Sports executive producer Bill Fitts. He headed the CBS production teams for Super Bowls I, II, IV, VI, and VIII. Fitts remembered how tight the tiny CBS mobile unit was with NBC's producer Lou Kusserow joining them to coordinate what was being fed to his production truck. Fitts said the truck was "a mad house, Kusserow was even louder than me!"

The CBS team took pride in their years producing live football games and in the fact that the television ratings for their NFL games were considerably higher than those for the AFL games on NBC. (Contributing to the numbers advantage was the fact that more NFL franchises were in larger cities than the AFL.) The CBS pride came across to many of NBC's production personnel as a patronizing attitude, and that led to friction which resulted in a few scuffles between CBS and NBC technicians at the broadcast compound outside the stadium. The solution was to erect a 10-foot chain-link fence between the two broadcast trucks. The forced cooperation between networks was unique to Super Bowl I, and it was never repeated. Starting with Super Bowl II in January of 1968, CBS and NBC alternated coverage with CBS doing games in the even-numbered years and NBC in the odd. This pattern continued until Super Bowl XX in January of 1985 when ABC's new NFL rights package gave it a place in what then became a three-network rotation.

One of the other elements that made the telecast of the first NFL vs. AFL championship different from previous title games was the pageantry planned for the pre-game and halftime. A flock of doves was to be released and two jet-pack pilots with "AFL" and "NFL" emblazoned on their respective chests would fly over the field and land at the 50-yard line where they would ceremonially shake hands to represent the joining of the two leagues. On the Saturday before the game, Fitts insisted on rehearsing the doves and the jet-pack pilots. He said he had to see where they would fly so his director would know how to follow them with which cameras come Sunday. The dove-wrangler did not want to rehearse: "They're not homing pigeons," he told Fitts, "they'll fly away, and I'll have to get more doves." Fitts was adamant, so standing on the field he learned two things from the doves' rehearsal, 1) the direction the birds would fly, and 2) as soon as doves are released, they all immediately poop. "I was standing on the field and was covered in bird poop," he said. "I won't ever rehearse doves again in my life!"

Neither CBS nor NBC saw their shared broadcast experience at the first Super Bowl as optimal, but both shows progressed without any major problems until halftime. The Packers led 17–7 at the break, and play was scheduled to resume exactly 20 minutes later. Over his years producing games for CBS, Fitts had come to know the NFL's head of officials Mark Duncan as "a hard-ass." Halftimes for regular season games in that era were set for 15 minutes, and Duncan did not like the idea of extending it to 20 minutes for this new championship game.

Fitts recalled Duncan telling him before the game began, "Halftime is 20 minutes. Then we're kicking off. I don't care what your red-hat is doing." The red-hat is the stage manager on the sideline who receives timing cues via headset from the TV truck so he or she can signal the referees that the telecast is back from commercial and play can resume. They always wore red hats to make it easy for the referee to pick them out among the many people standing along the sideline.

Fitts said he relayed Duncan's warning to his NBC counterpart, Lou Kusserow. At halftime, CBS got its required commercial breaks in early so they would have time for their commentators to discuss what to expect in the second half. But an interview NBC was doing had run long, and the network still had one more break to squeeze in as the 20-minute clock was counting down. "Lou, you better get your ass in commercial," Fitts remembered shouting at Kusserow.

With only a minute and 15 seconds left before the second half was scheduled to begin, NBC finally went to its last halftime break, which meant that the red-hat would have to hold the second-half kickoff for at least an extra 45 seconds after Duncan's watch hit 20:00. But the official was true to his word, and he signaled the start of the second half while the NBC TV audience was still watching commercials. Immediately after the Packers kicked off to the Chiefs, CBS play-by-play announcer Jack Whitaker said he saw flags thrown and heard whistles blowing as the ball hit the ground untouched. He didn't know why, so he turned to his analyst Frank Gifford who shrugged his shoulders, not knowing what had happened either. The officials signaled the ball from the first kickoff dead, and the Packers had to kick off a second time, and by this time, NBC was back from break. It was the only TV-related "do-over" in Super Bowl history.

The next morning *The New York Times* said of the first Super Bowl, "The contest was more ordinary than super." The Packers had proven they were the superior team, and their convincing victory reinforced the generally held public opinion that the NFL in its fifth decade of play had much stronger teams than the AFL, which was just seven years old.

The Nielsen Company reported that CBS won the ratings battle with a 22.6 rating, which represented an average of 26.75 million viewers per minute. NBC's rating was an 18.5 with an audience of 24.43 million. The combined audience of 51 million viewers represented more than half the television homes in the United States.

NOT A SURE THING

Pete Rozelle was determined that Super Bowl II, to be played the following year at the Orange Bowl in Miami, would be a sell-out. The league had more time to promote the game and ticket prices were reduced to increase attendance. A total of 75,546 fans turned out on January 14, 1968, making the game the first $3 million gate in the history of the sport. What fans at the stadium in South Florida and viewers at home saw was another dominant performance by the Green Bay Packers, this time over the AFL champion Oakland Raiders. The Packers had a 33–7 lead until late in the fourth quarter when Raiders' quarterback Daryle Lamonica hit receiver Bill Miller for a touchdown to make the final score 33–14.

Back-to-back lopsided wins for the Packers in this new championship between the two leagues underscored the common perception that the NFL and AFL were not equals. For Super Bowl III in January of 1969, most fans and media alike thought a victory by the NFL's Baltimore Colts over the New York Jets would be a foregone conclusion. The Colts were favored by as many as 19 points the week of the game, which would be played at the Orange Bowl for a second consecutive year.

Pete Rozelle was concerned about the long-term outlook and audience for the season-ending Super Bowl if the public began to expect an annual NFL beat-down of the AFL champions. He addressed the issue at his news conference the Friday before Super Bowl III, announcing that the league was considering a change in the post-season playoff structure after the 1970 season. A modification in the format would have allowed two NFL teams to meet in a Super Bowl game after the AFL-NFL merger was completed and teams from both leagues had begun playing a unified schedule. *The New York Times* sports headline on Saturday morning January 11,

1969, read: "Rozelle Indicates Tomorrow's Super Bowl Contest Could Be Next to Last."

Television viewers overwhelmingly expected an easy Colts victory, and the ratings were lower than for Super Bowl II. Only 36 percent of American homes watched the Colts vs. the Jets, the lowest-rated Super Bowl in the history of the series. But after Joe Namath and the Jets stunned the Colts with a 16–7 victory for the AFL, any talk of changing the playoff structure evaporated.

Namath had guaranteed a Jets victory, but almost no one took him seriously. He made the guarantee while accepting the "Player of the Year" award at the Miami Touchdown Club dinner the Thursday night before Super Bowl III. While Namath was at the microphone a Colts supporter in the audience yelled, "We're gonna kick your ass." To that Namath replied, "Wait a minute, let's hold on. You Baltimore guys have been talking all week, but I've got news for you, buddy. We're gonna win the game. I guarantee it." Namath said he made the comment as a response to the fan's taunt, not out of arrogance. But it touched off a media storm that set the stage for a Super Bowl that would have a more wide-ranging impact than any other before or since.

The Jets' victory over the Colts added drama and suspense to all ensuing Super Bowls. The game would never again be looked upon as a virtual exhibition game between the big boys of the NFL and their weaker stepbrothers that followed the more important league championship games. The stigma of league inequality would be laid to rest the following year when the Kansas City Chiefs defeated the Minnesota Vikings in Super Bowl IV for a second consecutive AFL triumph. Advertising rates for the Super Bowl telecast took off after Super Bowl III, making it economically more important and a much larger factor in future television rights negotiations for the NFL games. Television ratings bounced back for Super Bowl IV to a 39.4, a 10 percent increase in a year, and from that point, a steady rise continued unabated into the 21st century, making the Super Bowl the most-watched program on American television year after year: a ritual of TV viewing without equal in the United States.

When Joe Namath made good on his guarantee to win Super Bowl III, he ushered in a new era of individual star power in team sports and became the prototype for the modern television celebrity athlete. He combined success on the field of play with good looks, the latest fashions, a well-spoken easy delivery in the media, and speculation about his sex life as a rich, handsome bachelor who was often seen escorting photogenic women to the trendiest clubs and restaurants in New York. Namath's star power translated into commercial endorsements and wealth approaching the level of television entertainment stars. And it added to the collective power of all players who could rightly claim their share of the value they brought to team ownership. A shift in power from the owners to the players and their unions was underway.

"ARE YOU READY FOR SOME (PRIMETIME) FOOTBALL?"

On their run to Super Bowl III, the New York Jets played the Oakland Raiders at the Oakland Coliseum Sunday, November 17, 1968. The game had started at 1 pm Pacific Time, 4 pm Eastern on NBC, and it was running long. The program scheduled to start at 7 pm Eastern after the game was the children's classic film *Heidi*, and NBC's broadcast operations supervisor in New York, Dick Cline, had no network guidelines that would have allowed him to let the game continue on air past 7 pm. NBC's executive producer Scotty Connal was at his home in Connecticut watching the game and trying to get a phone call through to broadcast operations in New York with instructions to stay with the game until the conclusion. But the switchboard there was receiving so many calls from viewers who either wanted the network to stick with the game or were asking what would happen to the *Heidi* telecast if the game did spill over, that Connal could not get through.

At 7 pm sharp, after the Jets had taken a 32–29 lead on a field goal with 1:15 left on the game clock, NBC went to commercial and then switched to *Heidi*. What viewers didn't see was Daryle Lamonica throw a touchdown pass to Charlie Smith giving the Raiders the lead with 42 seconds left. The Jets fumbled the ensuing kickoff and Raider Preston Ridlehuber fell on the ball in the end zone for a second Oakland touchdown in just nine seconds. Final score: Oakland 43, New York 32. Cline, who went on to have a distinguished career as a television sports director, said that a call from NBC president Julian Goodman did get through, but by that time it was too late to carry out his demand to, "Go back to the game."

The story made the front page of *The New York Times*, Monday morning, November 18, 1968. The headline was: "Jets Cut for 'Heidi'; T.V. Fans Complain." And on NBC's *Huntley-Brinkley Report* that Monday evening, David Brinkley reported that "NBC apologized for the error but by then Oakland had scored two touchdowns in the last minute, had beaten New York, the game was over. The fans who missed it could not be consoled."

What would go down in history as "The Heidi Game" had several valuable lessons that would have an impact for years to come:

- Professional football on television was reaching and affecting so many millions of people that coverage on the front page of national newspapers and on nightly network newscasts was warranted. If a televised game had been similarly cut off five or 10 years earlier, there almost certainly would not have been the same level of public outcry or national media attention.

- TV truck, network operations, and programming executives would forever after be connected by telephone hotlines so that last-minute programming changes could always be made.
- And perhaps most importantly, the appetite for live football telecasts extended beyond Sunday afternoons into primetime where they could rival traditional entertainment shows.

THE BIRTH OF MONDAY NIGHT FOOTBALL

NFL Commissioner Pete Rozelle had seen primetime television as an opportunity for expansion in the early 1960s. As an experiment, the league scheduled its first Monday night game on September 28, 1964, for a game between the Green Bay Packers and the Detroit Lions that drew a sell-out crowd of 59,203 to Tiger Stadium but was not televised. It proved that fans would embrace games played on a weeknight. Now all Rozelle had to do was find a network partner.

When it still had the AFL package, ABC had proposed doing a weekly Friday night football game to replace its *Gillette Friday Night Fights* package that was not doing well in the ratings. The marketing manager at Ford, Lee Iacocca, who would later gain fame as the chief executive at Chrysler, had agreed to sponsor the new Friday night AFL series. But the National Collegiate Athletic Association (NCAA) got wind of the plan and spread the word that ABC was planning to put live football games on TV on Friday nights, which would cause people across the country to stay home and not support the local high school football games that were traditionally played on Friday evenings. It wasn't long before Congress amended the Sports Broadcasting Act to nullify the antitrust exemption for any professional football played on a Friday night after 6 pm local time or at any time on a Saturday between the second Friday of September and the second Saturday of December on "any telecasting station located within 75 miles of the game site of any intercollegiate or interscholastic football contest." That effectively killed ABC's Friday night football idea.

In 1966, the NFL began a four-year Monday night primetime experiment with its broadcast partners: CBS televised one Monday game in 1966 and one in 1967, and NBC did the same with AFL matchups in 1968 and 1969. None of the games was a huge ratings success, but Rozelle was not discouraged. The table was set for *Monday Night Football* to break new ground in American sports entertainment history.

Not long after the New York Jets victory in Super Bowl III, Rozelle had a series of lunches in Manhattan with ABC Sports executive producer Roone Arledge to talk about NFL football in primetime on Mondays. Arledge did not yet have the green light from his bosses to cut a deal.

ABC Chairman Leonard Goldenson reportedly liked the idea, but his new network president Elton Rule did not think it wise to disrupt the entertainment schedule in primetime.

Rozelle liked Arledge's proposed approach that would turn the shows into a mix of football and entertainment with the goal of attracting more women to the audience. But it was always the commissioner's intention to offer a Monday night series to his broadcast partners at CBS and NBC first. Rozelle knew that ABC was a poor third in the primetime ratings race, which meant cross-promotion for his new series of games would reach far fewer people on ABC than it would on either of the other two networks. ABC's standing was so dismal at the time that a TV insiders' joke was, "How do you end the Vietnam War? Put it on ABC and it'll be canceled in 13 weeks."

The NFL's other option that would not require a contract with CBS, NBC, or ABC was a syndication partnership with the Hughes Sports Network (HSN), which was bankrolled by reclusive billionaire Howard Hughes. HSN would offer to sell the NFL package directly to any television stations that wanted to buy the programming. Word quickly reached ABC that up to 100 of its affiliated stations, including powerful WPVI-TV in Philadelphia, were ready to drop their regular lineup of Monday night ABC shows and take the syndicated football games instead. This would have been a crippling blow to ABC. The network reacted swiftly out of fear that it would have to "go dark" on Monday evenings, and the board of directors approved spending $25.5 million for a three-year contract with the NFL.

But Pete Rozelle still insisted on giving CBS and NBC the right of first refusal. The ratings leader on Monday nights was CBS with a schedule that included *Here's Lucy* starring Lucille Ball, *Mayberry R.F.D.*, *The Doris Day Show*, and at 10 pm Eastern Time, *The Carol Burnett Show*. CBS network programmers decided to stand pat and pass on Pete Rozelle's *Monday Night Football* offer.

NBC did consider taking it, but the network would have had to move its hit show *Rowan and Martin's Laugh-In* from Mondays to another night. And an even greater stumbling block for NBC, where the scars from the "Heidi Game" were still fresh, would be that if any Monday night NFL game ran long, it would delay the start time of *The Tonight Show starring Johnny Carson*, which was NBC's biggest moneymaker. The programming department did not want to upset Johnny Carson, so they too turned down the NFL in primetime.

When the Commissioner and ABC resumed their talks, Rozelle made it clear that the network would have to change its three-year offer to a term of four years beginning with the 1970 season to coincide with the new four-year rights contracts that the league was negotiating with CBS and

NBC for its Sunday games and four Super Bowls. ABC secured the rights to *Monday Night Football* for $8.6 million per year for four years for a total of $34.4 million. When all three TV rights agreements were finalized, the NFL was guaranteed $176.4 million over the next four years. For their regular season and playoff games, CBS had agreed to pay $18 million per year and NBC signed for $15 million. CBS and NBC paid an additional $2.5 million per Super Bowl for the two they would each televise during the four-year term of their contracts.

Rozelle could rightfully return to his team owners with a broad smile on his face: the NFL would now be seen live on each of America's three major television networks, the league would have a weekly primetime television presence for a minimum of four years, and the league would set a new record for television rights income. Shared equally, the league's 26 teams would earn $1.7 million in rights fees per year for the life of the contracts.

The ink on the ABC contract was barely dry when Roone Arledge pitched one of his most revolutionary ideas to Pete Rozelle. Arledge wanted to use a three-man commentary booth for *Monday Night Football*, and his choice for "the third man" was former attorney and controversial ABC Sports reporter Howard Cosell who had gained national prominence covering Muhammad Ali's fights in the ring and in the courtroom. Arledge's argument was that Cosell would not let the audience ignore him, "he forced you to watch." Knowing how obnoxious some people found Cosell, the commissioner's response was, "Why not just dig up Attila the Hun?"

ABC's first choice for the expert football analyst position was Frank Gifford, but he still had one year left on his contract with CBS which he intended to honor. Gifford did however recommend a friend for the job who he said, "would really be great." That friend was recently retired Dallas Cowboys quarterback Don Meredith who had quickly decided that spending life after football as a stockbroker was not what he wanted. Arledge asked Gifford to have his friend give him a phone call.

Meredith phoned ABC four days in a row leaving a message for Roone Arledge each day, but he got no return call. His fifth message was that he was starting negotiations with CBS to work on that network's college football games. Arledge had a reputation for not returning phone calls promptly, but message number five got his attention, and a lunch meeting was set up with the assistance of Gifford.

In his autobiography, Arledge remembered that he had his apologies all prepared when Don Meredith showed up at Toots Shor's restaurant in New York City at the appointed hour. Meredith however did not sit down. He told Arledge, "The only reason I came is to tell you to your face what a horse's ass you are." Arledge's quick reply was, "And that, sir, is the kind of candor I want in an expert commentator."

The two men sat down and three hours later they had the details of an agreement written on a napkin. Arledge could not wait to see the chemistry develop between Meredith, the "good ol' boy" Texas football star, and the often-abrasive New York intellectual Howard Cosell. He paired these two opposite personalities with ABC college football play-by-play announcer Keith Jackson, and the first *Monday Night Football* three-man booth was complete.

The debut of *NFL Monday Night Football* on September 21, 1970, marked one of the most important moments in sports television history. It turned live sports into primetime TV entertainment. The city of Cleveland served as host for this historic coming-out party with the largest crowd ever to see a Browns' game, a total of 85,703 at Cleveland Municipal Stadium. The owner of the Browns at the time, Art Modell said that many of his fellow owners were wary of taking the first Monday night game for fear that attendance would not be as strong as it was on Sunday afternoons. Modell said, "Let me take a chance in Cleveland. Just give me the Jets," because of Joe Namath's popularity and the New York television audience he would attract. It was the beginning of what would become a *Monday Night Football* phenomenon: the tenor of the home crowds assumed a party or carnival atmosphere. Fans festooned the stadium with banners, many referring to Howard Cosell or "Dandy Don" Meredith, and hundreds more dressed in outrageous costumes in hopes of being seen on national TV. Meredith called the weekly *Monday Night Football* scene "Mother Love's Traveling Freak Show."

The live game that viewers watched that Monday night in September of 1970 was unlike anything they had ever seen. ABC's open made you feel like you were inside the TV truck watching the countdown to airtime. Director Chet Forte had more cameras in more places to provide shots and angles that had not been used before. It was all part of Roone Arledge's philosophy to "bring the viewer to the game," instead of bringing the game to the viewer.

The television audience that watched the Browns defeat the Jets 31–21 was much larger than ABC had projected. Thirty-three percent of the American viewing audience tuned in, giving ABC a ratings victory over the CBS and NBC entertainment lineups that those two networks had chosen to retain rather than take a chance with NFL football in primetime.

During the season the stadiums continued to sell out and record numbers tuned in to ABC to join the Monday night festivities and to hear the next outrageous thing that Meredith or Cosell would say. Their exchanges, with Meredith constantly ribbing Cosell or questioning his use of vocabulary that he had never heard before, became part of the "must-see" entertainment. Not everyone was an instant fan though. ABC Chairman Leonard Goldenson got a call after the first game from Ford Motor Company chairman Henry Ford II, one of ABC's biggest sponsors, demanding that

Cosell be taken off the show because "he's hogging all the time. He talks so much I can't enjoy the game." Arledge remembered being called into Goldenson's office to discuss Ford's criticism, but he convinced his boss to hold firm with Cosell by assuring him that, "It's only been one show. The audience needs to get to know him." Ford called Goldenson back a few weeks later and said he had grown to like the patter in the booth.

A *TV Guide* poll that first season found that Howard Cosell was both the "most-hated" and the "most-liked" sportscaster in the United States. The celebrity status of the TV talent was something completely new for American sports television. The game had always been "the thing" and the commentators were just part of the presentation, never taking the spotlight for themselves. ABC changed that forever in 1970. The network also welcomed celebrities from the entertainment world and politics to join the fun in the booth. In so doing, ABC broadened its audience. Perhaps the oddest pairing of celebrity visitors came during halftime of a Washington vs. L.A. Rams game on December 9, 1974, at the Los Angeles Memorial Coliseum. John Lennon and outgoing California Governor Ronald Reagan were in the TV booth together. "Now there's a pair," said Arledge.

So many people chose to sit in front of their televisions on Monday nights that attendance at movie theaters dropped significantly. Theater owners in parts of the country offered discounts or free snacks to entice custom-ers. Many bowling leagues abandoned Monday nights and moved their matches to later in the week. Process servers got busy knowing that most of the people they sought would be in their homes on Monday evenings.

In short order, *Monday Night Football* had become the NFL's premier showcase and most valuable property. The league's games on Sunday com-peted with each other for the television audience, and a million or more would-be viewers were sitting in the stands at the games. Other sports like basketball, hockey, and golf also competed for a piece of the Sunday afternoon TV audience. On Monday nights however, the lights were on in only one pro football stadium, which meant fans who had been in their stadium seats on Sunday were back home on their sofas on Monday. And even if the matchup was between two teams that a fan didn't follow, there were always Howard Cosell's halftime highlights of the best action from Sunday's games which itself became a major draw. In this era before ESPN or the internet, the only way to see all the highlights together was to watch halftime on *Monday Night Football*.

When Frank Gifford became available in 1971, Roone Arledge hired him to take over the play-by-play host role from Keith Jackson because he was looking for a "bigger personality" in the booth. Gifford would con-tinue with the series for 35 years, sharing the booth with a succession of broadcast partners who would eventually replace Howard Cosell and Don Meredith. Keith Jackson who anchored the *Monday Night Football* booth for just one year was reassigned as ABC's number one college football commentator.

In its 36 seasons on ABC, *Monday Night Football* became an institution. It changed Americans' expectations for all televised sport, creating what would become an insatiable appetite for more angles, more replays, more personality and entertainment, more drama, and more fun. The shows made NFL football more conspicuous and more important, a powerful presence on weekends and in primetime on all three of the nation's broadcast television networks. The huge audiences it attracted made NFL rights more valuable, and the commercials sold within the games more expensive.

And *Monday Night Football* brought people together through common experience: bleary eyes and yawns at the office or at school on Tuesday mornings, extra cups of coffee as they relived the latest comedy or controversy from Cosell and Meredith, and the sense of belonging with all their "rowdy friends." It was a weekly carnival that made people laugh, got their blood boiling, or had them jumping out of their seats to cheer an amazing touchdown run by Earl Campbell or pass from Dan Marino.

The television reviewer of *The New York Times* Jack Gould sensed a foreshadowing of what was to come in his column the morning after ABC televised its first Monday night game from Cleveland in September 1970. Gould wrote that this "innovation will be watched carefully by media students." He asked how sports would do up against the movies and situation comedies that were the staple of primetime? Would women surrender to their husbands' control of what the family watched on a weeknight, or would "the increasing prevalence of multiple-set households" divide families into separate rooms, creating a rift in the harmony of the "one-set home?" Gould concluded that "should evening network sports give entertainment a serious challenge, last night could be remembered as marking one more change in the course of television." That it did.

As the economic realities of the television industry changed in the decades following its 1970 debut, *Monday Night Football* moved from ABC to co-owned ESPN in the fall of 2006. ESPN's first contract for the series guaranteed the NFL $1.1 billion per year for eight years. In its 36 years on ABC, the value of the rights to *Monday Night Football* had grown from $8.6 million per year to $1.1 billion, a 1,279 percent increase.

THE NFL TODAY

The pre-game and post-game live studio shows that have become a staple of sports television trace their origins back to 1956, when CBS started doing a preview of their Sunday games simply called *Football Preview*. Before 1956, any show relying on video clips and highlights would have been impossible because that was the year that videotape was introduced by the Ampex Corporation. *Football Preview* preceded the CBS telecast of each Sunday's game, varying between 15 and 30 minutes in length. It became *Pro Football Kickoff* a year later, and in 1964, with a regular 30-minute time slot, it was remade and re-titled as *The NFL Today*.

The purpose of any pre-game show is three-fold:

1. Promote the upcoming game or event so that more people will be enticed to watch.
2. Introduce the storylines that are expected to unfold and the players who could control the contest so that when viewers decide to watch, they will stay tuned longer. The greater the time spent viewing by each member of the television audience, the higher the overall program rating will be.
3. Create additional advertising inventory for sponsors who have already bought commercials in the game and want to increase the number of times their message is presented, or for those sponsors who could not buy spots in the actual game because the existing inventory was sold out, or because the price tag was too high. Commercials in the pre-game shows are invariably sold at a lower price than those that will air within the actual game or event.

These early NFL pre-game shows consisted primarily of the network football analysts setting up that day's matchups. They were not a showcase for personality or entertainment. Frank Gifford did add some star power to *The NFL Today* when he took over as its host on CBS from 1966 through the 1970 season, after which he made his move to ABC's *Monday Night Football*.

The sports studio show changed forever in 1975 when the new president of CBS Sports Robert Wussler, along with producer Mike Pearl, totally re-built *The NFL Today* adding personality, interviews, style, and fun. Wussler assigned Brent Musburger as the host, Phyllis George as interviewer and co-host, former NFL player and coach Irv Cross as the football expert, and acknowledging the huge public interest in gambling on NFL games, Wussler hired Jimmy "The Greek" Snyder as the show's Las Vegas insider. Musburger had been doing a Sunday NFL post-game show in Chicago that brought in feeds from all the games around the country. He thrived on the fast pace of the show, quickly moving from one highlight to the next. The executive producer on the show, Bill Fitts said, "Brent was like a kid in a candy store."

Phyllis George was Miss America 1971, and during her reign was the guest on talk shows all over the country, including at least three appearances on *The Tonight Show with Johnny Carson* on NBC. Her personality and ease on camera caught Wussler's eye, and when he brought her to CBS Sports he told staffers "let's make her a star." George added character and charm to the football studio show, and her ability to put interview subjects at ease got many to open up and show a personal side that had never been seen by television viewers before.

In an interview that first season with Dallas Cowboys quarterback Roger Staubach, an Annapolis graduate and future Hall of Famer, Phyllis George said, "Roger you have an all-American image. You're kind of a straight guy. Do you enjoy it or is it a burden?" Staubach responded, "You interviewed Joe Namath. Everyone in the world compares me to Joe Namath. He's a single bachelor swinging, having all the fun, and I'm married," he continued, "but you know, I enjoy sex as much as Joe Namath, only I do it with one girl," referring to his wife Marianne. Phyllis George helped weave the human side of athletes into the story, adding depth and interest to the telecasts, and showing that, in the words of former NBC Sports president Dick Ebersol, "football was not just about men watching men."

When he joined *The NFL Today*, Irv Cross became the first African American studio host in the history of American sports television. Cross had been a defensive back for nine seasons with the Philadelphia Eagles and Los Angeles Rams. His deep knowledge of the game and the ease with which he interacted and shared a laugh with his *NFL Today* co-hosts has paved the way for African American sportscasters ever since. In 2009, the Pro Football Hall of Fame honored Cross with its Pete Rozelle Radio Television Award. "We were CBS's *Mod Squad*," said George, referring to a 1970s era TV cop show that featured a white male officer, a white female, and an African American male. "And we had the Greek," she added.

Jimmy "The Greek" Snyder, born Demetrios Georgios Synodinos, was an oddsmaker who set the Las Vegas betting line for football games. CBS was again breaking new ground when they hired Snyder because no one with professional gambling ties or expertise had ever been part of a network sports telecast. "The Greek" became a fixture for 12 years on *The NFL Today*, making his predictions and explaining how factors like a team's speed or defensive line would affect a game's outcome. Snyder was fired by CBS in 1988 after an interview in which he made racially offensive statements about what he called the "breeding" of African Americans during the days of slavery. The comments were in response to questions from WRC-TV in Washington, D.C., for a report to be aired on the Martin Luther King Jr. holiday that year.

By doing stories and interviews that went far beyond game highlights or strategy, *The NFL Today* changed the television audience for professional football. The goal of the show was to evoke emotions and make connections between the players and fans, and between the broadcasters and football fans.

Every sport has great stories and interesting performers. But for American audiences, the combination of stories and stars with powerful visuals and audio, and the inherent pacing of the game that punctuates every play, have made the NFL's partnership with television an unequaled success. This perfect marriage has set the standard for a broad spectrum of live sports media programming development and production innovation.

BIBLIOGRAPHY

Arledge, Roone. *Roone: A Memoir.* New York, N.Y.: HarperCollins Publishers, 2003.

Associated Press. "Act of Congress Paved Way for Saints, Super Bowl." *ESPN .com*, 2010. http://www.espn.com/espn/wire/_/section/nfl/id/4868499

Fitts, Bill. *Interviewed by the Author*, 2011.

Gould, Jack. "TV Review: Pro Football Kicks Off in A.B.C. Prime Time." *The New York Times*, New York, 1970, 91. https://www.nytimes.com/1970/09 /22/archives/tv-review-pro-football-kicks-off-in-abc-prime-time.html

Justia US Law. *American Football League v. National Football League*, 205 F. Supp. 60 (D. Md., 1962) US District Court for the District of Maryland - 205 F. Supp. 60 (D. Md. 1962), May 21, 1962. https://law.justia.com/cases/ federal/district-courts/FSupp/205/60/2181427/

Kornheiser, Tony. "Cosell Told it Like it Was, Only Like He Could." *The Washington Post*, 1995. https://timesmachine.nytimes.com/timesmachine /1966/06/09/82449917.html?pageNumber=78

Kriegel, Mark. *Namath: A Biography.* New York: Penguin, 2005.

MacCambridge, Michael. *America's Game: The Epic Story of How Pro Football Captured a Nation.* New York: Anchor Books, 2005.

Meserole, Mike. "Arledge Created Monday Night Football." ESPN.com, 2002. http://www.espn.com/classic/obit/arledgeobit.html

NFL Media. "HARRIS POLL: NFL Continues 42-Year Run as Most Popular Sport." https://www.nfl.info/nflmedia/kickoff%20weekend/2007/FINAL %20PDFs/Page%2028.pdf

Nielsen.com. "Historical Super Bowl Viewership." 2021. https://www.nielsen .com/us/en/press-releases/2021/super-bowl-lv-draws-nearly-92-million-tv -viewers/

Pro Football Hall of Fame. Congress Approves the AFL-NFL Merger, 1966. https://www.profootballhof.com/football-history/history-of-football/1960 -1979/1966-congress-approves-the-afl-nfl-merger/

Rogers, Thomas. "Jets Cut for 'Heidi'; TV Fans Complain." *The New York Times*, 1968, 1 & 61. https://www.nytimes.com/1968/11/18/archives/jets -cut-for-heidi-tv-fans-complain-telecast-of-jetraider-game-cut.html

Sheehan, Joseph M. "National and American Football Leagues Will Merge Into 26-Team Circuit." *The New York Times*, 1966. https://timesmachine .nytimes.com/timesmachine/1966/06/09/82449917.html?pageNumber=78

Time Magazine. "Sport: Vinnie, Vidi, Vici." *Time Magazine*, 1962. http:// content.time.com/time/magazine/article/0,9171,940172,00.html

Wallace, William N. "Football Merger Seen in Jeopardy: Rozelle's Try for Antitrust Immunity is Turned Down." *The New York Times*, 1966. https:// timesmachine.nytimes.com/timesmachine/1966/09/09/82904370.html ?pageNumber=53

Wallace, William N. "GREEN BAY WINS FOOTBALL TITLE; National League Champions Beat Kansas City, 35–10, in Super Bowl Game." *The New York Times*, 1967. https://www.nytimes.com/1967/01/16/archives/

green-bay-wins-football-title-national-league-champions-beat-kansas
.html

Wallace, William N. "Rozelle Indicates Tomorrow's Super Bowl Contest
Could Be Next to Last; REALIGNMENT DUE AFTER '69 SEASON." *The
New York Times*, 1969, 24. https://www.nytimes.com/1969/01/11/archives/
rozelle-indicates-tomorrows-super-bowl-contest-could-be-next-to.html

Weiss, Don, and Chuck Day. *The Making of the Super Bowl: The Inside Story
of the World's Greatest Sporting Event*. New York: McGraw-Hill, 2003.

Wojciechowski, Gene. "Q&A; WITH PETE ROZELLE: Former NFL
Commissioner Looks Back on First Super Bowl and Looks Ahead at
Possible Ramifications of New Agreement." *Los Angeles Times*, January
24, 1993. https://www.latimes.com/archives/la-xpm-1993-01-24-sp-2736
-story.html

ESPN: The First 24/7 Connection to Sports

"If you're a fan, *if* you're a fan, what you'll see in the next minutes, hours and days to follow may convince you you've gone to sports heaven." It is unlikely that very many people heard those words spoken by Lee Leonard at 7 pm Eastern Time on Friday night September 7, 1979, when ESPN debuted as the "Total Sports Network." Less than five million homes in the United States could receive ESPN's signal. Even fewer could have imagined the force that ESPN would become in the American sports industry "in the days to follow."

ESPN was a precursor to the internet, giving fans a taste of the future by providing access to sports events and sports news 24 hours a day. It was a revolutionary step toward the type of instant information access that is now commonplace but was unheard of in 1979. ESPN was the first constant connection to sports for fans in the same way that the debut of CNN in June the following year provided all-day and all-night access to news. The availability of specialized content regardless of the day or time is what we have taken for granted since the proliferation of the "worldwide web" took hold in the mid-1990s. But ESPN stood alone for 15 years, which made it the "must-have" channel for anyone who wanted sports action and information that would fit any schedule.

The creation of an all-sports cable television network in 1979 was dependent upon a set of technological advances that made cable networks possible and the dramatic expansion in the total number of live sports events that occurred in the years leading up to 1979. The network's successful launch required a set of specific conditions to exist concurrently, as well as considerable creativity, courage, and a sizeable investment of capital. Borrowing an albeit over-used term from sports broadcasting, let's call these conditions our "keys to victory" for ESPN.

KEY #1: CABLE TELEVISION

John and Margaret Walson owned a hardware store in Mahanoy City, Pennsylvania, called Service Electric. In 1948, the Walsons had a number of new General Electric television sets on the shelf, but nobody was buying them. The reason: Mahanoy City is 98 miles northwest of Philadelphia where the nearest TV stations were located, so reception in town was poor

DOI: 10.4324/9781003165590-5

to non-existent. If you lived in Mahanoy City you could not justify buying a television if you couldn't see any shows.

John Walson figured out a simple remedy that he was sure would help him sell TV sets. He put an antenna atop an old utility pole on the highest neighboring hill, then amplified and routed the signals he received to his Service Electric store via coaxial cable. When customers came into the store they could see and hear television programming, and if they bought a set the Walsons would offer to hook them up to their cable for an installation fee of $100 plus two dollars per month. *The first cable bill anyone ever paid in the United States was two dollars.* Service Electric started selling a lot more TV sets and cable television was born as community antenna television (CATV).

In the 1950s, 1960s, and 1970s, CATV spread to communities across the country that found themselves in the same geographic situation as Mahanoy City: too far away from television stations even for an antenna mounted on the roof of one's home to improve reception. By 1979, the year of ESPN's birth, a total of 14.8 million American homes were wired for cable, a national penetration rate of only 20 percent.

As it grew, the cable industry was strictly a hardware business, not a programming business. Cable was a means for people to receive programs produced by broadcasters until November of 1972 when Home Box Office (HBO) began distributing movies and some live sporting events without commercial interruption. The programming was delivered via microwave to cable systems for a monthly fee. Coincidentally, the very first HBO subscribers were 365 customers of Service Electric Cable in the Wilkes-Barre, Pennsylvania area. Within a year, HBO was sending its microwave feed to 14 cable systems that in turn sold the monthly service to 8,000 paying subscribers.

KEY #2: COMMUNICATIONS SATELLITES

The live transmission of television signals via satellite that had been possible across the oceans since SYNCOM 3 and Early Bird were launched in the mid-1960s would not become a reality for domestic TV distribution until Western Union sent Westar 1 into orbit in 1974, and RCA sent up SATCOM 1 in December of 1975. SATCOM 1 was America's first commercial communications satellite that could be used by broadcast and cable networks to distribute programming to their affiliates across the country. The efficiency and advantage of satellite transmission quickly became apparent. Before 1975, all television transmission was either by dedicated AT&T lines that could accommodate color video and two channels of audio or by microwave, which required hundreds of simultaneous feeds from an origination point to individual terrestrial antennas and repeating stations. One satellite transmission, on the other hand, could reach an infinite number of receivers with just one feed. HBO was the first cable programmer to lease one of the SATCOM 1 transponders, thereby expanding its reach from Pennsylvania to every cable system in the continental United States.

Ted Turner began using SATCOM 1 in 1977 to send his WTCG Channel 17 in Atlanta to cable systems making it America's first "super-station." A large portion of Turner's programming was Atlanta Braves baseball games. He owned the team and did not have to pay himself any rights fees.

With these small steps, cable television had begun the transition from a hardware business into a programming business. It had become a "video supermarket," and the challenge would become how best to fill the vacant shelves with a product that video consumers would pay for.

KEY #3: MORE SPORTS CONTENT

In the 20 years from 1960 to 1980, the United States population grew from 179 million in 1960 to 226.5 million. During that 20-year span, television and all communications media expanded their reach bringing live sports broadcasts into every community large or small. The increased exposure created a greater appetite for sport which was to be satisfied by leagues and investors who saw an opportunity in bringing more sports teams, stadiums, and events to an underserved public. With more teams in more places, the number of games being played increased and so did the number of fans. More sports content and more people caring about the results created a perfect climate in which ESPN could fill 8,760 hours of programming each year and expect enough viewers to watch for the new sports network to become profitable. (24 hours multiplied by 365 days equals 8,760 hours per year.)

In the same 20-year period, Major League Baseball expanded from 16 teams, eight in the American League and eight in the National League to 26 teams: 14 in the American League and 12 in the National. The baseball regular season increased from 154 games to 162 games in the early 1960s, and the League Championship playoff series was added in 1969. Before that, the team with the best regular-season record in the American League met the team with the best record in the National League in the World Series, which was the only post-season playoff.

In 1960, the NFL had only 12 teams and each played 12 regular season games. The AFL started play that season with eight teams, and they each played a 14-game schedule. The two professional football leagues had a total of 20 teams in the United States, and each league played exactly one post-season game: their respective league championship. Twenty years later, the combined NFL of 1980 had eight more teams for a total of 28, and each played 16 regular season games. By 1980, the number of post-season playoff games had risen from just one to nine, starting with two wildcard games – one in the National Football Conference and one in the American Football Conference – and ending with the Super Bowl.

The NBA and NHL each grew dramatically between 1960 and 1980. The NBA went from just eight teams in 1960 to a total of 23 in 1980. No NBA team was based west of the St. Louis Hawks or south of the Cincinnati Royals in 1960, but the league had reached across the country by 1980. The NHL only had six teams in 1960, none farther west than the Chicago Blackhawks and none south of the New York Rangers. In the ensuing 20 years, the league grew to 21 teams from coast to coast.

College football and basketball also experienced growth spurts. From 1960 to 1980, college football expanded from 10 regular-season games and only nine post-season bowl games to a regular-season schedule of 12 games per team and 15 bowls. (In the "ESPN-era" since 1980, the number of college football bowl games mushroomed to more than 40.) From 1960 to 1980, the number of universities playing at the top level of college football, then called Division 1-A, increased by 25 to a total of 139.

Only 25 teams made the post-season NCAA Men's College Basketball Tournament in 1960, and the top schools were playing regular seasons of 24 games each. The tournament included 40 teams in 1979 and then expanded to a field of 48 in 1980 with most universities expanding their regular season schedules to 30 games.

More teams playing more games represented a dramatic expansion of live sports content. But the time dedicated to sports telecasts on the three major broadcast networks in 1980 had remained virtually unchanged over the same 20-year period. Sports was scheduled in four-to-six-hour blocks on Saturdays and Sundays. More available games for the same number of hours allowed each network to be more selective, but as a result, a larger percentage of each sport's games was left un-televised. That would begin to change as ESPN, with its voracious appetite for sports content, became a player in sports television.

THE E.S.P. NETWORK

ESPN may have never been founded if Bill Rasmussen, the 45-year-old communications director for the New England Whalers NHL hockey team had not been fired. Rasmussen had been sports director and then news director at a TV station in Springfield, Massachusetts, before he joined the Whalers. He also had years of advertising and promotion experience along with an MBA degree from Rutgers. But as of May 27, 1978, he was unemployed.

Part of Rasmussen's job with the Whalers had been to produce a weekly promotional hockey highlights show on videotape that he and his son Scott would deliver by car to nine different cable systems in Connecticut for each to air at its discretion. When faced with deciding what to do with the rest of his life, Rasmussen began thinking about putting together a package of University of Connecticut live events and New England Whalers games to distribute to those nine cable systems and any TV stations interested in a syndication deal. At that time, the Whalers did not have a local television agreement to air their games in Connecticut.

Less than a month after being fired by the Whalers, Bill Rasmussen invited every cable operator in the state to a meeting on June 26, 1978, at which he planned to present his sports package idea and assess potential interest. About half the state's cable operators showed up at historic Cooke's Tavern in Plainville, CT, and they made it clear to Rasmussen that he would have plenty of obstacles if he chose to move forward. For one thing, the cable systems did not have a common source for receiving signals. The programming they got came directly from their multisystem operators (United Cable, Cox Communications, et al) via microwave, and local programming was amplified from their own antennas.

Rasmussen remembered Jim Dovey, the vice president of United Cable of Plainville, telling him at the Cooke's Tavern meeting, "You really ought to investigate satellite. I'm sure RCA would be happy to talk to you." Within a matter of months, the cable systems would all be installing downlink satellite dishes to receive program feeds, replacing the costly microwave system that required separate transmissions to every single system. By comparison, one satellite transmission could be received by any cable system in the contiguous 48 states, Alaska and Canada. But the men in that room did not know that. They were not sure if satellite transmissions covered just the Northeast or perhaps only the Eastern seaboard.

Bill Rasmussen set about finding answers. When he called RCA Americom in Washington, D.C., the marketing manager, Al Parinello, was so anxious to lease the vacant channels ("transponders" in satellite parlance) on RCA's SATCOM 1 that he told Rasmussen, "I'll come up to Connecticut to see you."

That presented Rasmussen with a problem: he couldn't be taken seriously if he had an important guest visit the temporary office he was using at United Cable. His desk was an old door from his son Scott's condo that was bolted to a set of legs they bought at a lumber yard. For $20 Rasmussen leased the conference room at the United Cable building in Plainville and prepared to host the RCA representative on July 20, 1978.

At that meeting, Parinello explained that indeed any program uplinked to RCA's SATCOM 1 could be received by any satellite Earth station in North America. However, there just weren't many Earth stations in place … yet. The cost to buy five hours of satellite time seven days a week from RCA would be $1,250 per night. The Rasmussens didn't have any money coming in yet for their proposed Connecticut sports package, but $1,250 for five hours every night sounded reasonable.

Rasumussen recalled that Parinello then told him, "There is one rate that's not on the card." RCA would lease a transponder for a year, 24 hours a day for 365 days, at a price of just under $35,000 a month. There had been so little interest in annual leases that RCA had stopped pitching this option to clients. That night Bill Rasmussen told his 22-year-old son about the day's meeting. Scott quickly did the math in his head. If they signed up for the annual lease, it would cost them just $1,143 per day, which was less than the five-hour nightly rate, and that would give them a 24-hour satellite channel.

The very next morning Bill Rasmussen said he called Parinello at RCA to tell him "We'll take one." Rasmussen didn't have to put any money down, but within 90 days he'd have to make his first payment. He figured that his sports package would have to be organized and sold within those three months, and if not, he would just walk away from RCA and say, "No thank you." More than 30 years later, Bill Rasmussen said he still remembered the exact amount that he agreed to pay RCA each month: $34,167.

It was Scott Rasmussen who first proposed turning their idea for a Connecticut sports service into a national network because any programs they sent up to SATCOM 1 could be seen across the country not just in Connecticut. And there was just no way they could generate enough revenue locally to offset the cost of producing games and make the monthly payment to RCA. That begged the question from his father, "What would we do for 24 hours a day?"

The answers started to flow on a hot day in the middle of August as Bill and Scott Rasmussen sat in a traffic jam on their way to the New Jersey shore. Bill's daughter Lynn was turning 16 on that Wednesday August 16, and she was at the beach in New Jersey, but Bill and Scott were stuck on Interstate 84 in Waterbury, Connecticut. Their conversation turned to college sports, and they realized that the NCAA played thousands of games each year in several sports that were not televised. If they produced even a few of those games each week, they could play them back on tape on their satellite channel.

This opened the floodgates and before they knew it, they were discussing how many remote TV production trucks would be needed, how many people including top-name sportscasters that they would have to hire, what kind of a facility they would need to build with how many control rooms and studios, and how they could attract the investment needed to finance the project. Bill Rasmussen said he and Scott were so preoccupied that once they got to the birthday party, they really didn't give Lynn the attention she deserved for turning "sweet 16."

On the drive back to Connecticut they came up with the idea that would become *SportsCenter*. Bill Rasmussen remembered his days at WWLP-TV in Springfield, Massachusetts, and how it bothered him that he never got more than three or four minutes in any newscast to do all the sports news, scores, highlights, and related stories. He suggested a format that would include four or five half-hour sports "roundups" every day, plus 10 or 15 "mini-updates" in and around the events they would televise.

The Rasmussens started calling their brainchild the "E.S.P. Network," for Entertainment and Sports Programming. At the time, every broadcast network used three initials for its branding, and there was a reluctance to break from that tradition. But the initials "E.S.P." could have confused would-be viewers because they more commonly referred to extrasensory perception. The bold move to four initials had to be made, and the network became ESPN. Regardless of its title, four difficult, interdependent challenges had to be faced if ESPN were to become a reality:

1. The NCAA would have to agree to sell them the rights to enough games and competitions to make the network attractive to investors and to the multisystem cable operators (MSOs) that controlled the majority of cable TV distribution in the United States.
2. Investors would have to contribute several million dollars with the expectation of making that much and more back. A loan from his father and the $9,000 line of credit on Bill Rasmussen's credit card could only take them so far. To advance the kind of money needed, an investor would have to be assured that there would be plenty of attractive NCAA programs and the network would have to reach enough homes to make it possible to charge for advertising.
3. The major cable systems would have to show enough interest in subscribing to the new sports service that sources of financial capital would see ESPN as a good investment. The interest of the cable operators would hinge largely on the content of the network's programming, and that relied heavily on whether the NCAA decided to negotiate a rights deal with a network that was not yet on the air.
4. Advertisers would have to commit in advance to sponsoring sports programming on the new, untested network. Bill Rasmussen had decided that his network needed to be advertiser supported because his initial contact with cable systems convinced him they were unwilling to pay a monthly per-subscriber fee large enough to offset his costs. Even his first suggestion of a one penny per day per subscriber fee, 30 cents a month, was flatly rejected across the board. But in 1978, there were no advertiser-supported cable networks. The only cable-specific network that most operators knew about was HBO, and it was supported by monthly subscription fees alone, not advertising.

Add to that the necessity at the same time of finding and securing a building site for the offices, control rooms, and studios that would be needed for the launch of a television network. These challenges would make a daunting "to-do list" for even the most seasoned television professionals let alone a few self-described "little guys from Connecticut." Many years later, Bill Rasmussen told me that "without A.B.C. and N.B.C. there would have been no ESPN." He explained that A.B.C. meant "always be curious" as he was when he began inquiring about satellite distribution. And N.B.C. meant "never be complacent." With that as his mantra, he set out to clear each of the four hurdles that lay between him and the establishment of the first all-sports television network. (Figure 5.1)

CHALLENGE #1: PROGRAMMING CONTENT

Rasmussen's long-term goal was to present college and professional sports around the clock on his new cable service. He started by contacting then University of Connecticut athletic director John Toner who was an influential member of the NCAA Council, a body that served very much like a board of directors for the organization. Toner connected Rasmussen with the man who had been the executive director of the NCAA since 1951, Walter Byers.

Beginning in October of 1978, Rasmussen made several trips to NCAA headquarters, which were then located in Shawnee Mission, Kansas, to present his plan for televising hundreds of hours of collegiate competitions that had never been shown on national television. Byers wielded a great deal of power in college athletics and was known as a man who was set in his ways, difficult to approach, and even harder to win over. He was the only executive director the NCAA had ever had. But Bill Rasmussen said that what caught Byers' attention was the fact that ESPN was offering to provide the first-ever nationwide television coverage for more than 30 NCAA national championships in sports from volleyball to lacrosse, plus all the early round games from the NCAA men's basketball tournament.

On Valentine's Day, February 14, 1979, the NCAA agreed to enter a contract with ESPN. Rasmussen returned to Shawnee Mission, Kansas, on

■ **Figure 5.1** ESPN founder Bill Rasmussen visited the network's newest digital center and the *SportsCenter* set in 2014, 35 years after the show premiered. (Photo by Rich Arden/ESPN Images)

March 9 to sign the document in which ESPN agreed to pay the NCAA for exclusive rights to televise a specified set of events either live or on tape delay, that in the network's first year alone would total 455.5 hours. When you see the huge popularity that *March Madness* now enjoys, it is hard to believe that before March of 1980, the early rounds of the NCAA tournament had never appeared on national television.

In the spring of 1979, Rasmussen carried his search for programming to the major American professional leagues. "We had a lot of enthusiasm, and we weren't inhibited by facts," he said, "so we went and told the story of what we wanted to do." He didn't get any immediate interest, but when he talked to NFL commissioner Pete Rozelle and the league's broadcast director Val Pinchbeck, he said they listened intently. Rasmussen said they told him, "It's a little too early in the development of cable, but one day you come back, and the NFL is going to be on cable television." His optimistic parting message to the league officials was "we assume that's going to be ESPN." Eight years later ESPN aired its first live NFL game, a preseason contest between the Miami Dolphins and the Chicago Bears on August 16, 1987.

CHALLENGE #2: FINANCING

Even the best of ideas cannot bear fruit without seed money. Bill Rasmussen's had to cover the cost of his flights and hotel rooms as he flew around the country making presentations. Not sure where to turn first for financial backing, he reached out to the real estate management firm that handled the complex where he had a condominium in Farmington, Connecticut. He knew that K.S. Sweet Associates, based in King of Prussia, Pennsylvania, just outside Philadelphia, handled capital for more than real estate investments, and he was hoping they could give him some advice. What Rasmussen eventually got from K.S. Sweet was a commitment of $75,000, which grew to a $200,000 loan by the time they had found a major investor for the project.

The Getty Oil Company had invested some of its vast profits in the insurance industry, real estate holdings that included pistachio farms in California, and communications. In December of 1978, the partners at K.S. Sweet put Rasmussen in touch with Stuart Evey, the vice president of Getty's Real Estate and Forest Products Division which oversaw all the company's non-oil investments. The division would soon be re-named as Getty Diversified Operations. Rasmussen flew to Los Angeles two weeks before Christmas, 1978, to make his pitch to Evey at Getty's main offices and then ask for $10 million, which would be split evenly between equity and long-term debt.

Stuart Evey thought the television network proposal was worthy of further evaluation, and he liked the idea of getting into the entertainment business. But as a clear example of how interdependent the challenges facing Rasmussen were, Getty waited until eight days after the NCAA agreement was reached to commit any funding to ESPN. The oil company paid off the $200,000 loan from K. S. Sweet and bought an option for 85 percent of the new network. Rasmussen had received the investment he needed, but he had effectively surrendered control of his creation.

One of the first steps Stuart Evey took was to begin searching for an ESPN president with a strong background in television network sports. Rasmussen's new title would become Chairman of the Board, and in July 1979, Chester R. "Chet" Simmons was lured away from his job as president of NBC Sports to join ESPN. Simmons had helped Ed Scherick found Sports Programs, Inc. in 1957, the company that would become ABC Sports. He worked there with Roone Arledge until 1964 when he joined NBC Sports, becoming its president in 1977.

CHALLENGE #3: CABLE DISTRIBUTION

In the first few months of 1979, Bill Rasmussen also started traveling the country to meet with the leaders of the multisystem cable operators (MSOs), from whom he needed commitments to subscribe to the new sports network and distribute its programming to their share of the 14 million Americans homes that had been wired for cable by 1979. Part of his pitch was that he was in negotiations to bring plenty of never-before televised college sports programming to his new network. Rasmussen admitted that his strategy was to take the potential positives from each of his concurrent efforts with the NCAA, cable operators, and investors, and use them to help convince whichever group he would be meeting next.

When his proposal for a fee of one cent per home per day was rejected by every MSO he visited, Rasmussen had to find a viable alternative. The solution was to *pay* the cable systems to carry ESPN instead of charging them a monthly rate. Once Getty's financial backing was secured, the network used part of its marketing budget to pay the cable systems to put the new network in their channel lineups. Imagine how persuasive this was for cable operators: an all-sports network offers to give you the service AND they will pay you a few cents per month for every subscriber you have. This inspired tactic led to ESPN's rapid subscriber base growth. Plus, ESPN allocated 30 percent of its total advertising inventory for the local cable systems to sell. That would allow cable operators to sell commercials within network games and events to local advertisers and keep 100 percent of the revenue from those commercial sales. At this early juncture in the history of cable television however, only about 10 percent of cable systems were actually selling local ads. In successive years, local ad sales became an important part of the revenue stream for every cable system.

Less than two weeks after signing the programming deal with the NCAA, Rasmussen had his first cable affiliate: Gene Schneider, the president of United Cable Television, which had its national headquarters in Denver, agreed to add ESPN to its station lineup. This was most satisfying for

Rasmussen considering the important role that the United Cable system in Plainville, Connecticut, had played in helping him when his idea for a cable sports television package was taking shape. This first cable affiliate agreement came on the same day, March 21, 1979, that the Bristol, Connecticut Redevelopment Authority gave ESPN its official approval to start building on a 10-acre parcel of reclaimed landfill on Middle Street across from a metal salvage yard and next door to a tiny family run restaurant called "Hamp's."

Over the course of the next few months, and after an enthusiastic response at the National Cable Television Association's annual Cable Show in Las Vegas in May 1979, ESPN had signed up enough cable partners to reach an estimated four million homes by the date of its premiere in September 1979.

Launching ESPN in the 21st century would have been a far more difficult proposition: with hundreds of choices now available on cable television, channel space is extremely precious, and the competition for slots is fierce and expensive. But in 1979 with a sparse lineup usually composed of about a dozen stations: the local NBC, CBS, and ABC affiliates, a few "superstations" like WOR, WPIX, and WNEW from New York, WTCG Atlanta, or WGN from Chicago, plus perhaps HBO, the cable systems had plenty of vacant channels.

CHALLENGE #4: ADVERTISING

Bill Rasmussen's cross-country odyssey took him to St. Louis where he convinced one of the largest advertisers in broadcast sports, Anheuser-Busch, to become ESPN's charter sponsor. In May of 1979, A-B agreed to pay $1,380,000 for one-eighth of ESPN's entire commercial inventory through the end of 1980. At that time, it was the largest advertising contract in cable television history. The agreement gave A-B "exclusivity," meaning that no other beer could be advertised on the new network. And if ESPN wanted to televise a sporting event that was sponsored or underwritten by a rival brewery, the network would need to get permission from Anheuser-Busch to exercise one of its small allotment of exclusivity exceptions. One year after ESPN went on the air, Anheuser-Busch renewed the contract for five more years at a significantly higher price: $25 million.

Other national advertisers that bought time on ESPN before it went live included General Motors Pontiac Division, Hertz, SONY, the Wall Street Journal, and not surprisingly, Getty Oil.

THE PREMIERE

On September 7, 1979, ESPN's building was not quite finished, the tape machines that would play out the network's recorded opening had not yet arrived (a truck delivered them at 2 pm that afternoon), the studio was still under construction, the control room for the first shows was in a rented television mobile unit parked outside, and the company's new president was saying he knew they should have postponed the launch until January 1, 1980. But at 7 pm that Friday evening, ESPN would start sending its programming to a little over 600 individual cable systems, and a new era in sports television would begin.

Producing the premiere was Bill Creasy, who had been hired away from CBS to become ESPN's first vice president for programming. Creasy had produced the football game in which instant replay was used for the first time in history, and he was the producer in the CBS truck for the very first Super Bowl in 1967. He had years of experience under every imaginable condition in studios and at live remotes. Creasy was handling the first day chaos as well as anyone could: dealing with technical problems, adjusting his show format, and taping segments with Bill Rasmussen, Chet Simmons, and Stuart Evey to be ready for ESPN's first show: a half-hour *SportsCenter* with Lee Leonard and George Grande. Conspicuous on the wall behind the anchor desk was an NCAA logo, symbolic of how important college sports had been and would continue to be for ESPN. The very first in-studio guest that night was the NCAA president at the time, Bill Flynn.

ESPN only had about 70 employees on the day of its launch. Grande said:

> We knew things were going to be chaotic. We knew things weren't perfect. Anybody who was there the first four or five years can attest to that – this was a magic carpet ride that started on that night. I think we all knew we were involved in something special. (Figure 5.2)

That first *SportsCenter* was followed by a half-hour *NCAA Preview* show to set up the fall 1979 college football season, and at 8 pm, the network aired its first live event: a game from the World Series of Professional Slow-Pitch Softball in Lannon, Wisconsin, outside Milwaukee. The

■ **Figure 5.2** George Grande (L) and Lee Leonard hosted ESPN's first *SportsCenter* show on September 7, 1979. The NCAA logo on the set was a testament to the importance of college sports as content for the new network. (ESPN Images)

matchup was between two teams called the "Kentucky Bourbons" and the "Milwaukee Schlitz," which caused a minor uproar in Bristol because the network didn't want the first day of its exclusive advertising contract with Budweiser to be the last. In 1979, Budweiser was the top-selling brand of beer in the United States, and Schlitz was a strong rival.

Kent Samul, the director at the game site in Wisconsin, came up with a simple solution: "We'll just call the teams 'Kentucky' and 'Milwaukee' during the show," he said. And that's how play-by-play announcer Joe Boyle and analyst Jim Price, a former catcher for the Detroit Tigers, referred to them for the entire telecast. One of Chet Simmons' first moves when he became president had been to hire NBC veteran commentator Jim Simpson to give ESPN credibility with sports fans as it got started, but the honor of calling the first live game in the network's history went to Boyle and Price.

On the phone to Samul the entire game was ESPN's new executive producer, Allan B. "Scotty" Connal, another veteran hired away from NBC. Kent Samul remembered it being a high-scoring game with runs coming too fast for the graphics generator in the television truck to keep up. Updating the score display was a painstaking process that required the operator to change functions, then build and store the updated graphic. "I need the score," Connal was shouting over the phone. "I do too Scotty," Samul replied. Kent Samul continued directing live and taped events for ESPN for decades.

Humble beginnings to be sure, but the "Total Sports Network" was on its way. For the first year, programming was scheduled from 6 pm to 4 am on weekdays and 24 hours per day on weekends. ESPN did not have sports 24 hours a day, seven days a week until September 1, 1980. Columnist Red Smith had foreseen that momentous day with comic fear in *The New York Times* of December 3, 1979. Sports on television every hour of every day, he said would represent "the ghastliest threat to the social fabric of America since the invention of the automobile."

NARROWCASTING

What ESPN did represent was a radical change from traditional broadcasting to "narrowcasting." Instead of building a schedule of programs that would appeal to the broadest possible cross-section of the viewing public, which was what CBS, NBC, and ABC were doing to attract large audiences, ESPN's mission was to target the narrower segment of the audience that followed sports and win their loyalty.

The target audience was men, especially young men who hadn't yet made lifetime choices as to which cars they would drive or beers they would drink. Delivering a small, homogeneous male audience meant that advertisers like beers, carmakers, automotive products, razors, and shaving gels could spend fewer dollars per commercial and reach a larger percentage of potential buyers. There was no need for them to buy more expensive commercials in primetime comedies or dramas on the broadcast networks if half or more of the mass heterogeneous audience was women who may have little or no interest in buying products that were most often purchased by men.

Another important advantage of "narrowcasting" to a targeted audience is that a network's promotional messages become that much more valuable. A captive audience of sports fans is far more likely to watch more sports than would a broad mix of all demographics. Therefore, promoting tomorrow's college basketball game to the fans watching tonight's game is a very effective use of time. The same holds true for promoting an upcoming tennis telecast to the upscale audience watching a golf tournament. Research shows that similar audience demographics will tune in to watch both.

Today, the American audience on any given day is fragmented into a myriad of special interests and program types on cable, subscription video services, and streaming digital apps. As a result, the total number of viewers watching narrow interest networks and platforms is far greater than the combined audience watching the four traditional broadcast networks.

ESPN'S RAPID GROWTH AND CHANGE

Getty Oil's Stu Evey and his appointed president Chet Simmons quickly decided that they needed to leave ESPN's founders behind. At a Sunday breakfast two days after the launch, Bill Rasmussen recalled Evey telling him, "Chet's in charge. You stay out of his way." By October 1, Scott Rasmussen was out of the picture, having had his salary cut by 75 percent. Bill Rasmussen was out of the decision-making mix at ESPN within a year after its premiere, and he sold his shares in 1984.

A caravan of old pros from broadcast network sports divisions in New York was making the move 120 miles northeast to Bristol, Connecticut, and they were taking over. Among them was Bill Fitts, the man who had been executive producer for Super Bowl I on CBS. At the beginning of 1980 Fitts was hired to lead ESPN's remote and studio productions. He had moved to NBC after Robert Wussler took over the sports division at CBS and had recently been working on various independent productions.

At the end of January 1980, Fitts had been at ESPN only a few days when Chet Simmons returned from Super Bowl XIV in Pasadena and excitedly announced, "We're gonna do the NFL Draft in April." In Pasadena, Simmons had run into Val Pinchbeck, the NFL's senior vice president for broadcasting, and asked him if there was anything the new Total Sports Network could do with the NFL. Pinchbeck told Simmons that the NFL was concerned that it disappeared from the public eye during the off-season, and perhaps the annual NFL Draft would be a way to get the league back into the TV spotlight in April.

Fitts' response to his new boss was, "Chet are you crazy? Have you been to a draft? There's nothing to see. There's nobody there, just a few people on phones." Fitts remembers Simmons telling him, "Bill, it's the NFL Draft. N-F-L. We've gotta do it to get the NFL on our air." Before he even learned his way around the brand-new building, Bill Fitts had called on his old NFL researcher Frank Ross and enlisted a couple of production assistants to help him start making phone calls to the major college football programs in the country to search for film or videotape of their respective draft prospects.

When draft day arrived on April 29, 1980, The NFL Draft became a televised event for the first time, and Bill Fitts had video of all but two players who were selected in the first two rounds. Every year since, the interest in the draft has grown along with the length and scope of the telecast. It marked the beginning of a programming vision that ESPN would expand in the years to come: create events like the *X Games* or *Espy Awards*, and produce coverage of existing events that had never before been considered as television content. These included the player drafts in the NBA and Major League Baseball, the Baseball Hall of Fame induction ceremonies, the *Scripps National Spelling Bee*, and the *NCAA Tournament Selection Show*.

While one small team was at work collecting video for the NFL Draft, Bill Fitts was faced with how to produce the NCAA championships, the acquisition of which had played such a pivotal role in the founding of the network. In its first *March of Champions*, ESPN would televise 20 championships from all three NCAA divisions and 23 early round games from the men's basketball tournament. The NCAA hired the production trucks and crews for each of the basketball games so it could syndicate the game telecasts to local TV stations in the markets that followed the specific teams. What Fitts had to do was take the signals from each game into ESPN's Bristol broadcast center and integrate them using a 25-year-old studio host fresh from his job as sports director at Suburban Cablevision in East Orange, New Jersey, Bob Ley. He paired Ley with the former coach of the University of Detroit men's basketball team and the Detroit Pistons, Dick Vitale.

For the first time in sports television history, viewers could watch multiple games at the same time on the same channel. ESPN began what would become the common practice of cutting from one game to another as tight contests developed, or blow-outs made other outcomes apparent. Bill Fitts was orchestrating all the switches from a small production control room, hoping to avoid having Bob Ley throw to a game where play was stopping for a time-out or a commercial break. But ESPN had no communications with any of the NCAA trucks, so a lot of the decisions were simply "best guesses." The following year, the NCAA was encouraged enough by the success of the shows that they allowed ESPN to put a phone and an associate director in each game's truck to better coordinate the tournament coverage.

THE DUAL-REVENUE STREAM

Word was starting to spread that there was a new channel on cable television that did nothing but sports all day and all night. By May 31, 1981, less than two years after its launch, the number of homes that could receive ESPN hit 10 million, and in October of 1983, it became the largest cable network in the United States when that total reached 27.5 million homes.

Chet Simmons had left ESPN after three years at the helm to become the first commissioner of the new United States Football League (USFL). He was succeeded at ESPN in June of 1982 by J. William Grimes who came to the network with a background in sales, unlike his predecessor who was a production executive. Grimes had been general sales manager then executive vice president of the CBS Radio division.

Just before Simmons left and Grimes arrived, Getty Diversified had commissioned McKinsey & Company consultants to do a study of ESPN's projected future. Getty's investment had gone from $10 million to $25 million in three years, but the network was not yet profitable with its only source of revenue coming from the commercial advertising it sold. McKinsey's lead consultant on the project, Roger Werner, projected that it could take five years and $120 million more to make ESPN profitable without changing the business plan. Werner recommended that ESPN stop paying cable systems to take the network and instead start charging them a monthly fee which would generate a consistent second stream of revenue. Part of his argument was simple human nature: if you have to pay for something you attach a greater value to it. And Werner said ESPN should be viewed as a valuable property, not as a give-away.

Bill Grimes was a strong proponent of the plan, and just a few months into his tenure, ESPN started charging its affiliated cable systems six cents per home per month. Some cable systems who were upset that the check they had been receiving from ESPN had just turned into a monthly bill, dropped the sports network from their lineup of stations. But the vast majority of cable operators had seen how important ESPN as a prime selling point to convince new subscribers to scrap their old antennas and sign up for cable. Many of the systems that dropped ESPN when the network started charging its monthly fee had to deal with irate customers, some of whom picketed outside cable offices demanding that they get their ESPN back.

Grimes said that there was also some resistance within ESPN among executives who feared that charging cable systems was the wrong move. They thought that cable operators who had been getting paid to carry the ESPN would never agree to pay for it and the network would lose subscribers as a result. That difference of opinion cost a few vice presidents their jobs. Roger Werner got a new job though. Grimes hired him away from McKinsey & Company and named him ESPN's vice president of finance, administration, and planning. When Bill Grimes left ESPN in 1988, Roger Werner became the network's third president.

The six-cent charge per home per month was adding $20 million per year to ESPN's bottom line by the end of 1983. The fee increased to 10 cents in 1985, and as ESPN added more desirable and expensive programming like NFL games, Major League Baseball, and the NBA, it in turn charged its cable affiliates more each month for what had become an even more valuable service.

In February 2011, ESPN's subscriber base hit its peak of 100 million American homes. The company does not publicly disclose the per-home fees that are written into its contracts with cable operators, but the monthly charge in 2011 had risen to over four dollars per home. Over the course of a year, $48 per home multiplied by 100 million homes equaled $4.8 billion in revenue for ESPN, and that was before the network sold a single commercial. By 2020, the monthly subscription fee was reported to be over nine dollars per home for ESPN's package of networks. Add that to the billions of dollars in advertising and sponsorship that ESPN sells each year, and it was clear that the dual stream of revenue from advertising and cable fees had become a formula for ever-increasing income. It was a primary reason behind the move of *Monday Night Football* from ABC to ESPN in 2006. ESPN could generate income by charging its cable affiliates higher monthly subscriber fees and collect more advertising and sponsorship revenue by creating 10–12 hours of programming to surround every Monday night game.

The dual-revenue stream has now become an economic imperative for virtually every network, not just cable networks. To survive in a very competitive television marketplace, networks need more than just the money they earn from advertising. The traditional broadcast networks have all put a price on the value of their program lineups that they now charge all cable and pay TV operators as part of their "re-transmission consent" agreements. In the past, networks like CBS, NBC, ABC, and Fox rarely if ever had charged cable systems or other distributors for their programming: the networks wanted the broadest reach possible via cable, satellite, and streaming services so they could charge top dollar for their advertising. That changed as the broadcast networks looked at their program lineups and said, "If ESPN can charge so much per month, our shows must be worth at least a fraction of that."

THE WORLDWIDE LEADER IN SPORTS

ESPN went from being owned by an oil company to being owned by a broadcast communications company in 1984, and the resulting changes and improvements set the network, then less than five years old, on a course to become "the Worldwide Leader in Sports." On January 4, 1984, ABC exercised an option that it had held since August of 1982 and bought 15 percent of ESPN from Getty for an estimated $25 million. Less than a week later, Getty merged with Texaco, so for a few months every ESPN employee was a Texaco employee. That did not last long.

In May 1984, Texaco agreed to sell the remaining 85 percent of ESPN to ABC Video Enterprises, a unit of ABC Inc., for $202 million. That brought the full purchase price for the network and its facilities to $227 million. Thirteen percent of that went to Bill Rasmussen and his family in return for his remaining shares. Later in the year, ABC Video Enterprises raised $60 million in cash by selling a 20 percent stake in ESPN to Nabisco Brands. (In 1988, Nabisco sold its portion of the company to the Hearst Corporation.) ESPN finally turned a profit in the fourth quarter of 1984 with a steady flow of monthly fees coming in from what was now a subscriber base of 34 million homes. If Texaco had held off on the sale of the network for even nine more months, the selling price would certainly have gone well above $227 million.

The combination of ABC and Nabisco put ESPN's ownership in the hands of television professionals: Nabisco had invested in Ohlmeyer Communications Company (OCC), and it chose to be represented on ESPN's board of directors by Don Ohlmeyer, OCC's founder, and his partner John Martin, both veterans of broadcast network sports. One of the first impressions the new owners had after visiting ESPN's Bristol, Connecticut, operations was, "How do they do so much with so little?" Herb Granath, the president of ABC Video Enterprises, and the team of Ohlmeyer and Martin set about making changes and allocating additional funds so that ESPN could do even more.

For example, *SportsCenter* had relied heavily on daily highlights that were edited from live games which were downlinked from satellites and recorded day and night in a small screening room with only eight videotape decks. Any other video stories came from a set of stringer reporters and video photographers who were paid a few hundred dollars each to shoot interviews and features and then ship the tapes with any scripts or notes to Bristol via overnight couriers for editing the next day. It was not long after Don Ohlmeyer saw this operation in action that money became available to start doing live satellite reports. Full-time reporters in the field soon replaced most of the stringers, and more travel dollars were freed up for *SportsCenter* anchors like Chris Berman, Bob Ley, and Tom Mees to get out from behind the desk and start covering events from sites.

Equipment was upgraded, workspace was expanded, and over the next year, ESPN started buying the rights to more high-profile sporting events and leagues: a primetime package of live college football games, Atlantic Coast Conference (ACC) college basketball, the National Hockey League, the Nabisco Masters tennis tournament, and the 1987 America's Cup yacht racing from Fremantle, Australia.

"A STORY BOOK YEAR"

As a gift for every employee at the end of 1987, ESPN published a thin, hard-bound story book that opened with, "Once upon a time in the land of Bristol a dream was born. A dream of sports. All the time. ESPN they called it and for seven years the dream grew. And in the eighth year, many magical things happened."

The magic that year began in January with live coverage of the America's Cup races between Dennis Conner's *Stars and Stripes* representing the United States, and *Kookaburra III*, the yacht that was defending the cup for Australia, the first time in 132 years that the defender was not an American boat and the races would be held outside the United States. ESPN received national attention for bringing live coverage from the Indian Ocean of sailors trimming their jib sails and scurrying across decks to viewers sitting at home in the wee hours of the morning. The America's Cup wasn't a ratings success, but it proved that ESPN could produce compelling live television from one of the most distant spots on the globe, and that elevated the network's standing with the public and within the television industry.

Every NFL game that had ever been televised beginning in 1939 had been on broadcast, over-the-air television until 1987. On March 15, the NFL reached a three-year agreement with ESPN to put 13 games for each of the next three seasons on cable television. As America's number one television sport, the NFL would add credibility and attract millions of fans to ESPN. The company "story book" called the NFL acquisition "ESPN's greatest moment." The first NFL telecast on ESPN was the August 16, 1987, preseason game where the Chicago Bears met the Miami Dolphins at what was then the brand-new Joe Robbie Stadium. The game immediately became the most-watched program to date on ESPN, gaining a 10.8 rating. Double-digit ratings on any cable network were unheard of in 1987.

But perhaps the most important event of 1987, and possibly in ESPN's first decade, occurred quietly on July 23, 1987. On that date, ESPN became the first cable network to achieve 50 percent penetration in the United States. It could now be seen in 43.7 million homes, more than half the television homes in the nation. From a curiosity in 1979, delivered via cable technology that was not even available to 80 percent of American homes at the time, ESPN had become a national television force.

The implications were enormous. ESPN's advertising sales force could now sell commercials that would go to a majority of American households. Clients who had previously not been interested in advertising on a minor network that could not be seen on most televisions were now buying time and targeting the sports audience on cable. Leagues and events that wanted national television coverage were now interested in talking with ESPN because the network had a national audience. In January 1989, a year and a half after hitting the magic 50 percent penetration mark, ESPN signed a four-year deal with Major League Baseball to televise 175 baseball games each year.

ESPN's *A Story Book Year* concluded with, "1987, a dream come true." The network had become part of America's sports media establishment, competing with the traditional broadcast networks for advertisers, audience, and the rights to events. It continued to grow in power, penetration, and public perception, adding the ESPN Radio Network in 1992, ESPN2 in 1993, and seven more domestic television networks since. ESPN International debuted in 1989, with limited programs fed to Latin America. It grew to become a multilanguage service seen in 71 countries and territories. ESPN .com was launched in 1995 and is now the nation's leading sports digital platform reaching more than 100-million unique users per month.

ESPN CHANGED EVERYTHING

The proliferation of ESPN and its success on multiple distribution platforms has had such an impact on the sports media that it is not an overstatement to say, "ESPN changed everything." It changed how people accessed sports content across multiple platforms and converted sports fans with ever-shortening attention spans from game watchers to highlight watchers. ESPN made sports bigger by producing thousands more hours of sports programming each year. The early rounds and matches from basketball, golf, and tennis tournaments that before ESPN had been limited to weekend coverage or the semifinals and finals were now available live. And the coverage of women's sports competition increased geometrically, thereby expanding the fan base and providing young women who love sports with role models to emulate, and perhaps one day surpass. The increased exposure has added to the public awareness and stature of sports, leagues, conferences, and events across the board. ESPN's bidding for the broadcast rights to high-profile series and events raised the stakes, adding significantly to the revenue collected by leagues, teams, and organizers.

The thousands of hours of sports content available to fans on cable television forced broadcast networks and local television stations to change their strategies. CBS, NBC, Fox, and ABC all consolidated their sports broadcast portfolios to approximately 500 hours per year or less, then launched sports-only channels and streaming services. Local TV stations had to shift their emphasis to the sports that viewers could not get from ESPN: coverage of local high school and college teams and players. No longer did anyone tune in to a local news program at 6 pm to catch highlights from the previous night's games because they were widely available all day on *SportsCenter* or the internet. The beneficiaries of this shift have been the high schools and local colleges that receive more attention and promotion on local stations.

The universal accessibility to sports highlights and news day and night has also been responsible for the growth of sports talk radio and the decline of newspaper and magazine coverage of sports. More people watching more highlights and consuming more sports news every day could share their observations and opinions about teams and players from distant teams and competitions by calling their local radio sports talk shows. The print media were put at a disadvantage because by the time they could publish, sports fans already knew the results and statistics from every contest. Newspapers and magazines shifted their focus to online delivery of content, in-depth stories about players, coaches, or issues, and investigative pieces that took a period of weeks or months to develop. The success of these investigative reporters however fueled a "brain-drain" from magazines and newspapers as ESPN, other networks, and websites hired away many of the best and brightest.

Perhaps more than anything else, ESPN changed what sports fans expected to see on television. We expect that every game that our favorite baseball, football, or basketball team plays will be televised. We expect to see every highlight from every game, not just those played by the league leaders or the nationally ranked college teams, but from *every* game. We expect to hear experts break down the important factors that will affect each game's outcome, and we expect that interviews, analysis, data, and debate will follow. We expect to get personal information about our favorite players, to see them laugh and cry and interact with each other on the field and off. And we expect all the sensational details whenever any player or coach steps out of line.

NEW CHALLENGES FOR THE WORLDWIDE LEADER

ESPN itself has not been immune to change. The same kind of technological innovations that made the network possible in the 1970s and 1980s have now changed the delivery of live sports. At the beginning of the 21st century, most homes in America with internet access had slow connections that were not suited for live streaming or playing videos. The first video highlights that were published to ESPN.com were compressed, which meant they would look okay on a small screen, but the quality was far inferior to the live pictures and sound fans could receive via cable TV. Access to high-speed broadband changed that, making it possible to watch internet video on a big screen with little or no degradation of picture quality.

When home access to high-speed broadband edged past the slower connection services in 2005, a new set of video options began to open that has seriously reduced the size of the cable television universe, eroding ESPN's television audience and cutting into profits.

The ESPN cable audience reached its zenith in the year 2011 with 100.1 million subscribers. That figure has declined every year since as cable "cord-cutting" gained momentum in response to the introduction of more digital delivery alternatives that were less expensive per month. ESPN did not automatically suffer a loss of revenue because its per-home fee charged to cable systems that started a $0.06 per month in the 1980s had exceeded $9.00 by the year 2020. When the network hit its highest audience total in 2011, the average monthly subscriber fee for cable and direct broadcast satellite (DBS) systems was less than $5.00. That meant that even after suffering the loss of over 15 million subscribers in a decade, ESPN was still collecting at least $3 billion *more* in annual fees than when it had a larger pay TV universe.

As its television audience steadily shrank, ESPN's reach on digital and social media platforms soared, making it clear to the network where the future lay. The network introduced ESPN+, its first digital direct-to-consumer (DTC) service, in March 2018 to offer original programming and a limited number of live streaming events directly to fans, bypassing the cable systems and the rest of the multichannel video program distributors (MVPDs) such as DirecTV, Dish Network, and Verizon Fios. The adoption of ESPN+ by consumers was so successful that it exceeded the 12 million subscriber figure in less than three years. However, priced at less than $10 per month, ESPN+ would have to extend its reach geometrically to support becoming the home of ESPN's highest-priced sports properties.

To offset the billions of dollars in annual rights fees that the network pays the NFL and NBA for live games and content and its high-priced long-term deals for Major League Baseball, the College Football playoffs, Wimbledon, and more, the network could not afford to abandon its traditional revenue model, but a period of transition is irrefutably underway. The availability of live sports events that are exclusive to cable networks has remained a prime factor in the retention of pay TV subscribers and one of the major deterrents against additional cord-cutting.

ESPN President and Co-Chair of Disney Media Networks Jimmy Pitaro said a multiplatform approach was the only way to fulfill the company's mission of serving sports fans anytime and anywhere they may be.

> The point is that we can be multiple things at the same time here and run parallel paths. We continue to invest in, and acquire content for, our traditional TV platforms, which are still quite valuable, and, at the same time, build out ESPN+ … And as consumers continue to gravitate towards DTC, we have the optionality and are well set up to serve them.

But as the number of cable subscribers continues to dwindle by several million per year, a tipping point looms on the horizon where ESPN may be forced to move more of its live content to ESPN+ and increase the fees for that digital service to offset the corresponding reduction in total people reached.

Virtually nothing in the live sports media business has been untouched or unaffected by ESPN's presence, power, and influence since its "Storybook Year" of 1987. The network has gone from an unlikely underdog to one of the most recognizable and valuable brands in sports. It is consistently at or near the top in primetime viewership among all cable networks, but the proliferation of new digital video services that accelerated during the COVID-19 pandemic splintered the sports audience and has forced ESPN to reinvent itself and diversify its offerings across multiple platforms. Despite the challenges it faces, there remains an enthusiasm for sports at "The Worldwide Leader" that thrives on competition. At the end of the tumultuous year of 2020 that brought the cancellation or rescheduling of hundreds of events and upheaval in the subscription video business, Pitaro said it is "inspiring to witness the amazing ESPN team display remarkable strength in the face of adversity, turning outsized challenges into opportunities to fulfill our mission of serving fans."

The entire network was re-energized in the spring of 2021 when it announced a new 11-year $2.7 billion per year rights agreement with the NFL that will bring the Super Bowl to ESPN and ABC and the first live NFL games to ESPN+. "When ESPN and the NFL work best together, the results are transformational for sports fans and the industry," said Pitaro. Fans can expect that ESPN and ABC will put their full complement of broadcast, cable, and digital platforms to work creating the biggest multi-platform "Mega-cast" ever for Super Bowl LXI in February of 2027.

This landmark agreement made Bill Rasmussen think back to the meeting he had with NFL Commissioner Pete Rozelle 42 years earlier when he was in search of live programming for ESPN's 1979 launch. He recalled Rozelle's words, "Not today, but someday Bill." That "someday" had arrived, and ESPN's visionary founder could not have been more elated.

BIBLIOGRAPHY

Adler, Kristie. "ESPN Digital Celebrates Three Years as the No. 1 U.S. Sports Property, Logs Best February on Record." *ESPN Press Room*, 2021. https://espnpressroom.com/us/press-releases/2021/03/espn-digital-celebrates-three-years-as-the-no-1-u-s-sports-property-logs-best-february-on-record/

Evey, Stuart. *Creating an Empire: ESPN-The No-Holds-Barred Story of Power, Ego, Money, and Vision That Transformed a Culture*. Chicago, IL: Triumph Books, 2004.

Fitts, Bill. *Interviewed by the Author*, 2011.

Nagle, Dave. "ESPN, Inc.: 2020 in Review." *ESPN Press Room*, 2020. https://espnpressroom.com/us/press-releases/2020/12/espn-inc-2020-in-review/

Pitaro, Jimmy. *Interview Notes Provided to the Author*, 2021.

Rasmussen, Bill. *Sports Junkies Rejoice! The Birth of ESPN*. Hartsdale, NY: QV Publishing, 1983.

Rasmussen, Bill. *Interviewed by the Author*, 2009.

Rasmussen, Bill. *Twitter Post*, March 18, 2021.

Service Electric. "History." *ServiceElectric.com* https://www.sectv.com/Web/aspFounder.aspx?strSystem=LV

Smith, Red. "Cable TV for Sports Junkies." *The New York Times*, 3, 1979. https://www.nytimes.com/1979/12/03/archives/cable-tv-for-sports-junkies.html?searchResultPosition=1

Worster, Hannah. "Hailing ESPN's 09/07/79 debut with SportsCenter original George Grande." *ESPN Front Row*, 2013. https://www.espnfrontrow.com/2013/09/icymi-the-week-on-front-row-plus-hailing-espns-090779-debut-with-sportscenter-original-george-grande/

Programming Sports for Viewers and Advertisers

Every year there are more than 400,000 hours of sports programming available to fans in the United States. Considering that each of us lives a total of only 8,760 hours in a year (multiply 24 hours a day by 365 days) a person would need almost 50 screens, each tuned to a different channel, and never sleep to consume it all. ESPN alone has nine networks, the NFL, MLB, NBA, and NHL each fill their channels with 24 hours a day of live and edited content as do the sport-specific networks such as the Golf Channel and Tennis Channel. There are over 30 regional sports networks, and several college conferences such as the Big Ten and Pac 12 each televise hundreds of games and events each year. Turner Sports distributes hundreds of hours of content annually as do the broadcast networks: CBS, NBC, Fox, and ABC. In addition, CBS, NBC, and Fox expanded their sports offerings by establishing branded 24-hour sports networks. (NBC decided to shutter the NBC Sports Network in 2020 and move its live events to the USA Network and the Peacock streaming service). Selecting which events and programs to broadcast on each channel or streaming service, then acquiring and strategically scheduling them is the job of the live sports media programmer.

In the fourth century BC, the Greek philosopher and teacher Aristotle said, "know your audience." It goes without saying that the means of communication have changed dramatically in the centuries since Aristotle, but the elements of effective communication are remarkably unchanged. To attract viewers and deliver content that will hold their interest, Aristotle's lesson still holds true: you must know your audience. You need to know who they are, which includes the demographics of age, gender, education, ethnic background, and income level. Where do they live, where did they come from, what do they like, what moves or entertains them, how much time do they spend on leisure activities, at what time of day or night are they watching, and on which devices? The more answers that a media sports programming department has to these questions, the more likely they will be to aggregate a set of events and shows that will attract their targeted audience.

DOI: 10.4324/9781003165590-6

The programming department for any network or digital video service has four primary functions: research, acquisitions, relationships, and scheduling. You can think of live media programmers as social and cultural interpreters who analyze the research they gather and put it into the context of evolving social trends and cultural preferences. It is their job to interpret information and data about their viewers and those who watch other networks or digital services, then project forward to make decisions as to which new programs should be planned, acquired, or created that will appeal to the audience they want to attract. Those selected programs must then be made readily accessible in either a linear network's schedule or as part of the on-demand menu of choices available to viewers whenever, wherever, and however they want to consume sports media.

Each network that presents shows and live events scheduled one after the other over a 24-hour broadcast day is "linear." Shows leading into and following one another require programming executives to consider how best to transition audiences from one to the next, aligning their schedules for maximum viewership and a minimum of abrupt changes of course. Online digital networks such as ESPN3 and every subscription video-on-demand digital services like Netflix, Prime Video, Peacock, or Disney+ are "non-linear." They offer multiple live or recorded events and shows all available simultaneously as a menu of choices designed to appeal to a variety of audiences regardless of the day or time. Viewers can customize their media experiences by exercising the kind of personal control over their content consumption that was not possible in the days before online or streaming distribution.

The other side of the programmer's responsibility is deciding which series or shows should be discontinued, moved to other platforms, or relegated to a lower priority. Factors taken into consideration for these decisions include changes in how people consume the content they choose, audience rating declines, an increase in the average age of viewers, or shifting demographics that make the program or series less attractive to advertisers. This is particularly important for linear networks that show only one program at a time, making their prime viewing hours very precious real estate. Non-linear services that offer programs for viewers to watch whenever they choose can retain an under-performing or niche series, but it is unlikely to get prominent promotion or be placed at the top of the menu. The quality of their research and how well programmers use that information can determine the success or failure of a network or streaming service. The consequences for misreading viewer preferences and appetites, or failing to see trends developing are smaller audiences, reduced advertiser interest, and lower revenues.

Clearly, the role of the programming department is critical. At every step of the way, from before a sports event is acquired for distribution through its entire life being presented to the viewing public, the value of the relationships forged and maintained by programmers is paramount. Establishing a partnership with the sports league, conference, or organizer that is based on mutual benefit and success is an important beginning that must be maintained for as long as events continue to be televised. When programmers openly share their information and objectives with their network's producers, advertising sales force, marketers, and affiliate relations group they build relationships that are vital for the coordination of resources and the overall product of the content game after game, season after season.

At no point in television history was this proven to be more important than during the COVID-19 pandemic of 2020–21, when the entire sports industry was affected by the cancellation, postponement, or rescheduling of so many games and events. Burke Magnus, ESPN president of programming and original content, explained that the multiyear agreements that networks have with leagues and major events must go much deeper than purely transactional relationships. Magnus said that during the upheaval of the pandemic, "We saw the best side of people come out. People took a collaborative and cooperative approach to these unprecedented situations. Everybody understood that the crisis was not good for anybody's business." Douglas White, the vice president of program planning for Turner Sports said the pandemic was "a masterclass in dealing with your partners externally and internally. You had to think about your personnel, that came first and foremost, how do we keep them safe as productions continued to happen."

"Force majeure" clauses are written into every contract for live sports to cover each party's liability in special circumstances such as a hurricane blowing through a city and forcing a game to be canceled as a result. But this contract language covering what were commonly called "acts of God" was never meant to be a remedy when every game was canceled or postponed due to a multiyear pandemic.

However, because of the mutual trust that sports network programmers had built up over several years with the NBA, the NHL, Major League Baseball, and other sports providers, Magnus said, "almost without exception there was a way through a contractual mechanism or just through good faith business conversations" to account for changes in the number of games to be played and their scheduling. There were many conversations with leagues, conferences, and organizers about the game inventory that was owed to the networks in terms of the number of games and the money involved. White said that every solution had to be equitable for all parties involved. "On one hand you obviously have an obligation to protect your company from any exposure," he said, "but you also don't want to put your partner in a position where you're going to bankrupt them or put them out of business."

Leagues, conferences, and organizers did refund huge sums to the networks to make up for games and events that were not played during the pandemic. In some cases, a portion of the refunds was committed to creating new programs for various network platforms that served to further promote the partner's sports content. Arrangements were also worked out that required the league or conference to purchase thousands of subscriptions to digital services operated by the network which helped increase their distribution and promotion. As the world, and along with it the sports industry, moved forward from the COVID-19 shutdowns, enduring lessons were learned from the crisis. "We are going to learn a lot from this ultimately in terms of how leagues and organizations value their fans, how they value their players, how they work with their media partners, how they interact with their local communities," said White. "I think there will be long-term benefits and long-term consequences for some people. Some leagues have done it better than others and they are going to come out of it stronger than others."

THE PROGRAMMING MARKETPLACE

Live sport has proven to be an important and lucrative programming strategy in an era of both expanding subscription video-on-demand services whose content is overwhelmingly recorded, scripted entertainment, and the wide proliferation of digital video recorders (DVRs). The advantage for sport as programming is that the games and events are a perishable commodity. If someone knows the final score or result, the overwhelming percentage of people will not watch a recording of that game. They may go to their smartphones, to online sports websites, or watch *SportsCenter* for a highlight, but very few will devote two or three hours of their time to watch an event that has already been decided. As a result, well over 90 percent of all sports viewing occurs live as it happens. By comparison, the percentage of entertainment programming that is viewed at its scheduled airtime has continued to decline as more people either record their favorite shows onto a home DVR for "time-shifted" viewing later or go to subscription video and streaming services that aggregate the entire series. The significant difference is that when you watch sports live you cannot fast-forward through the commercials like you can on a DVR, computer, or mobile device. Advertisers know that there is a far better chance their messages will be seen by prospective customers in sports programming than in any other genre of entertainment. As a result, advertisers are charged premium prices for commercials and sponsorship elements in sports programming, and that increases the value of sports as a media property.

Every time a new non-linear, on-demand entertainment service is introduced, a new social media network is launched, or a new video game hits the market, the competition for audience share intensifies. Anything that has the potential to take people away from watching sports must be seen as a serious competitor. ESPN's Burke Magnus maintains, "It's all about share of time. If you can attract as many people as possible, then hold them for as long as possible, then you have succeeded." With only 24 hours in a day and an ever-increasing number of options for people to spend their time, the battle is over how much of that time a network or digital service can control.

In this highly competitive arena, the elite leagues and events that perennially attract the largest audiences despite all the competing distractions are separating themselves from the rest of sports properties. Premium content has become "super-premium." The NFL, NBA, college football, and Major League Baseball in the United States, and the most popular soccer leagues, motor racing, and cricket around the world are more valuable because of the relative size of the live television audiences that they reliably command. They can continue to charge higher fees every time their media rights come up for negotiation regardless of whether their ratings are climbing or not.

Consider this disparity between soaring rights fees and slumping audience delivery: in 2018, the Fox Network extended its contract for Major League Baseball games for the years 2022 through 2028 at a reported price of $729 million per season. That was an increase of 39 percent over the $525 million that Fox had paid each year from 2014 through 2021. But from 2014 to 2018, the audience for the deciding game of the World Series fell from 23 million to 17.6 million viewers per minute, a decline of 23 percent. Each new programming deal that a major sport does with its media partners now includes expanded online, streaming, and highlights rights to justify the higher prices, but this MLB example is emblematic of the gulf that is widening between the most popular sports at the top and all the rest. "I think the premium properties will become more premium and continue to command escalating fees for the most part," said Magnus.

> I think there will be a lot of sports that previously were either in the middle or the lower end or in slow-growth mode that will feel a little bit of compression. The more you're forced to escalate fees on that premium cut of properties, the more everything else gets squeezed in a declining environment.

That "squeeze" is not only putting pressure on the prices that sports below the "super-premium" tier can charge for media rights fees, but it is also accelerating the migration of content from broadcast and cable networks to the expanding online and direct-to-consumer services. In 2021, NBC Universal announced that it would shut down its NBC Sports Network (NBCSN) and move some sports programming over to share time with scripted dramas and comedies on the co-owned USA Network and move other properties to the Peacock streaming service. In the final year of its exclusive rights contract with the National Hockey League, NBC designated a portion of its live hockey games to move from NBCSN to Peacock. The streaming service was launched on June 15, 2020, by NBC Universal, which is owned by Comcast. In its first six months, Peacock had amassed 26 million subscribers, far surpassing Comcast's total of 19 million cable homes.

The NHL is part of an expanding tier of cross-platform sports properties that are relying upon a combination of linear networks, online streaming, and direct-to-consumer services to distribute their live games. With an average audience of six to eight million viewers per minute in the United States for its top-rated Stanley Cup Finals games in the decade from 2010–19, the NHL is not in the "super-premium" category. Moving a substantial number of its live games to a streaming service could help cultivate a new set of fans who have abandoned cable. That is precisely what is expected under the new seven-year rights agreement estimated at $400 million per year that the NHL signed with ESPN in March of 2021. Approximately 75 games each season are designated for distribution on ESPN+, the network's direct-to-consumer service, and more highlights will be available on ESPN internet platforms. Turner Sports agreed to pay the NHL an additional $225 million per year for games and coverage on TNT and Bleacher Report.

Sports programmers at NBC, ESPN, and all the major multiplatform media conglomerates find themselves straddling two different worlds as they try to react to where the market is going. One foot is the linear world as we have known it, and the other is in the non-linear, digital streaming, direct-to-consumer world that may become the dominant form of distribution going forward. They are simultaneously serving two priorities: one is to continue to have the best portfolio of live rights content blended with original content and news and information. But the other is to expand their appeal to new audiences on new platforms and react to changing demographics, whether that is the elusive chase for younger adults, women, or multicultural viewers. To use a hockey metaphor, the programming departments cannot skate to where the puck is, they have to "skate to where the puck is going."

No media conglomerate has more rights deals for more programming than The Walt Disney Company's ESPN. With eight English-language networks available to US domestic subscribers, plus ESPN Deportes in Spanish, the ESPN3 online network, its ESPN+ direct-to-consumer service, and ESPN International reaching 71 countries, the company simply has more hours to fill than any other sports media distributor. The depth of the ESPN rights portfolio allowed its programming department to be nimble and flexible in dealing with the uncertainties and upheaval in sports during the COVID-19 pandemic. Take college football as an example. There are over 700 games scheduled on ESPN networks every autumn, so during the COVID-19 pandemic any game moved or canceled on the ABC or ESPN schedule could be replaced by the programming department with a game from ESPN2 or ESPNU, or a game that might have been designated for streaming on ESPN3 or ESPN+.

Every week during the college football season of 2020 presented a different circumstance with games canceled, games rescheduled, even games with two teams matched up that weren't supposed to play each other originally, but they met because each had their opponent drop out at the last minute for quarantine or health safety reasons. ESPN's programming chief Burke Magnus said, "We were dealing with circumstances that were previously unheard of. Reacting on the fly became almost commonplace. We had one game canceled at 9 a.m. on the day of the game." Having the deepest portfolio of rights and so many platforms from ABC on the broadcast side to its cable and streaming platforms was an advantage during what was an unprecedented set of circumstances in the sports industry. It was a lot of work for the 350 people in ESPN's programming department, but for them, it became the new normal.

When media companies like ESPN started expanding from just one network to two or three (or eight), "cannibalization" was the term that programming executives used to describe how much audience an attractive event or show on a co-owned network might take away from their primary network. They measured how much a show on ESPN2 or ESPNU would cut into the ratings for the games airing at the same time on ESPN. Fox would want to know how their events on Fox Sports One (FS1) would "cannibalize" their programs on Fox. However, as the number of networks ballooned in the 1990s and 2000s, aggregating the largest cumulative audience at any one hour became the overriding goal. A big college basketball game on ESPN2 scheduled up against an important NBA game on ESPN might cut into the ESPN rating, but, combined, the two shows give the company a larger share of the audience, and that is the prize. No one worries about "cannibals" anymore.

The scheduling advantage that ESPN had during the pandemic with so many networks and so much content available may not be as valuable when the world has left the tumult of COVID-19 behind. Sport as a social activity was hurt because gatherings of any size were discouraged and limits on a person's ability to watch a game with friends or go to a bar or restaurant to see a live event disrupted how we customarily consume sports content. The disruption of personal routines, the new digital entertainment options that have become widely available to people, and the revenue losses incurred by live sports media companies during the pandemic are continuing to adversely affect total viewership and profitability. The demise of the NBC Sports Network raises the question as to how many co-owned networks may be too many. In this era when more Americans every year are cutting the cable and moving to subscription video-on-demand services, we may very well see some networks do the same: abandon cable and adopt a streaming-only distribution model.

People will always gravitate toward quality products at competitive prices, and technology will always force the issue. In the early days of the internet the only video that could be accessed was compressed (only one pixel where a regular television picture would have eight) so its quality was diminished on any screen larger than a laptop. But as technological advances made the online transmission of high-definition video and stereo sound possible, new services crossed that threshold and changed the television marketplace. The rate of change continues to accelerate every year. There is no going back to the "old normal."

THE ACQUISITION OF SUCCESS

In the live sports media business, the acquisition of just one major property can bring immediate success and change the entire brand image of a broadcaster or digital distributor. One well-timed, wisely spent, significant investment can turn an also-ran into a powerful force in the industry. The emphasis is on the timing, the wisdom, and the size of the financial commitment.

The prime example of success through acquisition is the first rights deal that the Fox Network signed with the NFL in late 1993 for four years of National Football Conference games that CBS had been televising since 1961. Fox agreed to pay the NFL $395 million for each of the four years, $100 million more than CBS had offered to retain their incumbency. A headline in *The Washington Post* that December read "And the Fourth Shall be First." The Fox Network, cobbled together from a group of previously independent TV stations only seven years earlier, was in fourth place in the ratings race behind NBC, ABC, and CBS. The debut of NFL games on Fox in the fall of 1994, called by Pat Summerall and John Madden who Fox hired away from CBS, gave the network instant credibility and an important platform upon which it could promote the other shows in its schedule. The wisdom was in how Fox looked at the NFL as an asset not simply as a set of games every Sunday in the fall. This one acquisition changed Fox from ragged renegade to respected competitor in the television establishment.

The acquisition of sports events and series that bring with them a huge loyal following of fans will increase viewership for networks no matter how they are distributed. The sports media marketplace, however, is driven by profit and loss just like any other business. The programming department must estimate how much profit it can generate from higher subscription levels and fees plus advertising and sponsorship in and around the live games and events. To that is added the value of the promotional time in those shows that will drive an audience to the network's other shows and series.

On the opposite side of the ledger are all the costs associated with acquiring, producing, and delivering the programs. These include the rights fees, talent and production costs, location and travel expenses, any staging or sets required, and marketing fees and sales commissions, plus the costs associated with transmission and distribution. If the projected revenue offsets the cost of the programming by a margin large enough to make a profit, the network will likely make a competitive bid for the property and block out time for it in the on-air schedule. However, not all programs need to have a bottom line that is in the black. The value of certain properties like the NFL for Fox or the Olympics on NBC as they become part of a network's brand identity can actually exceed the value of the actual dollars returned from advertising, sponsorship, and/or subscriptions. The prestige and the promotional value that these properties hold for a network or digital service, along with the opportunities presented at each event for hosting major clients and advertisers, can outweigh the deficit on the "profit vs. loss" statement.

Enhancing the reputation of the network is one of the three primary reasons for acquiring a show or series along with boosting audience ratings and increasing revenue. The programming department therefore needs to judge how many marquis properties that will build reputation but may not necessarily show a profit it can afford to present and still end each year in the black. Regardless of the prestige and other benefits accrued from televising premiere events, the goal of any network or digital video service is never to lose money.

The networks compete for ratings when they schedule sports programming head-to-head, and when they bid against each other for choice television rights properties that come up for renewal. Most rights contracts allow the incumbent rightsholder the opportunity to negotiate first for renewal and should that fail, the first right to match or beat a competing offer. It's called "FNFR," first negotiation, first refusal. The importance of signature sports events and series to a network's brand identity and its standing in the business and with the public can be seen in the trend in the 21st century for longer rights agreements, many now covering eight to ten or more years. Most of those long-term deals are now renewed well before they expire in order that the partnership between a network and a sports league or organizer and the co-branding they share will extend for years to come. Its identity as "The Network of the Olympics" was so important to NBC, that in 2011, the network paid the International Olympic Committee $4.38 billion for the rights to the next four Olympics, then just three years later extended that deal until the year 2032 by agreeing to pay the IOC $7.7 billion more. Choosing which events and series to bid for that will add value, viewers, and generate revenue for a network or digital service is the most important decision that will be faced by a sports programmer. Just as critical is deciding how high to bid for each rights package without putting the network into the red.

When a competing network wins a premium sports property, the job for programmers at the networks that did not make the acquisition becomes counterprogramming. When NBC schedules Olympic programming, which traditionally attracts more female viewers than male viewers (the ratio is consistently about 55 percent female to 45 percent male), the competing networks will counterprogram with shows proven to draw large percentages of men like NBA games or sports news and talk shows. When *Monday Night Football* was still on ABC, ESPN had some success counterprogramming with figure skating events to draw females who were not NFL fans.

The real fight is for your time. People have far more choices today. The hours that someone spends on Facebook, Instagram, or Tik-Tok, or watching streaming video services such as Netflix or Amazon Prime are all hours not spent watching sports on television. However, as more individuals simultaneously watch television and visit online sites, and as internet-enabled television sets become more commonplace in homes around the world, the challenge for sports media services is to develop programming that takes advantage of this two-screen trend, exploiting the interactivity and rewarding the "co-viewing" audience with more layers of sports content and entertainment.

PROGRAMMING SOURCES

There are a variety of means by which a network, digital service, or local television station can secure sports programming.

1. *Rights contracts*. The television network or digital service pays a contracted amount of money to the organizer/ owner of the event(s) for the exclusive rights to air a set number of games or shows over a specified number of years in a defined geographic territory. (An example would be an agreement to pay $20 million per year for five years for the exclusive rights to televise 20 games per year in North America.) The International Olympic Committee owns and organizes the Olympic Games. FIFA is the owner/organizer of World Cup Soccer. Professional leagues and their teams own the product that they present: every game, every season. Annual events like The Masters golf tournament are the property of their organizers, in this case, the Augusta National Golf Club.

Organizers negotiate to sell the broadcast and media distribution rights to the highest bidder. This is how networks acquire most of the major sports properties that attract their largest audiences: NFL games including the Super Bowl, the Olympics, the NBA, international soccer, Major League Baseball, college football and basketball, golf and tennis tournaments, NASCAR, NHL games, and many other sports that don't reach the mass audiences commanded by these properties.

To prevent the value of their rights from being diluted, virtually every programming contract now extends the exclusivity well beyond television distribution to include "all means and media" so that fans do not have the option to watch proprietary content anywhere but on a co-owned or affiliated channel, digital service, or website.

2. *Barter agreements*. These deals may represent a sizeable portion of a network or digital service's sports programming depending upon how it chooses to do business and how much money it wants to spend. Unlike rights contracts that tend to be fairly uniform in structure and content, barter agreements come in a variety of shapes based upon specific situations and agreements.

   a. In a straight barter deal, an organizer or advertiser can agree to finance the production of a program or series then provide it to the network free of charge. In the agreement, the organizer or advertiser retains a specified amount of the commercial time available in each program. In the case of an advertiser, those commercial availabilities will be used to sell its product. The goal for a sports organizer doing a barter deal with a network is to build its audience and fan base with the media exposure, and it will sell commercials to sponsors to help offset the costs of production. The network gets free programming in which it can sell the remainder of the advertising time and keep that revenue.

   b. Cash barter. In this variation, a certain amount of money does change hands, and the network divides the total commercial time with the organizer or advertiser, more than likely retaining a larger percentage than in a straight barter. That ratio is subject to negotiation as is the responsibility for who pays all or part of the production costs. When a network or digital service puts its own money into the budget, it can be assured of greater control over the end-product, the quality of the coverage and editing, and the level of commercialization within the show. An example of a barter deal was the Korean baseball coverage that ESPN aired during the pandemic of 2020. The network took the produced coverage from the Korea Baseball Organization, and its staff commentators voiced over the games.

3. *Time-buys*. The owner or organizer of an event or series essentially buys a block of time on a network or other distribution service to make sure that the shows will be seen by their targeted audience. This type of arrangement can be very desirable for networks or individual stations because they are guaranteed a profit that is not contingent upon them selling a single commercial. The event organizer is responsible for selling all the advertising and paying for the production of the telecast(s). Networks that sell programming time maintain a set of guidelines covering what type of advertising is allowed and how the shows should be produced. These will almost always include:

   a. The number of minutes per hour that can be allotted for commercials.

b. The number of program segments per hour. (Example: A show broken into eight segments will have seven internal commercial breaks, each of a pre-determined length.)

c. The type of content and language that the network will allow. Most sports programming is G-rated so that it will attract young and old viewers alike.

d. Power of approval over all the talent who will appear in the program and what they will be allowed to wear. Viewers do not distinguish between client-supplied programs and shows produced by the network itself, so the professionalism of the commentators must meet network standards. And any talent apparel that has visible advertising, political logos, or personal messaging may be prohibited.

e. Certain products or services will not be allowed to advertise in the program or sponsor any segments or features within. Most networks maintain a ban on ads for firearms or other weapons and any controversial political advocacy that could alienate segments of the audience.

f. Production elements that affect the final look of the program must conform to network style guides. These include any graphics or animations to be used in the show, the music that is licensed for or played in the program, microphone flags that identify the network and/or event, in what form the finished program will be delivered to the network, and which legal entity is entitled to the copyright.

An example of a "time-buy" is the *Ironman Triathlon*. Timex, the maker of Ironman wristwatches, organizes the annual competition and for many years has purchased time on NBC to televise its event. Timex can use all the advertising time for its products or sell some of the commercial time slots to other approved advertisers. The watchmaker hires an independent production company that will provide the personnel and technical equipment necessary to record the video and audio, then edit it together into a finished package that NBC will accept and air.

A time-buy does guarantee the network or station a profit, but its level of control over the finished product cannot help but be diminished when an event organizer or its naming sponsor assumes responsibility for producing and selling that program. The vigilance of the network's assigned programming and production watchdogs will determine to a great degree whether the show that is delivered meets the specified standards and therefore looks to the viewer just like any other game or event that the network would produce itself.

4. *Owned programming.* This is any event or series that is created or owned by the network or station for which no rights fee is paid to

an organizer or other third party. ESPN created the *X Games* and annually stages summer and winter competitions. The network enters lease agreements with venues, pays to build all the ramps and jumps, pays for the transportation and housing of all the athletes, and covers the cost of their services, plus all the management, marketing, security, prize money for the medalists in each event, and every other function required to put on an event for the public. But ESPN never has to negotiate with a league or organizer for *X Games* rights fees.

SportsCenter and all other sports newscasts on any network or digital video distributor are another example of owned programming. The network enters into reciprocal agreements with other sports programmers allowing them to use highlights from each other's events. Beyond that, no rights deals need to be drawn, and the amount of money the network or distributor collects from the sale of advertising and sponsorships in the sports news shows almost always far exceeds the cost of production.

Each of the league-owned networks such as NFL Network and MLB Network, as well as the more than 30 regional sports networks that are owned in whole or in part by teams, fill their schedules with owned programming. The NFL does not pay rights to televise its own games or highlights, but the league could make more money if it chose to sell the rights to those games to other networks. An example is the shift of Thursday Night NFL games in 2022 from the NFL Network to Amazon Prime Video in exchange for $1 billion per year. The New England Sports Network (NESN) televises over 140 Boston Red Sox games and most of the Boston Bruins games without paying a dime for rights because the Red Sox ownership group controls 80 percent of the network, and the Bruins' owners hold the other 20 percent.

These four categories account for the vast majority of sports programming that we see each year, but there are a number of other variations that help fill out network schedules and digital menus. They include 1) revenue shares, 2) co-productions, 3) team or organizer productions given free of charge to the network, and 4) infomercials.

A revenue share agreement is what the National Hockey League used to get back onto American television screens following its lost season of 2004–05, which was canceled due to a disagreement with the NHL Players Association over salary caps and other collective bargaining issues. The NHL had been collecting approximately $120 million per year in broadcast rights from ESPN, but after the year-long interruption, the reliability and value of the NHL as a media property fell dramatically. Instead of signing a new rights contract at what would have been less than half the previous $120 million rate, the NHL entered a two-year revenue-sharing partnership with NBC in 2005. The NHL and NBC agreed to pool the profits from television advertising and league sponsorships, then divide that revenue according to an agreed-upon formula. After two years, the NHL had demonstrated its renewed stability and regained enough audience to again offer its games to media rights bidders.

PROGRAMMING: WHAT'S THE JOB?

The programming department is at the center of any television network or digital service: its programmers must interact with almost every other department and with the network's most important partners: its content providers and advertisers. Think of the programmers as being at the hub of a wheel. They must acquire and schedule games and additional shows before:

a) The production department can produce the content.
b) The sales department can sell any commercials or sponsorships in the shows.
c) The marketing team can do any promotion.
d) Affiliated stations or services will consider distributing the network.

Every program acquisition must be made with an understanding of how each show or series will fit into the network's air schedule or subscription service's menu of offerings as part of its overall strategy to attract and build viewership. Reaching an agreement for the rights to televise a series of events or for the production of any new programming can be a laborious process mired in detail, but the signing of a contract is not where the programming department's work ends. The implementation of the agreement, the maintenance of the relationship with each partner league, organizer, or producer, and the development of new shows or specials to expand a successful franchise for maximum value are also important parts of the programmer's responsibilities.

The basics of the job do not vary much from network to network. What does vary is the scope of the job. The traditional broadcast networks, NBC, CBS, and Fox, each televise approximately 500 hours of sports per year. For them, sports are a "picture window" in which they show off a set of prestigious acquisitions that help define their network brand and image.

By comparison, the programming departments at 24-hour sports networks must fill thousands of hours each year. ESPN has over 350 fulltime programming staffers. They perform the same tasks and go through the same processes that programmers at the broadcast networks do, but they program 8,760 hours per year on ESPN, another 8,760 hours each on ESPN2, ESPNews, ESPNU, ESPN Classic, ESPNdeportes, the Longhorn Network, the SEC Network, and the ACC Network, plus hundreds of hours on ABC every year. That is over 75,000 hours of sports programming per year before you add any of the events that are on ESPN3 or ESPN+. For media conglomerates that create entertainment content, every new platform, broadcast or streaming, represents opportunity. And every new opportunity to distribute content in more and different ways is another avenue to enhance viewership and collect more advertising revenue.

Building a successful programming franchise out of any sport or series requires tremendous effort, the coordination of multiple, parallel, and intersecting tasks, a multiplatform vision, and one more thing: the creation of "shoulder programming." If the primary program is the "head," for example *Monday Night Football*, all the programs preceding it with previews and following it with interviews and analysis are the "shoulders." The game telecast may start at 8:15 pm Eastern Time every Monday, but ESPN starts its shoulder programming five hours earlier with *NFL Rewind* at 3:00 pm ET. Coverage continues for hours after the game on *SportsCenter*, ESPNews, ESPN Radio, and ESPN.com. ESPN sells advertising in every shoulder program on every platform to advertisers that want to connect with *Monday Night Football* fans.

The combination of all these revenue streams is what made it possible for ESPN to pay $1.1 billion per year when it first moved the series over from ABC in 2006. For the 36 years that ABC had the franchise, it could sell commercials in only one three-and-a-half-hour game each week. ESPN greatly expanded that window with its shoulder programming and multiple platforms. ESPN's annual rights fee moved up to $1.9 billion for each of the next eight years and then to $2.7 billion per year in the contract that The Walt Disney Company signed with the NFL for the 11 seasons from 2023 through 2033.

THE DISINTERMEDIATION OF SPORTS TELEVISION

Earlier in this chapter when we discussed "owned programming," we quickly alluded to the sport-specific cable networks that each of the major professional leagues has established, starting with NBA TV in 1999, the NFL Network in 2003, NHL Network in 2007, and the MLB Network in 2009. It is very common for regional sports networks to be owned by the teams they cover. And college conference networks that appeal to large audiences across several states have joined the "owned programming" ranks, led by the huge success of the Big Ten Network, which was founded in 2007 as a partnership between the Big Ten Conference and Fox Cable Networks.

When a league, conference, or team owns the media that televises and reports on its games and players, it has a much greater degree of control over what is said and shown than when that coverage is provided by independently owned media. Delivering your message directly to your audience without an intermediary to analyze, question, or criticize your words or actions is a public relations dream come true. Opposing opinions need not be solicited.

If a team's general manager makes a stupid trade that hurts the franchise, how much will he or she be criticized by the commentators who are fellow employees of the same owner? Will you see a graphic comparison showing how much better the traded player is doing for his new team than the player your team got in exchange when you are watching a regional sports network telecast that is controlled by that team? How much does a network controlled by a college conference criticize its commissioner or member schools?

Such is the effect of "disintermediation," which in economics refers to the elimination of an intermediary in any transaction. Without unbiased analysis by production teams that owe their allegiances to an independent media outlet and NOT to the team or league they cover, the tendency is for the messages delivered to sports audiences to become more one-sided and suffer from the lack of an intermediary.

No one is more sensitive to this than Mark Quenzel, who is responsible for programming at the NFL Network. "People have to believe they will get accuracy from us," he said. "Any time someone can point to an example of the NFL Network soft-peddling a story, it's going to hurt our credibility." Quenzel said that the key for his network is to report stories and add opinions based on fact. Covering labor disputes represents a very clear dilemma for any network that is owned by a league. The league's position and point of view will get preference, even if it's only subliminal, when the reporters, producers, and editors' paychecks all come from the league. Fair and equitable reporting is more likely to come from independent media that are owned by third parties, not by the leagues or teams.

This is not to say however that the intermediaries, which are the networks, and media not owned by leagues, teams, or conferences, do not play favorites. Networks such as NBC, CBS, Fox, and ESPN are all partners with the leagues and conferences whose games they televise. The rights agreements that bind them together are worth hundreds of millions, and in some cases, billions of dollars per year. They rely upon each other for mutual success.

PRESSURING THE PROGRAMMERS

There is an understanding that networks cover news and that their analysts will criticize and foster debate, but there is sensitivity to what is said and by whom. A league or any other organizer that is the target of criticism can bring pressure to bear in ways both subtle and overt. The programming department can feel that pressure when it is negotiating with its league partner for the best games or favorable start times. It may find that the best matchups are finding their way into other rights holders' air schedules or are being retained by the league as content for its own network. Under that pressure, networks must weigh their options carefully: do they maintain a hands-off policy and give their reporters and analysts complete freedom, or do they come down on the side of protecting their partnership and put a lid on critical coverage? It is a tricky balance with the programmers at the fulcrum.

ESPN surrendered to the pressure of its partners at the NFL when the network canceled its *Playmakers* series in 2004, after just one season. At the time, ESPN was airing NFL games on Sunday nights and was making plans for its *Monday Night Football* bid. *Playmakers* was a dramatic series about a fictional professional football team that used controversial storylines like drugs and sex in its scripts. It got many good reviews and had attracted a respectable but not huge audience. However, complaints from the NFL to Disney executives helped hasten the cancellation of the series. *Playmakers* was not a sports news or analysis program, but without saying the words "National Football League," it did put professional football in a harsh and at times unsavory light. The lesson is never to underestimate the power of a partnership between a network and a league when billions of dollars are at stake.

ESPN did not lose its share of the sports television audience when it canceled *Playmakers*. Nor did its programming department feel the need to replace it with another dramatic series. That is because the events and shows that filled the empty slots in the schedule contained the "drama of athletic competition," and the compelling, unscripted stories of live sports that attract fans. A scripted dramatic series can never approach the spontaneity or offer the unique twists and turns that are at the heart of live sports programming.

As long as games continue to be exciting, rookies and veterans alike remain interesting, teams are the object of lifelong love, hope, or scorn, and live competition arouses passion, millions of people will continue to make the conscious choice to spend a portion of their leisure time watching sports programming on television, the internet, or on any device known or not yet invented.

BIBLIOGRAPHY

Armour, Nancy. "NBC Universal Pays $7.75 Billion for Olympics Through 2032." *USA Today*, 2014. https://www.usatoday.com/story/sports/olympics/2014/05/07/nbc-olympics-broadcast-rights-2032/8805989/

Lewis, Jon. "FOX Extends MLB Deal Through 2028." *Sports Media Watch*, 2018. https://www.sportsmediawatch.com/2018/11/mlb-fox-deal-extension-2028/

Magnus, Burke. *Interviewed by the Author*, 2021.

Palmeri, Christopher. "NFL Signs $105 Billion TV Deal, With Amazon Taking Thursdays." *Bloomberg.com*, 2021. https://www.bloomberg.com/news/articles/2021-03-18/nfl-signs-historic-tv-deal-with-amazon-taking-thursday-rights

Quenzel, Mark. *Interviewed by the Author*, 2019.

Shapiro, Leonard. "And the Fourth Shall Be First: How Fox Stalked the NFL and Bagged TV Deal." *The Washington Post*, 1993.

Sports Media Watch. "World Series Ratings Chart (1972-present.)." https://www.sportsmediawatch.com/world-series-ratings-historical-chart/

White, Douglas. *Interviewed by the Author*, 2021.

Producing Live Sports Broadcasts

Life is a day-by-day, minute-by-minute, ever-renewing series of stories. Stories of success and failure, of challenges and obstacles, of goals achieved or never met, of renewal and redemption, work done well or never well enough, of people who play by the rules and those who push the limits or do not play fair. In each life, there are beginnings, middles, and ends. There is celebration and despair. And the optimist in us hopes that each life is enriched by love and at least one passion to pursue.

When lives intersect, where passions and goals collide and compete, the result is drama, suspense, and new stories. Live sport attracts millions of passionate fans who feel a connection to their favorite teams and athletes or are curious about how the people who set the highest standards, who work the hardest to overcome all obstacles and achieve their individual and collective goals, will perform when competing against each other.

Telling these stories as they play out live in the electronic media requires creative production teams that will research all the stories that are at work or could possibly arise during each contest, then use every tool of sight and sound at their command to present the events in a manner so entertaining and informative that the audience will enjoy the time they spend watching and eagerly anticipate the next competition.

TELLING STORIES

Every game, match, or event has a multitude of stories, big and small. It is the responsibility of the producers as journalists to uncover and report them. For example, a producer may be assigned to a boxing show whose headliners are unknown outside their home regions. Simply presenting each fighter's record and the basic "Tale of the Tape" information such as height, weight, and reach will not attract or hold an audience. But by spending the time to do some research on each fighter the producer may find that "Boxer A" works fulltime in a warehouse, makes breakfast every morning for his three children before they head for school, and trains on the nights and weekends because he just does not make enough money in the fight game to support his family.

Now you have a story, and you have given your viewers a reason to root for this hard-working man. His name may not be famous, but the audience can relate to him as a human being. Anyone who has struggled to make ends meet, who cares for his or her family, or who has worked overtime to pursue a passion can identify with "Boxer A." What happens to him, whether he wins or loses the fight, now has meaning for the viewer.

Within each game or match, there are stories that are constantly changing. The rookie who has worked hard to crack the starting lineup gets his first chance to shine, a veteran player who has made changes in her game or in her life to ensure her continued success, or the team that finds the solutions to its scoring drought in the first quarter to catch up and take the lead in the second. These storylines and so many more embody the human experience and our social values: tangible achievements that we can see and measure that are the result of intangibles like determination, perseverance, commitment to common goals, the impact of mentors, or the sacrifices made by parents and athletes alike.

People as social beings are always interested in other people. It is part of what defines us as human. What else could explain our fan culture where stars become household names overnight, and celebrity TV shows and social media pages have millions of avid followers? Our interest in each other is what makes us want to know about the lives of our favorite players, what they did when they were growing up, how they got to the highest levels of their sport, and how they cope with the competition and the pressure in each contest and in their professional and personal lives.

Sports media production then has three goals: 1) to document what happens in each event; 2) to inform the viewer about what is at stake in the event and what stories are developing or being rewritten before their eyes; and 3) to entertain the viewers with the best pictures, both live and via replay, the most authentic sound that makes one feel as if he or she is in the arena or at the stadium, and commentary that adds meaning and fun to the event. Every sport, whether it be individual or team, is overflowing with wonderful stories of people chasing dreams that first took root when they were children.

Many sports broadcasts however live only in the moment. If the production team focuses solely on the documentation of an event, they will deliver plenty of details on that day's performance such as a running back has 86 yards rushing, a batter is 1-for-3 with one RBI, or the point guard has made five assists and has scored nine points. But the best producers and commentators go deeper to bring players and teams to life, humanize them and make them more interesting. The addition of a simple descriptive phrase, a lower third graphic, or a quick anecdote will give a viewer that extra bit of information that can transform an athlete from just another performer with a number on his or her back into someone whose success or failure makes a difference to those of us watching.

The goal is to produce "a telecast that people will stick with and enjoy," says Fred Gaudelli, NBC's producer of *Sunday Night Football* and a member of the Sports Broadcasting Hall of Fame. Achieving that goal requires four basic elements: time, people, resources, and information.

- *Time.* The more lead time that producers have before an event, the better they can plan and develop new strategies, do more research and interviews, edit compelling profiles and video packages, and search for the best talent and give them ample training. The entire process starts with putting the time into research.
- *People.* Creative, intelligent, inquisitive, and resourceful people who are willing to work hard for long hours are vital to the success of any live broadcast, or for that matter, any professional endeavor. The quality of the people working on a project is always more important than the quantity. Gaudelli said that the people in the announce booth at his games are "far and away the most important factor. Nothing makes the game more or less enjoyable than who the announcers are."
- *Resources.* A large budget will provide all the resources one needs to produce the best possible show. That includes hiring the best people and assembling the optimal complement of physical resources such as additional cameras and microphones in unique places, innovative technology that provides new eye-catching ways of analyzing action, editing video, and animating graphics that will improve the overall look of shows and how stories are presented.
- *Information.* Every telecast provides information to heighten interest and frame the importance of an event: team and individual records and histories, rivalries, biographies, anecdotes, live scoring data, and statistics. The production team must anticipate all the different directions a game could go, then prepare far more content and information than they will ever use in a live broadcast. This would include when the teams or competitors met previously, their history, analysis from previous matchups, and trends that could affect the outcome. As storylines develop in a game, producers can tap into the graphics, background information, and the visual elements that they have prepared prompting many viewers to ask, "how did they come up with that?"

A deficit in any of these four areas can diminish a live sports telecast. However, the producers who are resourceful and organized will always make the most of what they have and never settle for something that they would not be proud to share with their viewers.

THE PRODUCTION TEAM

"Producers are really the lifeblood of the broadcast," says veteran CBS commentator Ian Eagle. They take the lead on what research needs to be done and what questions need to be answered because they are responsible for the content of a telecast. And they set the tone for how an event will be presented to the viewing public. You can think of a producer as the "coach" of a team. He or she is the creative planner and administrative leader of the production crew, providing direction and guidance for all assigned personnel. The producer establishes the game plan that includes a detailed rundown of which elements will air in what order or in what situations, how the show opens, and how every successive segment should be structured. He or she then assigns duties based upon the storylines that need to be developed and the elements that need to be built such as pre-produced interviews, highlight packages from past games, and graphic panels or animations.

The best coaches and leaders in any profession must be masters of the four Cs: communication, collaboration, creativity, and coordination. There are so many moving parts in a live sports broadcast that producers need to be effective communicators who can simultaneously coordinate the efforts of dozens, sometimes hundreds, of people in multiple locations. That requires them to confidently delegate hundreds of tasks to their crew and trust those people to get the job done on a deadline so that each individual piece fits into the whole of the telecast. A producer who can establish a collaborative climate will encourage every team member to contribute ideas and creativity in the preparation for the event and in the moment when it is live on the air. A producer can have a great plan on paper, but if he or she cannot communicate or can't bring together a team effort where everybody wants to be involved, potentially great ideas won't be shared, and the show is likely to fall short.

The decisions that a producer makes as to which stories, words, and pictures will be used to document an event will define how that game or contest is perceived, and how each participant is perceived by everyone in the viewing audience, potentially millions of people. The stories, words, and pictures that the producer fails to include, or chooses to omit, carry almost the same importance. If information is left out that could explain why a team or player failed to perform up to expectations, or why they exceeded expectations, the factors that contribute to the public's perception will be incomplete or worse, inaccurate. The producer is responsible to every viewer for making the best choices that will tell the full, unbiased story of an event.

During a live event, the producer is the primary storyteller, leading the commentators to explain key points, selecting replays that will emphasize or analyze why and how plays succeeded or failed, and choosing when to insert graphics and all other pre-produced elements such as interview excerpts that will add to the viewer's understanding of what just happened, what it means as the game or season progresses, and who the players are who made it happen.

Producers need an almost super-human level of awareness to make split-second decisions as to which elements to choose and which ones to delay. Bill Bonnell, the lead producer of college football on ABC and ESPN, said:

You have to be aware of everything that's in front of you on separate monitors, aware of what the commentators are saying, aware of what the assistant director behind you is pitching for a sponsored element, aware of what an associate producer is pitching you as far as what graphics to get in.

The producer must maintain this heightened level of awareness, listening to eight people at once, communicating succinctly with very few words, and making decisions on the fly assertively for two, three, or more hours without melting down. "The best quality a producer can have is to be a really good listener," said Bonnell. "Always be aware of everything that's going on around you and read the room."

It is a demanding job that requires a high level of commitment and sacrifice. "I don't have a day off during the football season," said Phil Dean, the producer of ESPN's *Monday Night Football*. "My wife and my two kids wish I had a day off. I do try to sneak hours here and there." For this high-profile primetime series, Dean travels from his home in Connecticut to the game site every Friday. On Saturdays, the production team starts work in the television trucks and Dean attends meetings that he has set up with the director and commentators to talk with coaches and selected players from one of the two teams to get their storylines and perspectives on the upcoming game. These meetings continue on Sundays with the other team, and the producer has separate planning sessions with the associate producers and directors who will be contributing graphics, video, interview excerpts, and other pre-recorded pieces to the broadcast.

Game day on Monday starts at 11 am Eastern Time with a 90-minute production meeting to go over the storylines and goals for the telecast along with all the elements they have produced and discuss how to handle any eventuality that could arise. The game kicks off at 8:15 pm that night and concludes around midnight. Tuesday is a travel day home usually spent sitting on an airplane with a laptop or tablet reviewing the recording of the previous night's game to see what worked well and what needs improving. The planning and preparation resume in earnest on Wednesdays and Thursdays for the next game for which Dean will travel out again on Friday.

Producers work in tandem with directors who are their bridge to the audience (Figure 7.1). The director of a live sports telecast is the "quarterback" who executes the game plan devised by the producer in his or her "coach" role. Drew Esocoff who has directed multiple Olympics, Super Bowls, and Kentucky Derby telecasts for NBC said:

My job as a director is to take the guidance of the people sitting next to me and sitting in an announce booth, and make sure that the subject matter that's being discussed by the on-air talent is being visually portrayed by me.

■ **Figure 7.1** During a live sports broadcast, the producer, left, and the director work in tandem making dozens of decisions every minute that affect how the story of each event is presented to viewers. (Photo by the author)

The director is responsible for the visual coverage and the look of a televised event. He or she plans where cameras should be placed to capture shots of every action from the best angles. Before every game or event, the director leads a meeting of all the camera operators to present the coverage plan and explain what is expected of them in every situation. There are specific assignments for each camera in every game or match in every sport. For example, in football, each operator needs to know what to shoot when the football moves inside the 20-yard line nearest their position or inside the 20-yard line at the opposite end of the field. After a touchdown is scored, the director has a plan for which cameras will shoot the player who scored, the jubilant crowd, each of the coaches, the defensive player who was beaten on the play, and how wide or tight these shots need to be. The director's work provides answers to the questions that could decide who wins or loses a game. Their camera placement provides the producer with definitive replays in critical game situations to show whether, for example, a receiver had both feet in bounds, a runner's knee was down before he crossed the goal line, or in hockey and soccer if a player was offside.

The director is the leader of the technical crew and as such works with the operations manager to set the production schedule leading up to the game and troubleshoot any operational issues that arise. The director takes the producer's rundown for the show and oversees the pre-production of all packaged elements, mixing video with natural sound, narration, music, graphics, and visual effects.

During the telecast, the director is also listening carefully to the announcers who are calling the action. "For the broadcast to be in synch, the words the announcers are saying should match our pictures," said Esocoff. The director makes instantaneous decisions as to which camera to take live to air and instructs every camera operator as to the framing and/or movement of their shots. At the prompting of the producer, the director also calls for every replay and every graphic or packaged element. The director's voice alone is what commands the technical director to push the right button for every visual input and effect that the viewer will see.

Producers and directors have a great resource in the sports veterans and experts who serve as the on-air analysts for their assigned shows. These people who have played or coached a sport at the highest level see things in real time that someone without their experience would have to go back and review many times over to see. Their knowledge, together with the expertise of the producer, director, and the entire production team will combine with the passion for the sport that they share with fans to heighten each viewer's enjoyment of the live broadcast. They can predict outcomes and point out subtleties that most fans would not see on their own such as a tendency to be exploited, a move that telegraphs what is coming next, or slight shifts in momentum. Sports telecasts become more meaningful when they reveal the exquisite intricacies of a game being played at its highest level. When viewers' eyes are opened to distinguishing characteristics such as how an all-pro receiver changes speed when he changes direction on a pass route, how a boxer slightly drops his shoulder to change the angle of his next punch or the deep knee bend that puts added power and speed into a tennis champion's serve, the audience becomes more engaged and begins to appreciate the action on multiple levels.

"A producer will never know as much about the sport as the expert analyst does," said Bonnell, "so you take the value and resources that these smart people bring to a show, and you get a better show by listening and drawing them out and using their expertise and contributions and suggestions." It is not enough to tell the viewer *what* has happened. It is just as important to show and explain *why* and *how* plays, players, and teams succeed or fail. Once the fans become aware of the factors that separate success from failure and the nuances and intangibles that distinguish good performances from great, viewers will start to pay attention to more of what is happening before their eyes, which can make their experience more enjoyable, informative, and entertaining.

THE UNPREDICTABILITY OF SPORT

The compelling nature of sport is its unpredictability. The heavy favorite does not always win, so you must watch to see what happens. Ask the heavily favored Baltimore Colts who lost to the New York Jets in Super Bowl III. Or ask the top seed who gets beaten by an unknown at the NCAA Men's or Women's Basketball Tournaments or at a Grand Slam tennis event. You never know what's going to happen so the producer needs to be prepared for every possible eventuality. Despite all the meticulous planning by top producers like Bill Bonnell, he always tells his crew, "Don't forget it's the unexpected, the things we can't predict that will make the game special. We'll be judged on how we respond."

Every sporting event starts out with a set of "knowns" that provide the broadcast crew with storylines and production possibilities. In most cases, the "knowns" include:

1. *The venue.* The arena or stadium, indoors or out, at which the event will take place. Research will reveal any noteworthy events that have taken place there in the past, or if this is the first time the venue has hosted this sport or contest.
2. *The competitors.* The teams or combatants facing each other. Stories can be developed on the background and history of each team and player and when they have met or interacted before. In individual sports like golf or tennis however, the big star could miss the cut or lose in the early rounds so they do not wind up appearing in the live television coverage. That puts lesser-known players into the spotlight, so background information must be compiled and ready to go for every competitor, not just the established stars.
3. *What's at stake?* What will the outcome of this contest mean? Does the winning team move into first place or clinch a playoff berth? Will a winning streak or losing streak be broken? Is a starting player in jeopardy of losing his/her position if they do not perform well? Is this the first opportunity for a rookie and how will he/she deal with the pressure?
4. *The rules.* How the sport is played, what is legal, and what will be penalized.
5. *The start time.* When the event is scheduled to begin and how much time you have between the opening of your show and the first ball or the start of each race or contest.
6. *The scheduled length of the show.* The total number of hours that are allotted for the event, along with instructions for what to do if the contest ends early or runs long.
7. *Your personnel.* You know who is assigned to your team in every role: producers and directors, play-by-play hosts and analysts, technicians, production assistants, statisticians, runners, and everyone in between.
8. *Scheduled travel times.* When the teams, players, your crew, and your production truck or facilities are scheduled to arrive. If the team or players are arriving from a great distance or from having just played an important or overtime game, that may be another story to pursue.

9. *The weather forecast*. This affects all outdoor events but is especially critical for golf tournaments, auto races, outdoor tennis matches, and horse races. The producer will want to know which competitors do best in the weather conditions expected: which horses run better on a sloppy track, which football teams have better records in freezing temperatures. The threat of bad weather can force delays or suspensions of play for which the production crew needs to prepare contingency plans.

10. *Camera and microphone positions*. In a site survey prior to the event the producer, director, and operations manager will have scouted the venue to select the best places for cameras and microphones to provide the viewers with the views of every critical action and the sounds of the game. Making it possible for audiences to feel like they are at the event and to see and hear everything that could affect the game's outcome is an important part of storytelling.

11. *The content and length of pre-produced elements*. Packaged teases and animations, interview segments, edited highlights from previous games or matchups, and graphics panels and animations with biographical or statistical information. These are all built to add context and interest to the telecast.

12. *Total commercial time and the number of breaks*. How many times the show is required to take breaks in action and how long each break must be.

13. *Sponsored features*. The elements that must play in each show with sponsor identification and how each is to be executed. For example, "The Play of the Game presented by Sponsor A," or "The Sponsor B Sky-Cam." Money has been paid to the network or station in advance, so these must be incorporated into the show.

14. *Promotional elements*. The visuals and scripts for each upcoming program that must be promoted during the event, when these need to run (first half/ second half/ pre-game or post-game), and how often during the show.

15. *The next show*. On linear networks, the crew at each live event knows what program they precede. There are also guidelines explaining how that may change if an event is suspended, runs short, or runs past the scheduled off-time.

These are the givens, the starting line from which the production crew moves forward. Research and materials need to be gathered and prepared on deadline to be ready for what is required and expected. But it is remarkable how many elements are prepped and ready to go ahead of time in anticipation of every possible eventuality. A tremendous amount of work goes into preparing for what is known and expected. But just as much or more goes into preparing for the unexpected, how to handle the "unknowns":

1. *Venue problems*. The production team should know how to deal with technical, mechanical, or access problems at the venue. What

to do if the lights go out or the backboard breaks or how to fill time if the game or match is delayed while problems are fixed. There is an inventory of pre-recorded packages and replays of previous games or matches that are ready for playback.

2. *An unexpected star steps into the spotlight.* A player coming off the bench could be the hero, which means that the producer needs to have information and stats for every player who could possibly get into the contest, not just the starters. Graphics need to be built beforehand for each player with details on his/her current statistics, best past performances, career highlights, hometown and college, or other biographical information.

3. *The story of the game.* The producer works with the entire broadcast team to anticipate every possible outcome. The contest could be an offensive exhibition or a defensive struggle, a 10-stroke victory or a "nail-biter" that goes down to the final playoff putt. If the underdog wins, how does that affect the standings, the coach and players, the losers? Each scenario requires preparation so that the audience continues to get information and entertainment regardless of who is winning or losing or what the margin of victory may be.

4. *Rule violations.* Dealing with a common penalty is easy, but information and expertise need to be ready if a rare penalty is called or an official's call is challenged. The last thing any network wants is for its commentators or shows to appear confused or uninformed, so many have added rules specialists to their complement of announcers.

5. *The actual start time.* A game may be scheduled to start at five minutes after the hour, but if one of the two tennis players decides he or she needs to run to the bathroom, the start time is going to change. The pre-game pyrotechnics may leave behind too much smoke to start the game on time, so the producer needs to be prepared to fill extra time before kick-off or first tip without making the viewer think that something has gone wrong. And everyone on the crew needs to know in advance what to do if plans suddenly change.

6. *The actual length of the show.* When baseball games go into extra innings, football games go into overtime, golf tournaments end in playoffs, or tennis matches go past 6-6 in the fifth set, every production team needs to have guidelines from the network programming integration group as to how to proceed in any situation. Do satellite or fiber transmission times need to be extended, how many more commercials will run, do promos get repeated or are new ones added, how do you arrange bathroom breaks for crew members who have not left their posts in three or four hours?

7. *Personnel substitutions.* Illness, family emergencies, canceled flights, or bad weather can prevent assigned crew members from making it to the venue. The producer and operations manager need to have options ready and available so that a local freelancer or back-up commentator can be brought in on time for the show.

8. *The weather.* Even if the forecast had been for sunny with cloudless skies, a thunderstorm or stray shower could affect an event staged outdoors. (I once had an indoor event that was delayed by rain because the roof leaked.)

9. *Technical problems.* One or more cameras could go down, so the best directors know how to cover an event with only one or two cameras functioning. Microphones stop working without notice, so spare microphones need to be at the ready with enough audio personnel to respond and do repairs. Recorded interviews may not playback, so notes on what the player or coach said should be ready to prevent important storylines from being abandoned just because of a technical glitch.

10. *Impact on the next show.* If the live event on the air runs well short of its expected time, the network may require the production team to fill the extra time with post-game interviews and analysis segments, or it may call for an early throw to the next event for "bonus coverage." The producers of both shows need to be ready. Or if the first show runs past its scheduled off-time, the talent there may be required to start updating the audience on the progress of the game that is being pre-empted or toss to quick updates from the venue of that next game. Planning for these possibilities will make the on-air execution seamless. Sitting at home watching the live telecast, it can be painfully obvious to everyone when this kind of planning and preparation for the unexpected has not taken place.

The best sports telecasts combine commentary and astute analysis with great pictures (live and on replay) and sounds from the field of play to give viewers the sense that they are on top of the action, plus graphics and live data displays that add information and context. Mix in live or pre-recorded interviews to explain what is behind certain actions or reactions, music to add feeling, identity or a sense of drama, and new technologies that can improve a viewer's understanding of the action. The result is a symphony of sight, sound, stories, and information that connects with fans and enhances the entertainment value of the live coverage.

In a symphony full of passion and excitement, every instrument plays a vital part, and timing is critical. An orchestra has only one conductor and one baton. For sports telecasts, there are two leaders. The producer and director work together to cue each instrument, get the most out of each section, and blend them all together into a cohesive art form that communicates a variety of messages designed to engage the intellects and emotions of every person watching.

THE NEW NORMAL FOR SPORTS PRODUCTION

The COVID-19 pandemic and the social distancing that came with it forced changes in live sports production that will remain part of the profession moving forward. Traveling large numbers of personnel to the site of events where they would spend hours if not days in close quarters with dozens of other people in broadcast mobile units, edit suites, or control rooms was no longer feasible, nor in many cases, possible during the pandemic that began in 2020. Alternative methods needed to be employed to televise the events that continued to be staged regardless of whether they had been rescheduled or were being contested in empty stadiums or arenas.

Operations and engineering professionals worked closely with producers and directors to find solutions. What emerged were variations on the remote integration model that had been adopted more than a decade earlier by ESPN and other networks for the telecasts of games that were of regional interest but would not attract a large national audience. Nicknamed "REMI" (pronounced REM-ee) productions, these shows have taken advantage of expanded high-speed broadband and optical fiber transmission capabilities to send separate live feeds from every camera and microphone, along with communications lines from the site of an event back to a production control room at the network's primary digital broadcast center. From that control room, the director can communicate with every camera operator at the game site to cut a live show by switching from one camera feed to another. The producer located in the same control room calls for graphics and replays to be added, and the commentators describe the action that they see on a monitor in their announce booth down the hall or from their homes, not at the site of the game. Only a few people are needed on-site for a REMI production: a handful of camera operators, an audio technician or two, and an operations manager to coordinate the separate feeds and communications links from a small, virtually deserted TV truck.

It quickly became apparent that the commentators did not even need to travel to a network production facility if broadcast quality microphones and an array of monitors could be installed at their individual homes. The play-by-play announcer and analyst could be hundreds or thousands of miles apart and both simultaneously hear directions from the producer, see the action taking place at the distant game venue, and they could watch each other on dedicated monitors so they knew when each could talk without stepping on their partner's words.

The millions of dollars saved traveling crews to venues and paying for their hotel rooms, meals, and expenses convinced all the national and regional sports networks that remote integration was a means to achieve higher profits. As a result, we will never return to the old model of sending commentators, analysts, and production teams to virtually every game that is broadcast. It will save money, but it comes at a cost. "If somebody says it's just as good having announcers calling it off tube from a control room or their house, it's not just as good," said Esocoff. "If you are doing a basketball game and you didn't go to the shoot-around that morning, then your preparation is not as good as it could have been." The broadcast product cannot help but be diminished if the commentators who fans rely upon to be their eyes and ears at an event are not actually at that event.

"You can only see so many things on so many monitors at one time," said NBC's Mike Tirico. "Your peripheral vision cannot pick up things that the camera is not showing you." He sees remote integration as a detriment to the lower and mid-level televised events. "As a fan I expect it to be really good, and if the broadcasters aren't there, I expect them to make up the difference, and it's just impossible." He continued, "That is a part of this that will stay with us and hurt the quality of the product going forward."

Calling a game from home forces commentators to work harder to find their authentic voice. "You're experiencing a game the way the viewer is, which is you're watching it on the screen, but you're still expected to document it as well as you possibly can, to have genuine enthusiasm," said Chris Fowler, ESPN's primary announcer for college football and tennis. "A great play isn't less great because you're not in the press box. Whatever happens out there it's still your responsibility to document it." Many announcers find that they are yelling in their basement office or apartment, and that is hard to do with other people in the house. "It's not how we all learned and prepared," said CBS commentator Ian Eagle.

> It's now more challenging than ever to figure out the energy level that you need, the concentration level that you need and the ability to connect with not just your audience, but your analyst who's not in the same room with you.

An equilibrium is being found between the cost savings of remote integration for lower-tier or regional broadcasts, and the importance of sending a full production crew to big events like the Super Bowl and NBA Finals that attract the most viewers. Some events of national interest will be produced from the venue but with smaller trucks and reduced complements of cameras and crew. As media rights fees continue to soar, the pressure will increase to reduce production budgets and do more telecasts with fewer people at the event venue.

Another casualty from the pandemic era of social distancing is the access that sports broadcasters and journalists have to the athletes. Teams and players who got comfortable doing Zoom interviews and not having reporters in their locker rooms may or may not re-open those doors. The leagues, teams, and players have much more control of their message in a Zoom interview, and their face-to-face interaction with media reporters is limited. Sometimes players turn their cameras on and sometimes they do not, depending upon what mood they are in. The new normal is never going to be the old normal.

WHEN THE GAME IS OVER THE SHOW IS NOT

When the game is over, the job of the production team is not. In fact, the precious few seconds or minutes between the end of the play and the end of the show are crucial. Ending strong is just as important as starting strong. Every storyline that was set up at the top of the telecast should be wrapped up by the time the event ends. As a prediction either comes true or is turned upside down, the producer and commentators should be explaining how and why it happened.

A show should never raise a question that it does not answer. If it tells you that the team now has the second-best record in the month of June, that begs the question, "who has the best record?" If at the top of the show a star was introduced as "number three on her university's all-time rebounding list," has she now moved into second place? And how close is she to surpassing the rebounding leader? The viewer deserves a finished product, so the best producers do not leave loose ends.

It's vital for a successful sports telecast to put each result into perspective. What does the victory mean? What doors will open as a result? Will the next fight be for the world title? Is the next match against an old rival or the defending champion? Is the team one step closer to the playoffs or to leveling their record at .500? What individual achievements did we see that may put an athlete into a whole new realm of recognition? And what does the defeat mean for those who lost? Is a successful season now out of reach? Will the starting lineup change, or is the coach or manager now in jeopardy of being fired?

In whatever the television sports production team does, it should never shortchange the viewer. I have always told my producers and students to make all their decisions on behalf of the fan. The person who spends his or her valuable time watching an event should always come away feeling that it was time well spent, that they were treated with respect, and that they were entertained and informed. If they enjoyed the experience, they will always come back for more.

BIBLIOGRAPHY

Bonnell, Bill. *Interviewed by the Author*, 2021.
Dean, Phil. *Interviewed by the Author*, 2021.
Eagle, Ian. *Interviewed by the Author*, 2021.
Esocoff, Drew. *Interviewed by the Author*, 2021.
Fowler, Chris. *Interviewed by the Author*, 2021.
Gaudelli, Fred. *Interviewed by the Author*, 2020.
Tirico, Mike. *Interviewed by the Author*, 2021.

Live Sports Commentary and Analysis

"You are the fan's eyes and ears at an event," said Mike Tirico, NBC's host for Olympics and NFL coverage, when asked to explain his role.

> You have the responsibility for documenting the game, and it has evolved into documenting, informing and entertaining. You have to document, inform and entertain, but you and your production team are controlling which one you do at which time, and that's hugely important for the fan.

Chris Fowler started doing play-by-play for ESPN in 2003. He defined the job by saying, "I document an event. I describe what's going on filtered through my own sensibilities and observations built over time and through experience." Fowler, whose work as ESPN's lead play-by-play announcer for college football and tennis has reached millions of viewers, said that it is vitally important, "to convey the excitement that you feel about being at a live event to the fans."

"We're on the same team with the fans," said Rob Stone, the host of World Cup Soccer for Fox who also does play-by-play for a multitude of sports. "We're there to help them understand what is happening on the site and why things are important and why they should care and why they should look forward to being entertained."

Many of the most successful sports broadcasters of this generation watched Keith Jackson on ABC Sports as they were growing up. Jackson was one of the pre-eminent and most admired sportscasters in America until his passing at the age of 89 in 2018. He described what he did for 50 years in one simple line: "Amplify, clarify and punctuate, and let the viewer draw his or her own conclusion." Jackson always wanted to share his enjoyment of the game with viewers. His concise definition of the role still fits perfectly even as the live sports media have expanded, and the number of different on-air talent roles has multiplied. No sports commentator regardless of his or her assignment will ever fail to responsibly serve the audience if they adhere to Keith Jackson's eloquent job description.

THE SPORTS COMMENTATOR'S JOB

Amplify. Sportscasters amplify each event or story by providing details that will expand the viewer's understanding of what is happening. They incorporate background and statistical information, critical analysis of the competitors, the history of rivalries and venues, the strategies being used in each play, series of plays or games, and provide educated assessments of the quality of each player or team's performance. The sportscaster's sense of the stories at work and the drama within each sporting event, coupled with their explanations of what motivates each athlete and team, add to a telecast and make it more meaningful.

"You want to set the story up early, you want to describe the action, you want to stay out of the way when the moments get big," said Fowler.

> You want to rise to the moment when a voice on top of the pictures is called for, and then sum it up at the end while being very tuned in during a game to the body language and the moods of the athletes, to changes in momentum.

One of the great arts of the job, he said, "is being tuned in to the flow and perhaps anticipating something that's about to happen based on your experience and your gut feeling."

The details and storylines that amplify and enhance a sports broadcast are what set the television commentator apart from the public address announcer whose basic job is to tell the spectators in a venue who is coming to bat in a baseball game, the down and distance in gridiron football, and who just scored regardless of the sport.

Clarify. The sports commentator is a guide who tells the viewer *what* is happening, *who* is responsible, *how* it happened, *when*, and *why*. Anyone whose job is to answer these questions is a journalist plain and simple. For the journalists who commentate on live television, their stories are narrated to video most often without a script. The work they do is simultaneously produced and consumed, so they need to take greater care in what they say, how it is phrased, and the tone they use than reporters who have editors or producers reviewing and improving their written or recorded stories for presentation sometime after they are produced.

To competently clarify, the commentator must have a deep knowledge of the sport, its teams and/or participants, its history, and its rules. It all starts with curiosity. Asking plenty of questions in the days before an event and doing the research to find answers will prepare the commentator for the role of "clarifier." The best sports announcers are those who do their homework. Mike Tirico said that it takes him a full 70-hour week to prepare for doing the play-by-play on a three-and-a-half-hour live NFL telecast. As a journalist, it is his or her responsibility to put each live event into context and frame the significance of what is happening with the facts and history that apply. "The fan doesn't have all day to go back and watch past events and to be able to make the connection to what has just happened in a game," he said.

The best talent and production teams will always dig for and prepare much more information than they could ever use in a broadcast. "You have to do your research and dig deep," said Rob Stone. "The audience will call you out if you haven't done your work, and you can't have that. You absolutely cannot have your audience saying, 'why are you here, because I know more than you do?'" In each telecast, there is a delicate balance between not enough information and too much. The commentator along with the producer need to exercise their judgment so as not to spend too much time on what may be interesting but insignificant facts, and in the process miss the bigger story or diminish the beauty or greater significance of the play.

The successful play-by-play announcer's knowledge should include an understanding of how the entire broadcast team functions and interconnects. "It's a team, it's always going to be that way in television, and you have to have a real understanding of what everybody does," said Ian Eagle who calls NFL and college basketball games for CBS and NBA games for Turner Sports and the YES network. That means working with producers so that they share the same vision for a broadcast, but it goes well beyond that. Eagle said:

> It means getting on the same page with the graphics operator, knowing their top graphics that they're looking to feature that night. And getting to know the associate director and the video that they have accumulated for the game so that you can weave in the story and get there seamlessly, so you're not waiting for them to lead you.

Punctuate. Think of how different it would be to read a book that had no punctuation marks. No commas or periods for pauses that separate one thought or topic from the next. No exclamation points to add emphasis. No underlining to add importance or question marks to raise an inquiry or doubt. Sports commentators add the punctuation marks to live events by changing their pace, inflection, tone, and volume. They communicate the importance and drama of individual plays and then connect them into the story of that quarter, half, period, game, or an entire tournament. They build suspense as contests move toward a conclusion, accentuating the key components that move an event forward, and then put the result into its proper perspective.

Some of the best punctuation in sportscasts comes when the commentators stop talking to allow the power of the pictures and the sounds of the event to tell the story. When a hard-fought championship is decided the viewer wants to hear the athletes' cries of exultation and the roar of the crowd, not a continuing narration that forces the sounds of the event into the background. Knowing when to "lay out" and when it is appropriate to speak again comes with understanding the significant impact that punctuation has in live televised sports.

The best play-by-play commentators develop the confidence to trust their own instincts and identify the moments that need punctuation. In the context of a game or event, they can judge when something has a greater meaning than the viewer might realize and underscore its importance with their voice rising to the moment or artfully pausing for the scene to play out.

"That is what separates the greats," says Fowler.

> What I appreciate when I watch a game is not necessarily an announcer bellowing over a touchdown or punctuating it with a catch phrase, or trying to immortalize some 15 seconds of language that's going to live forever over a piece of video, because not everything is, "Do you believe in miracles? Yes!"

That call by Al Michaels from the 1980 Lake Placid Winter Olympics, when an American team of amateur and college hockey players defeated the mighty Soviet national team, is still widely regarded as the best spontaneous commentary in the history of live sports television. It put an exclamation point on one of the greatest upsets in Olympic history as it happened, and Michaels' words to a great degree have helped this moment live on in our collective memory.

In every profession and every walk of life there are obvious distinctions between those who truly enjoy their jobs and those who just go through the motions wishing they were somewhere else. The same is true in sports commentary. The audience can tell which talent has a passion for telling stories and reporting on events. You can tell if they love their sport and respect the skills, determination, and sacrifices being made by each participant on the field of play or on the sideline. The pleasure and excitement of these commentators are contagious. Their enjoyment becomes the viewer's enjoyment in a very personal form of one-to-one communication.

The presentation of sports is a massively important endeavor for the people involved, the athletes, the coaches, the broadcasters, and advertisers. There are billions of dollars invested in the industry, but sports are meant to be fun especially for the viewers. "Fans have more choices than ever to get away from watching a sporting event," said Tirico, "but they are choosing to spend their entertainment dollars and their time with you when they watch your broadcast or watch an event." He continues, "So you can't make every snap, every play as if it is the end of the world. You have to keep it in context and have some fun along the way."

Chris Fowler said his favorite thing in a live sports broadcast is

> once the game is going and you're in the flow you are totally present and it's exactly what you've always wanted to do. There are those moments when a game or a match is evolving into a classic and you just realize that what you're watching is something special. And you get the chance to be the one in this chair with the headset on. That's priceless.

Consider the commentator who gets paid to watch sporting events, who has perhaps the best seat in the house with access to the most in-depth research and accurate information, but who does not sound as if he or she is enjoying the experience. They may be amplifying, clarifying, and punctuating, but if they are not communicating enjoyment, they are not doing the job the way it should be done.

The play-by-play job changes with each sport. Calling a professional or college football game that has 22 players on the field at once presents a greater challenge because of all the variables that can happen on every play: run, pass, tipped ball, interception, fumble, gain or loss of yardage, sack, kick return, or mistake. And each of the 22 players and their coaches has a distinct history and unique personal stories to tell. The structure of American football creates space for announcers to handle all these moving parts. "Football is a perfect television sport in many ways because of how it's set up," said Eagle. "You run a play, there's time before the next play, you can run a replay, you can add a graphic, go to a promo. You have time and space to work with." But sports like basketball, hockey, and soccer do not have as many natural breaks so information either gets jammed into a telecast or left out.

There are far fewer variables in individual sports such as tennis and boxing, which allows for a clearer focus on the competitors and provides a greater platform for the analyst in each telecast. It is the job of the play-by-play person to bring out the best in their analysts, make them feel comfortable, and weave their expertise into an on-air conversation that viewers will enjoy.

LIVE SPORTS ANALYSIS

The role of the analyst evolved in the 1950s, starting out as a "color" commentator. The original assignment for this second announcer in the booth for a big event telecast was to talk about the pageantry surrounding the competition and the characters on the fields and sidelines. During the game, they were called upon to add "color" to the lead commentator's call of the action. After the game, they were usually dispatched to handle locker room interviews. Even after "color" commentators started adding their analysis of the play to telecasts, most were still required to leave the announcer booth with a couple of minutes left on the clock so that they could be at field level for the post-game interviews.

The introduction of instant replay in 1963 forever changed the analyst's job. When an expert in the sport, a former player or athlete, could use a replay to explain plays and the intricacies involved that distinguished an athlete or team's performance, the networks left the old "color" commentary behind.

The key elements of a live sports analyst's job are:

Explain how and why. This is most often done using instant replays. How did a play work? What are the moving parts? Why was a certain play chosen at this point of the game? Why did it succeed or fail? How does one athlete's level of performance set him or her apart from another?

Anticipate change. Use current facts, trends, and statistics plus past histories and tendencies to project what the viewer can expect to see unfold in the upcoming contest, half, or on the next play. This is far more than just predicting who will win. It adds the *how* and *why* to the equation. And during a telecast when that anticipated change does not occur, the analyst can use the new evidence at hand to explain what did happen and why.

The responsibility to anticipate change also requires the analyst to help the director and producer make their coverage plans. Sharing information about how teams will deploy their players, how certain players match up against their defenders, or the specific moves or footwork athletes use to improve their performance will help the director determine which cameras to use in specific situations. And the producer can determine which players or units to focus on for replays that will add to the story of how a game is won or lost.

Explain change. To detect a change in momentum or spot a trend is reporting. Describing what caused the change is analysis. The best analysts can quickly spot tendencies as they develop during an event. For example, "with third down and less than four yards to go, they have handed the ball to this running back nine out of 10 times." Then showing the audience how the defense adjusts or fails to adjust to this tendency will make the game more interesting to watch.

Take a stand. When players or teams fall short of their goals, it is up to the analyst to describe to the viewer what needs to change for failure to become success. The analyst's vision should take in not just what is happening on the field or court, but what *is not* happening. They must apply their knowledge of all the pieces necessary to win championships to prescribe the preparation or the adjustments required for athletes and/or teams to achieve and maintain success. And they can't straddle any fences. Analysts should tell viewers what is being done well and what isn't. Rob Stone says that an analyst

> has to make a point that perks people up and gets them out of their seats to say "right" or "wrong." And they need to be true to who they are and

pure. There are some actors and actresses out there, but the audience is so smart and savvy these days that they see right through them.

Analysts more interested in putting on a show than clearly telling viewers how or why things are happening tend to hit a professional ceiling very quickly. Successful analysts are true to who they are, whether you agree or disagree with them, and will tell you what they see and what they believe.

Add depth and texture. Information and anecdotes about players, teams, venues, and rivalries that are not readily available to the average fan make live sports broadcasts more interesting. Analysts glean information from their years of experience in the sport, from interviews with players and coaches, from attending practices, from professional researchers, and from simply walking onto the field or around the stadium.

When John Madden was doing analysis on NFL telecasts, he would take a yellow legal-size pad to each team's practice leading up to a game and fill it with notes and observations. It did not matter if he had seen one or both teams earlier in the season, he would always see something new that would add depth and texture to the game telecast. And he shared that insight with his producer and director to help them plan and prepare.

Make distinctions. The trained eye of the expert analyst can spot the "exquisite intricacies" that distinguish the most elite athletes from their teammates and opponents. They can show us how a player or team's attributes, tactics, strengths, and weaknesses separate perennial winners from also-rans. In many sports broadcasts, you are watching the best in the world do what they do. When the analyst can dissect a performance and make the viewer aware of the subtleties that separate an exceptional player or team from all the rest, you will start to notice these details. Learning what specifics to watch for makes the viewing experience more meaningful and enjoyable.

Compare and contrast. Analysts have the advantage of attending practices and screening video clips from virtually every game or match played by the competitors leading up to a live broadcast. They have observed past performances, past seasons, different combinations of personnel, and different opponents. On the air, the analyst can then compare what he or she is seeing with how the player or team handled the same situation in the past against the same or different opponents, or at an earlier juncture in the very same game being televised.

Analysts can point out what is working from what they saw in practice, and what is falling apart. They can show the viewer the contrast between different coaches' strategies, the actions and reactions of different players on the same or opposing teams, even how competitors deal with pressure, victory, and defeat in their own unique ways.

Athletes or coaches who leave the game after retirement or injury to become television analysts can suddenly find themselves on "the other side," playing for a different team. Their live sports media job requires them to criticize the performances of former teammates and colleagues who may feel betrayed and react emotionally. Players and coaches who had friendships or professional relationships with the analyst often feel entitled to some protection from criticism, or at least to a little favorable treatment. When current competitors hear someone who they consider to be a friend or colleague point out their failings to millions of viewers, they may get very upset. Several have refused to do any future interviews with the critical analyst who they now consider a "traitor."

The job of the analyst in many ways is to represent the viewers. He or she must anticipate, ask, and answer the questions that viewers have about a contest and its players, show them how the game is executed, and specifically what it takes to win. To do that well, analysts must make the break from past ties and honestly evaluate every player and coach. Those who take it easy on friends and overlook flaws that impact the competition will almost always be forced by demanding producers to make early exits from the broadcast booth.

Former athletes who have made successful careers as television analysts draw comparisons between their current jobs and their playing days. The intense preparation for each event is similar: watching game video, studying past performances and tendencies, meeting with players and coaches, and planning strategies with a team of professionals. The build-up to game day can have the same kind of adrenaline rush that the analyst felt when he or she was wearing a uniform, not street clothes. When the analyst has that kind of excitement and love for the game, it comes through on the screen.

A constant challenge for the live sports analyst is keeping up to speed with the ever-expanding knowledge of the viewers. More channels and platforms make more games available for fans to watch, and they have access to so much more data and information than ever before, that their expectations are far greater. The commentators in the booth or in the studio can assume that a sizeable segment of the audience has tapped into many of the same resources that they use. They have heard a lot about the game at hand, they have plenty of data, and they may even be checking for updates online while they are watching the broadcast. Analysts must keep up, and as the pace of the sport accelerates and the pace of the broadcast picks up, they must learn how to be concise and how to prioritize their analysis.

THE EVOLUTION OF THE AUDIENCE AND TALENT

The evolution of a more educated, tuned-in audience has dramatically affected how sports commentators approach their jobs, but it has also fostered the development of new talent roles to feed the fans' heightened expectations for more and better information and insights. Live events that are presented on national platforms must serve three different audiences at the same time. There is the national audience, every person from one corner of the country to the other, who watches the same broadcast with varying degrees of interest. The second audience is the home team and its fans, and the third audience is the road team and its followers. The audiences following each team are more loyal, and they almost always watch in greater percentages than fans who do not have a regional interest. Commentators should consider how their words will be interpreted by all three sets of fans and artfully balance each telecast so that it becomes neither too provincial nor too broad. Either of the two extremes can drive away fans who are important customers for the network and its advertisers.

As the coverage of sports has expanded the past few decades and the fans' knowledge and appetite for information have grown, so has the need for commentators with a wide variety of skills. Every network has added to its rosters a set of event and studio hosts and analysts, sideline and specialty reporters, experts on rules, safety and player injuries, and/or gambling, as well as investigative journalists, essayists, and provocateurs.

The role of the host has evolved to become separate from the play-by-play commentator. For example, when NBC televised Super Bowl III in 1969, Curt Gowdy hosted the show and did the play-by-play. That was the norm well into the 1970s. But as pre-game, halftime, and post-game shows were added and expanded to provide viewers with more features, interviews, and data, as well as create additional commercial inventory for networks to sell more sponsorships, studio hosts and on-site event hosts were added to the list of sports talent job descriptions.

The pre-game host, whether in a studio or at the site of the event, helps introduce viewers to the players and coaches who will be competing. A half-hour or hour of pre-game allows for longer interviews that would never fit into the live game coverage itself where the only breaks in the action are the few seconds between plays or the few minutes between periods. The host can take a broader approach than the play-by-play commentator whose focus is the game at hand. The host's role is to look at the game as part of something larger: the league, the impact of other games or of this game on others, and issues within the sport itself. The host can also provide any number of tangential stories on related topics that deserve to be told but would not be appropriate in the flow of live play-by-play action.

The pinnacle of the profession for a live sports host is the Olympics, which spans 18 days of coverage and reaches huge audiences each day. Mike Tirico, NBC's Olympic studio host, says the job would be impossible without a strong research team digging deep for information and traveling to world championships and other qualifying events for months before the games begin.

There is no way as an individual that you can prepare for the incredible volume of athletes, over 10,000 for the Summer Games and of sports, between three and four dozen, and have a full grasp of what you need at a moment's notice.

So much information is gathered and available that Tirico says one of his primary responsibilities as host "is knowing how to control the flow of the 'fire hydrant'. You can't just open it up and try to take in everything. That would be overwhelming."

When you compare the host role to play-by-play it is macro vs. micro. The host is at a level above the event where he or she sees the big picture and puts into context what is happening, why it is important, and what it means to the viewer. The play-by-play person for individual events is at ground level and needs to be ready with all the granular details of each specific contest, its history and rivalries, the athletes, coaches, and the venue.

One of the most important things that hosts do is set the table for their studio analysts, which is another category of sports television talent that has evolved over the past few decades. It is a hybrid of the game analyst position, but with more latitude and time to tell stories than the analyst in the booth whose comments must be confined to a short sentence or phrase between plays. The lineage of studio analysts goes back to the debut of *The NFL Today* on CBS in 1975 (Figure 8.1). Brent Musburger was host to studio regulars Irv Cross, Phyllis George, and Jimmy "The Greek" Snyder. Irv Cross brought his experience as a player, coach, and game analyst to the CBS studio. Phyllis George specialized in interviews and features, and Snyder's narrow focus was the effect of personnel and game decisions on the betting line. The number of specialties has multiplied in the years since 1975, and nothing would indicate that this diversification will end until sports themselves stop evolving.

■ **Figure 8.1** The original cast of *The NFL Today* on CBS. Pictured from left: Brent Musburger, Phyllis George, and Irv Cross. (CBS photo/Getty Images)

Sideline reporters made their debut in the 1960s when producers, searching for new stories and frustrated by having their only commentators isolated in a small booth high above the action, extended their reach to field level. Limitations are still imposed by leagues and organizers who want reporters and microphones to keep their distance from active competitors, but the information that can be gathered close to the action adds dimension and supplies answers when the unexpected occurs.

There is a distinction between the skill sets of sideline reporters in live broadcasts and the reporters who cover stories that are separate from live game coverage. Sideline reporters in a live game need to be constantly aware of change as it occurs, and they should be strong "self-editors" to keep their comments and interviews short, so they do not take time away from the play out on the field or court. For broadcasts or platforms other than live games, reporters need to be excellent interviewers, writers, and editors. Their "beat" is defined either by sport or by region, and their reports are seen on daily, weekly, or other regularly scheduled sports news and magazine shows, on television and online. They too will do their share of live reports, but most are stand-ups that lead into or wrap up produced and edited packages that do not have the time constraints imposed by live games.

The live sports media as part of the entertainment business has been home to "provocateurs" since the first time Howard Cosell needled Muhammad Ali or railed against "Dandy" Don Meredith and the "jockocracy" of athletes-turned-analysts that to him Meredith personified. The provocateur pokes and prods and sometimes intimidates guests and fellow commentators which can make for very entertaining programming. When the sparks fly and sometimes erupt into full-fledged fireworks, they draw attention to important issues and attract viewers who love spontaneity and confrontations. The by-product is more platforms and more shows for provocateurs on national networks, across the internet, streaming services, radio, and in local television markets.

The challenge for producers is to select the proper roles and the best people to fill them based upon the requirements of their specific events or series and the expectations of the audience. There are pitfalls in choosing either too few or too many commentators for any particular program. If the producer puts a play-by-play commentator and two analysts in the booth, but does not use a sideline reporter, he or she could be vulnerable when news breaks down on the field or courtside.

At the other end of the spectrum, a studio show with one host and four, five, or more studio analysts can lead to confusion as to who talks next and about what. And because each one has to get a share of airtime, the show can suffer from the under-utilization of one analyst who may have the best angle on that game or topic. One or two insightful analysts will usually make a studio show better than a panel of four or five analysts, some of whom may be there only because they are famous.

THE PIONEERS

For the first 26 years of television sports, from 1939 until 1965, every face the public saw doing sports commentary was white. No member of any minority group had ever been hired to do sports on TV. Jackie Robinson broke the color barrier in major league baseball when he took the field for the Brooklyn Dodgers in 1947. And he broke the barrier in the announce booth in 1965 when he sat down behind the microphone for ABC Sports as an analyst for its *Major League Baseball Game of the Week*. Robinson had been inducted into the National Baseball Hall of Fame in 1962, six years after his retirement from the Dodgers. He worked just one season on the air for ABC before accepting a job as general manager of the Brooklyn team in the short-lived Continental Football League. Jackie Robinson returned to the microphone to work as a part-time commentator for Montreal Expos games during the 1972 season only a few months before his death that October at the age of 53.

The groundbreaking work begun by Jackie Robinson was continued by Irv Cross who spent 23 years as a pro football commentator for CBS beginning in 1971. Cross had played defensive back for the Philadelphia Eagles and the Los Angeles Rams from 1961 to 1969. He was the first Black analyst on a nationally televised NFL game and made a lasting impact as the original studio analyst for *The NFL Today* pre-game show. In 2009, Irv Cross was honored by the Pro Football Hall of Fame with the Pete Rozelle Radio-Television Award. His work inspired generations of young people of color to apply their knowledge, education, and communications skills to careers in broadcast sports.

Young women have been able to do the same thanks to Jane Chastain and Donna de Varona. Jane Chastain started doing a weekly sports report on WAGA-TV in Atlanta in 1963, just two years after she graduated high school. She was called "Coach Friday," and she made her predictions for Saturday college football games. When Chastain moved to WTVJ-TV, the CBS affiliate in Miami in 1971, she became a respected sports reporter and got her first network sports assignments. CBS hired her in 1974, making her its first woman sports commentator. Chastain stayed at CBS for just one year, unhappy with assignments that she said were mostly interviews with cheerleaders and athletes' wives.

Donna de Varona was only 13 years old when she swam for the United States in the 1960 Olympics in Rome. She won two gold medals at the 1964 Olympic Games in Tokyo and was named the outstanding female athlete in the world by the Associated Press. When de Varona retired from competitive swimming in 1965 at the age of 17, ABC put a microphone in her hand to do reports on the network's *Wide World of Sports* program, making her the first female sports commentator on any American television network.

Donna de Varona covered every Olympics for ABC through 1988, also doing reports for the *ABC Evening News* and *Nightline*. She was the co-founder of the Women's Sports Foundation along with tennis legend Billie Jean King, and she served as the foundation's first president from 1976 until 1984.

BECOMING A SPORTS COMMENTATOR

Getting a job broadcasting sports on television is the dream of young male and female sports enthusiasts regardless of where they grew up. For a few talented individuals, the dream will come true. But only a very small number have everything it takes and will be lucky enough to find themselves at the right place at the right time, to get that on-air job. The baseline for success as a television sports commentator begins with having an interest in and knowledge of a broad spectrum of sports. An important asset to have is an expert knowledge of one or more sports that comes from being a lifelong fan or participant who studies players past and present, teams, history, rules, venues, and contemporary issues. In addition, commentators need:

- *Self-confidence.* When the lights and the camera come on, the successful on-air talent have the confidence that comes from knowing they have prepared exhaustively. They are self-assured, knowing that the information they have is solid and authoritative, and that giving the best they have from within themselves will be good enough and better than imitating any other commentator. Chris Fowler's advice is, "Be true to yourself, be authentic, be yourself because everyone else is already taken."
- *Dynamic personality.* When the red light goes on, you need to come out and play strong. "You have to be brave enough and strong enough to shove yourself in front of a camera and talk to potentially millions of people as if they are one of your best friends, and that can be daunting," said Rob Stone. Viewers want to like the people who deliver their sports. They want credibility, but they also want to feel that the commentator loves the sport just as much as they do and that it would be fun to meet and just "talk sports."
- *Sincerity.* Television viewers can spot a phony in five seconds or less. The successful sports commentator has sincerity in his or her voice, face, and most importantly, in the eyes. Virtually everyone watches the eyes of whoever is talking, in person or on video screen, so if the commentator is sincere and believes what he or she is saying, it will be there in their eyes.
- *A quick wit.* Live sports media is full of unexpected turns and events. It is nearly impossible to teach someone how to respond quickly and appropriately to events with a phrase that will add context, relax tension, or cause viewers to smile. "Bob Costas is a brilliant adlibber," said Fowler, "but it always sounds well-thought-out because he is able to keep his brain two seconds ahead of his mouth. If you can do that

while speaking extemporaneously for long periods of time, that's how you can approach the level of smoothness that Bob has."

- *Patience*. The very best commentators let live scenes play out, take the time to get the story right, and never sound rushed or out of breath. Patience reinforces their command regardless of how fast things are happening.

- *Humility*. "I think you have to do this job with humility, understand that you are always a work in progress," said Fowler. "You should always feel that improvement isn't just possible, but it's required." Admiring the work and skill of others, not yourself, is what sports reporting is all about. Sports commentators will always be interacting with colleagues on the production team, players, coaches, and team, conference, or league officials. Through it all, the key is to treat every individual with genuine respect. "You have to be a good person and a team player," says Ian Eagle. "You better have a collaborative spirit and understand that you're no more important than anybody else on your crew." That means whenever you need help you ask for it, you never demand it. And you thank those who provide their services, never take them for granted as if you were entitled.

The people who will succeed as sportscasters are those who work the hardest. It is true in school and in every profession. It takes dedication and an unswerving love for sport and the profession to put in the hours preparing and studying for each assignment. Travel from home to game to game to studio and back is not in the least glamorous or easy. Nor is sitting in front of a bank of monitors in a studio or at your home for several hours while you call a live event with an analyst who may or may not even be in the same room or time zone.

There are early morning meetings for games later that night and late-night meetings for shows the next day. There are assignments like basketball tournaments and tennis grand slams that require working several games or matches on the same day, with barely any time in-between to eat or visit the bathroom. It is hard work, and it always should be if you set high standards and strive to always improve. What will sustain you is your life-long love of sports and the joy you derive from just talking sports with your friends.

When you have finally made it into the ranks of live sports broadcasters, how do you know when you have done a good job? That the show is a success? Stone says:

The elements of a great show are: it moved, it made you laugh, it brought up some point you hadn't thought about before, there was definitely some form of improv or adlibbing going on. It wasn't pre-produced, but it did include creativity that was put in days beforehand. You added a new angle to a conversation or a theme, and it worked. When all those elements come together is when I walk back and I say, "that one worked, it had a good pop and a good rhythm to it."

BIBLIOGRAPHY

Eagle, Ian. *Interviewed by the Author*, 2021.

Fowler, Chris. *Interviewed by the Author*, 2021.

Kupper, Mike. "Keith Jackson, Homespun Voice of College Football, Dies at 89." *The Washington Post*, 2018. https://www.washingtonpost.com/local/obituaries/keith-jackson-homespun-voice-of-college-football-dies-at-89/2018/01/13/06f9c916-f893-11e7-a9e3-ab18ce41436a_story.html

Stone, Rob. *Interviewed by the Author*, 2021.

Tirico, Mike. *Interviewed by the Author*, 2021.

Sports Coverage That Spans the Globe

The American appetite for sports from around the world was whetted by the coverage of the Olympics from foreign venues that began with Rome in 1960, followed by the 1964 Winter Games in Innsbruck, Austria, and the Summer Games that year from Tokyo. The 1964 Summer Olympics, which were held in October that year, became known as "The TV Olympics" because they were the first to feature live coverage via satellite. The signals were transmitted using NASA's Syncom III satellite which had been launched into a geostationary orbit 22,300 miles above the Pacific Ocean just two months before the opening ceremonies were held on October 10, 1964. *ABC's Wide World of Sports* started "spanning the globe" in search of what the show open described as "the constant variety of sport, the thrill of victory and the agony of defeat" every weekend from the summer of 1961 until 1998. The launch in the 1960s of more communications satellites over the Atlantic and Pacific and the laying of trans-oceanic fiber cables along the ocean floors that began in the late 1980s also fed the craving for more sports from more places, which was shared by millions of viewers.

The sports programs coming back to the United States from foreign countries however had a different look than the games and events that originated in the United States. The pictures and sound were never quite as clear and synchronized as they were on American shows. The European networks used a technical broadcast standard called PAL that had more lines of resolution than the American NTSC standard. Any show that was recorded using PAL cameras and tape machines had to be converted to NTSC to make it compatible with American television sets and transmission equipment. And the sports themselves were different, sometimes bordering on exotic, definitely "foreign."

What international sports programming did for American television viewers was to open eyes and broaden horizons. Americans found that several sports considered minor in the United States such as tennis, soccer, and horse racing were the major sports in many countries overseas. Some sports with virtually no domestic US television coverage like cricket, rugby, and Formula One auto racing had millions of devoted fans on continents other than North America, along with iconic celebrity stars and lucrative TV rights contracts. The major American sports with the largest fan bases and most valuable TV deals, gridiron football and baseball, were

DOI: 10.4324/9781003165590-9

of limited interest in only a few scattered countries around the globe, and they were played in even fewer.

Regardless of the sport or where it is played, the basics of live sports media product are the same: words and pictures telling dramatic and entertaining stories as they happen. The terms we use may be different: our commentator or announcer is called a "presenter" in many countries. When the presenter is seen on camera, he or she is "in vision." Our TV truck is their "OB van," for "outside broadcast," and what American television professionals call a "site survey" is a "recce," short for "reconnaissance," in English-speaking countries outside the United States. Translations and variations abound in the non-English-speaking world. The terminology may differ, but the goal of sports production personnel worldwide remains unchanged: deliver compelling live games and events to engage an audience of eager viewers.

With different cultures come different approaches to televised sport, which makes it all the more interesting when American TV networks go overseas to originate programming for their audiences back home in the United States, or when foreign broadcasters come to the United States to send coverage of events here back to their home countries. Every nation and every network does business in its own fashion. When they work together to televise international events to multiple nations, there are three universal common denominators: 1) international rights agreements, 2) host broadcasters, and 3) international broadcast centers.

INTERNATIONAL RIGHTS AGREEMENTS

In an earlier chapter, we discussed how television rights agreements work: a media network or television station pays an amount of money specified by contract to an event organizer or league for the exclusive rights to televise a set number of games or shows over a specified period of time. For domestic events, the network or station that pays for the broadcast rights to games or other events is responsible for producing the coverage, providing all the necessary personnel and technical equipment, and transmitting all programs to its affiliated stations, systems, and viewers.

Many international rights agreements work differently. A network or consortium of networks will pay the organizer for the exclusive rights to televise an event in a specific territory, which could be just one country or several countries that may or may not be contiguous. In return, each network that buys a media rights license gets 1) access to the world feed of that event which can be transmitted live back to their country or territory, 2) a fixed number of credentials for their personnel who will be on-site, and 3) the exclusive rights to sell advertising in event programming and to promote it on their network. Obtaining the international rights to an event such as the FIFA World Cup, the Olympic Games, or Wimbledon does not automatically come with permission for a network to set up its own cameras or bring in its own personnel or technical equipment to each venue. That would be impossible to control if only for space considerations. Imagine if each of the more than 200 nations and territories that pay for the rights to televise a FIFA World Cup soccer tournament could send their own cameras, microphones, and crews to each soccer stadium. There would be a lot less space available for spectators or players.

Instead, the organizer, which in the case of the World Cup is the Federation Internationale de Football Association (FIFA), establishes an International Broadcast Center (IBC) and makes available a host feed of the event to those networks that buy the rights. The feed is produced and directed by crews hired directly by the organizer to provide video and audio coverage with scoring graphics of all the action from every game. Access to host feeds is available at the organizer's IBC and as a menu of digital feeds that can be downloaded by rights-holding broadcasters around the world. As the world feed arrives at a rights-holding network's production facility in its home country, the coverage can be customized for that nation's audience with the addition of a native language voice-over by announcers watching the competition on a monitor and by the insertion of graphic titles, animations, and commercials also in the language of that home country. It is important to note that feeds delivered via satellite, fiber, or internet connection travel at the speed of light, which is 186,000 miles per second. Viewers watching anywhere in the world are therefore seeing all the action virtually live as it happens with a delay of perhaps only one or two seconds as the pictures and sound are augmented then retransmitted to their homes.

If a network wants greater access with its own studio, technical facilities, and production personnel on-site, these expanded rights come at a greater cost. NBC, for example, has paid the International Olympic Committee (IOC) $7.75 billion for exclusive TV, internet, and mobile rights in the United States for the six Olympic Games from 2022 through 2032. The rights payments from the American broadcaster customarily represent roughly half of all the revenue that the IOC collects in television licensing fees. The payments from every other country in the world, a total of just under 200 territories, combine to make up the other half.

It is very common for broadcasters from individual nations in Europe, Africa, and Asia to band together into a consortium to buy rights to major international sports events. The aggregate size of the consortium gives them more bargaining power and influence than if dozens of nations of varying sizes tried to negotiate one-on-one with an international organizer such as FIFA or the IOC. In 2015, Discovery Communications, the parent company of the Discovery Network, acquired the exclusive rights to televise the Olympics from 2018 through 2024 across 50 countries and territories on the European continent. Discovery has never televised the

Olympics in the United States, but the company paid 1.3 billion euros (roughly $1.5 billion) for all the free-to-air television, subscription/ pay television, internet, and mobile phone distribution to those 50 countries in every language. Discovery expanded its global presence in 2021 when it merged with WarnerMedia, which includes HBO, CNN, Warner Bros., and DC Comics, to form Warner Bros. Discovery.

A basic international rights agreement gives broadcasters license to televise the event just once: live or on a delayed replay, the choice based upon how many time zones the venue is from their home region. Almost invariably, broadcasters do not get the rights to re-air games or shows, and their use of highlights from the event is also limited to a set period of time after which the rights to all video revert back to the organizer. NBC may air the Olympics in the United States, but the IOC retains ownership of all the video, audio, and data.

The rights-holding network follows the organizer's guidelines to determine whether any other video platform in their country or territory will be allowed to use recorded highlights from the event on their competing stations or websites, and what restrictions are placed on that usage. These parameters and prohibitions are distributed to all news and sports media in the form of "embargo notices" in advance of events. Normally, news coverage by non-rights-holding networks or stations is strictly forbidden until after the rights holder's show goes off the air. (For example, if NBC had bought the rights to an event, ESPN would not be allowed to show any highlights on *SportsCenter* until after NBC concluded its show.) There are also limitations on how many seconds of video can be used by non-rights holders in bona fide news programs during any 24-hour period. It is not uncommon for rights holders to also put expiration dates on their video. NBC has historically not allowed the usage of any Olympics highlights after 48 hours have elapsed from the time the event occurred live. Highlight usage on internet video platforms is now usually included in a media rights license, so clips and excerpts may not be published to sites that are not controlled by a rights-holding network. This encourages fans to look for video on their proprietary websites or social media platforms, not on those owned by any competitor or third party.

The networks representing the largest countries that pay the highest broadcast rights fees for major international events have the option of setting up a dedicated studio and commentary positions and installing their own "unilateral" cameras and microphones at one or more venue sites. Paying over $1 billion per Olympiad, NBC has traditionally added studios, multiple control rooms, edit facilities, and offices staffed by hundreds of network personnel, all of whom receive credentials issued by the International Olympic Committee. That has been changing in recent years as NBC found it more economical to send the world feeds from several Olympic sport venues back to its production center in Stamford, Connecticut, for remote production integration and announcer voice-overs there.

The COVID-19 pandemic and the travel restrictions that came with it accelerated the move by networks to reduce the number of people they send to international event sites and expand the coordination of productions from crew members at their homes or in the network's domestic broadcast facilities. As an example, in January of 2021, ESPN had only two commentators in Melbourne for the Australian Open, both Australian citizens. Most of the hosts, announcers, and production personnel were on the air for two weeks from an ESPN Digital Broadcast Center in Bristol, Connecticut. However, John McEnroe called several days of matches from his home in New York, Cliff Drysdale was in Austin, Texas, and analyst James Blake was in San Diego. The operations manager coordinated all the on-site facilities and technical personnel in Melbourne from his basement in London. And the person who set up all of ESPN's post-match player interviews was in Ponte Vedra, Florida. Everyone working on each show installed the Unity Intercom® app on their phones, tablets, or computers making real-time communications possible regardless of where in the world they were sitting.

HOST BROADCASTERS

The amount of work involved in organizing international sporting events such as the Olympics, World Cup soccer, tennis Grand Slams like Wimbledon, or major golf tournaments from around the world is monumental. The International Olympic Committee must work with the sport federations from every nation that sends athletes to the Games. It works with the host city on the design and construction of arenas, stadiums, athlete housing, and amenities. And it does the marketing and licensing of the Olympics and its merchandise. FIFA coordinates the three years of international competition that yields the 32 teams that will compete for the World Cup. Then it works with the soccer federations from all 32 nations in much the same way the IOC connects with the governing bodies of each individual Olympic sport. And there are stadiums to build or renovate and marketing to be done. Staging events and competitions is the specialty of these sports organizing bodies. Broadcasting is not.

To handle all television production matters and relations with broadcast rights holders, international organizers such as the IOC and FIFA contract with third-party production entities or set up subsidiaries to serve as the host broadcaster. The role of the host broadcaster is to produce all the television and radio coverage of an event and make the feeds available to every network that has paid for broadcast rights. To do so it must:

- Design, build, install, and operate the IBC. And then dismantle it when the event has concluded.

- Design, build, install, operate, and then remove broadcast facilities and equipment at the competition venues and select non-competition venues such as medal stands or news conference and interview rooms. For a Summer Olympic Games, this would include over 1,000 cameras to cover all the competition venues, 15,000 miles of cables (25,000 kilometers), and over 7,000 personnel.
- Coordinate and provide various facilities and services to each rights-holding broadcaster. These can range from the distribution systems that allow a network to select various venue or camera feeds to the rental of office furniture at the site or catering for production personnel.
- Represent the needs of the rights-holding networks to the organizer. For example, a Japanese network may want a match at Wimbledon that features its number one tennis player to be scheduled for a time that coincides with prime evening viewing hours back in Japan. The host broadcaster cannot guarantee that the All England Club will adjust the schedule, but it is responsible for taking that request to the club's scheduling committee.
- Produce various features, animations, video teases, and show opens that any network can use as part of its programming from the event.
- Assist the organizer with the design and construction of infrastructure needed at the venues to accommodate broadcasting needs. These could include camera towers for the coverage of expansive outdoor events such as an Olympic stadium or a major golf tournament, as well as enlarged press boxes or additional commentary positions in stadiums or arenas.
- Provide all the data and scoring feeds that include race timing, game clocks, leader boards, entry lists for every heat, and every statistic that is tracked in the sport from every court or arena. In the case of tennis, this data would include game, set, and match scores plus serve percentages, total aces, unforced errors, backhand winners, and much more from every match currently in play or already completed. These data feeds are part of the graphics that are incorporated into the basic world feed, and they are also available for the right-holding networks on-site to interface into their own network graphics machines for use in their broadcasts at the discretion of each producer.

The host broadcaster template dates back to the 1972 Olympic Games in Munich where an international signal that was separate and distinct from the domestic broadcast of the nation hosting the Olympics was first produced for global distribution. The German broadcast networks created a separate unit to produce the international feeds because requests coming in from rights-holding networks had increased to the point that they could not be handled by the staff whose primary responsibility was producing the live telecasts that would be air on ARD and ZDF. Prior to 1972, the primary network in the host nation, NHK for the 1964 Summer Games in Tokyo for example, was responsible for providing a clean feed of their domestic coverage to any network that had paid the International Olympic Committee for a television broadcast rights license. For smaller, less complex international competitions such as a three-day Davis Cup tennis event called a "tie," the home nation's primary network is still responsible for acting as host broadcaster and making a feed of its coverage available to any foreign network that has purchased rights from the organizer, which in the case of the Davis Cup is the International Tennis Federation.

At the largest international sports events, the host broadcaster provides a variety of feeds and options to every network that has purchased the television rights. A rights-holding network can simply air the coverage of games and matches that is produced by the host broadcaster with its scoring and timing graphics and commentary, which is available in multiple languages most often including English, Spanish, French, and Mandarin. Or it can customize the program for its home audience by taking several separate and distinct feeds into a production control room located either on-site or back at its home country broadcast center. These feeds are available in four configurations:

- *Dirty feed*. This is a produced feed that contains all video as cut by a host director live on-site, with the ambient sound from the venue, announcer commentary, and all world graphics including scoring data. There is no network branding, only the logos of the organizer such as the Olympic rings.
- *Clean feed*. This includes all the directed video, venue audio, graphics, and scoring data that come with a "dirty" feed, but there is no commentary audio.
- *Clean/clean feed*. Only the directed video and the venue audio. No graphics (except scoring and clocks as desired) and no commentary.
- *Discrete feed*. This is a direct signal from a selected camera, such as the camera in an interview room, or a wide panoramic shot from a specific venue at the event like the figure-skating arena or the ski-jump at a Winter Olympics.

A network may choose to add its own commentators' voice-over in their native language to a clean feed, or it can take the dirty feed with a separate announce track in English, Spanish, or French for example. The native language commentator will listen to that "guide track" in his or her headset and simultaneously translate the description of action into the language that the network's viewers will understand. The world graphics and scoring data are designed to be understandable in most languages that use the Roman alphabet. The commentators can be at the site of the competition, in a studio in the IBC, back in their home studios, or even at their individual residences watching the video feed on monitors and adding their voices to the final product. Calling the show "off the tube" is the most cost-efficient method of customizing a feed, saving the network travel costs and any fees associated with setting up production equipment on-site or in an IBC.

DISCRETE FEEDS

At an event such as the Olympics, Wimbledon, or major golf tournaments there is simultaneous action at several venues, arenas, courts, and locations on a course. The rights holder can select which competition to broadcast back to its home country based upon who is playing where. If the champion shot-putter from Croatia is competing on the athletics field, the Croatian television network can choose the feed from that venue, even though the rest of the world may be focused on a swimming race underway simultaneously at the aquatics center. Or if the number one ranked tennis player from Japan is on Court 13 at Wimbledon, NHK as the rights holder for Japan can punch up "Court 13" in their router and show it to all their viewers regardless of who is playing the match over on Centre Court. These discrete feeds from arenas or courts are directed and produced by professionals hired by the host broadcaster.

Discrete feed offerings include continuous feeds from specific cameras, such as a fixed aerial beauty shot of the grounds that can be used when the network chooses to break away from action and go to a commercial, or as the background shot for graphics that promote what is coming up next. An ambitious rights holder may request several discrete camera feeds which it can use to cut into and augment the host feed, further customizing the coverage that it delivers to its home audience. The host broadcast director has instructed each camera operator as to their coverage assignments so discrete camera feeds tend to be very reliable for a rights-holding network to take live to air. But with several different network programs directed by people speaking a variety of languages all integrating that camera's pictures into their feeds, the camera operators at international event venues can take direction from only one voice: the director of the host broadcast feed. They have no way of knowing if other networks are showing their camera live when they pan right or left or adjust focus.

The host broadcaster charges extra for every additional discrete feed that a rights holder adds onto the basic coverage feed. It can also set up studios, provide production and office space in the International Broadcast Center, assign and equip announcer booths, provide interview rooms, relay any rights-holding network's signal to the nearest uplink or fiber terminal, and supply computers, furniture, even catering. When you add up every item selected from the host broadcaster's rate card, a large production over several days or weeks can be very expensive. And the unknown variable is how much the international exchange rate may have changed in the weeks or months since your initial budget was approved. A weaker dollar will result in higher costs abroad, which could force a network to spend more, or its producers to cut back on travel, personnel, and/or equipment to stay on budget.

THE HOST BROADCASTER MODEL CHANGES

In 1984 at the Summer Olympics in Los Angeles, a new option was added to the mix for international broadcasters. For an additional fee, a rights holder could add one or more of its own "unilateral" cameras at an arena or other venue to further customize coverage for its viewing audience. This allowed networks for the first time to focus their coverage even more specifically on athletes from their home nations. These unilateral signals can now be added to the set of feeds being sent directly back to that rights holder's home broadcast center, or they can be added to programs being produced on-site by that network through the use of a small production integration facility at the International Broadcast Center.

Until the 1992 Olympic Games in Barcelona, serving as host broadcaster had always been the responsibility of the rights-holding network that was based in the host country. For example, ARD and ZDF worked together in Germany in 1972, and ABC was the host broadcaster for the 1984 Los Angeles Olympics. The International Olympic Committee changed its rules in 1992 to allow a broadcast organization that was *not* from the host country to serve as host broadcaster. In that year, Radio Television Olimpica (RTO '92) was set up by the Barcelona Olympic organizing committee to serve as host instead of the Spanish television rights-holding network. For subsequent summer and winter Olympics, the IOC solicited bids from independent production groups to fill the host broadcaster role. That ended with the Beijing Olympics of 2008 and the Vancouver Winter Games of 2010. For these and all Olympics since, the IOC established its own subsidiary to serve as the permanent Olympic host broadcaster. This entity called Olympic Broadcasting Services (OBS) gave the IOC more control over the content and tone of its television product, and it established production continuity from one Olympics to the next regardless of which country would be hosting the Games. The same model of host broadcasters that are independent of domestic networks has been embraced by FIFA for soccer World Cups as well as by several other international event organizers.

THE INTERNATIONAL BROADCAST CENTER

When hundreds of television networks have all paid for broadcast rights to an event and they or their representatives all come together in the same place at the same time speaking different languages and serving different audiences in widely separated time zones, the result can be chaotic. To control if not eliminate the chaos, the organizers of major international events work with their host broadcasters to build an IBC or designate an international broadcast compound.

That center or compound is the locus of all the production facilities, services, communications connections, and signal feeds for an international sports event. Every offering made by the host broadcaster is available in one place. How each rights-holding network or consortium of networks decides to use the facilities and services varies widely. When ESPN took over the US cable rights for Wimbledon in 2003, we knew we would need plenty of space for control rooms, edit suites, offices, and a studio. We therefore contracted with the All England Club (AELTC) and its host broadcaster, the BBC, to use virtually an entire wing of the broadcast center building, upstairs and down. The network paid an established fee per square meter for the space. Then we hired production equipment from vendors to outfit the rooms we had rented at an additional expense. We selected which discrete court and camera feeds we wanted to be routed to our control rooms from the BBC distribution center, nicknamed "Oscar." Then we populated our wing of the IBC with well over 100 people to work two weeks or more on the ESPN coverage, which in the first week of play ran to 10 hours per day.

By contrast, some networks from Europe and Asia only assign one person to work for them on-site. Their purpose is to make sure the right feed from the courts where their players of interest are competing is routed onto the correct transmission path that will deliver that audio and video back to their network's home base. That is where their tennis commentators watch the feed as it arrives and add their voices to the coverage. Fans in their countries see live tennis matches and so do fans in the United States, but very often they are different matches from different courts with varying levels of production customization.

At many international venues, there is no permanent building for an IBC. At these events, an open area or parking lot adjacent to the venue is secured as the broadcast compound. Individual rights holders can hire all the technical facilities they need from the host broadcaster, or in many cases, from independent vendors. The video and audio feeds, electrical power, communications lines, portable offices, and restrooms are all moved in, and surcharges are added to the bill for each network that puts them to use. These broadcast compounds are by their nature less organized than a permanent IBC, but they have the same function: for organizers to serve all the rights-holding broadcasters who are providing coverage of and publicity for their events around the globe.

PRODUCING SPORTS TELEVISION OVERSEAS

It takes a special set of skills to successfully produce sports programming from foreign countries for broadcast in the United States or to produce events in the U.S for distribution in various other nations. Adaptability and resourcefulness are paramount. Broadcasters in different countries do things differently. That does not mean they are wrong. It just means they are different. Learning how to work within new systems that come with a variety of challenges and limitations will make all the difference. No amount of complaining or tantrums will get a foreign nation or network to change its ways of doing business.

In my two decades of producing international sports television, one of the most challenging events was the 1995 Davis Cup Final in Moscow where we produced three days of coverage fed live back to ESPN. We brought our tennis commentators, Cliff Drysdale, Mary Carillo, and Fred Stolle, along with our producer, director, operations manager, associate producer, and a translator from the United States. We hired Woods TV from Paris to provide the necessary technical personnel and broadcast equipment. They trucked everything across several borders and set up our control room in one of the backstage rooms at the massive indoor Olympic arena that had been built for the 1980 Moscow Olympics.

The day before play was to begin our ESPN crew was anxious to do test feeds back to our base in Bristol, Connecticut, from the cameras installed by ORT, the Russian television network that was serving as host broadcaster. When ORT kept delaying us, we offered to make the connections ourselves, but we were advised through our translator that "that could be dangerous." Late the Thursday afternoon before matches were to begin on Friday, our exasperated technical director, an American named Bernie Kraska who was living in Germany, had had enough. He made the connections, we successfully tested the cameras and audio feeds, and our crew all went back to our hotel.

On Friday morning we arrived back at the arena to find that our cables had been physically cut. We were due to start feeding live tennis back to the United States just a few hours later. When our translator and I went to our ORT contact to find out what was going on, the response was, "We told you it could be dangerous for you to connect your cables." The Russian director had an assistant at his side who clearly explained in English that he needed "one grand" in cash before the connections could be restored. I had expected that I would have to grease some palms in Moscow, but I did not have $1,000 in cash.

My solution was to go to the executive director of the International Tennis Federation, Christopher Stokes, who had traveled in from London. I had worked closely with Christopher many times before, and our good relationship made all the difference that day. He agreed to take the cash out of his fund for local expenses. We paid off the Russians, our cables were restored, and that afternoon we went on the air with live tennis from Moscow.

A few years later it was my responsibility to set up ESPN's first-ever event broadcast from Zimbabwe. It was a Davis Cup weekend of five matches featuring a US team led by Andre Agassi and captained by John McEnroe versus the best players from Zimbabwe. The Zimbabwe Broadcasting Corporation (ZBC) had rarely originated live tennis coverage, whereas our ESPN team was turning out 100 days of live tennis programming every year. Early on I diplomatically proposed to the ZBC that we at ESPN would be happy to serve as the host broadcaster and deliver to them three days of superior tennis coverage, to be directed, and produced by some of the most experienced professionals in the world.

After a series of conference calls, the ZBC agreed to take the secondary role and let ESPN serve as host broadcaster. One hurdle was cleared, but the next would be finding the necessary production equipment in or near Harare. There were only two mobile television production trucks in the entire country, one of which the ZBC was using to produce programs and the other that was being used for parts to keep the first truck operational.

We needed two functioning television mobile units for the tennis coverage: one in which our ESPN crew would produce three days of tennis matches and the second for ZBC to add their own graphics and commentary audio to the clean feed we would provide so they could deliver their customized coverage to viewers in Zimbabwe. When I arrived at the Harare Sports Center arena, I saw only one truck. I asked about the second truck and was told that since there was only one good battery, a couple of ZBC staffers had driven the first truck to the Sports Center, removed its battery, and put it into the trunk of their car to go get the second TV truck.

We were fortunate to have again hired Woods TV from Paris to provide technical assistance and personnel. The company had experience in Africa working on broadcasts of the South African Grand Prix. They were able to obtain the blueprints of the two trucks from Paris-based Thomson Electronics (now Technicolor SA) which had built the trucks. And they brought along a French engineer who used every ounce of his resourcefulness to get both trucks up and running in time for our telecasts.

International broadcasting can be compared to learning a new sport. You have a new set of rules, there are different players, and you may have to use different equipment and put new resources to work for your advantage. And just like sport, it can be exciting and extremely rewarding, providing you with a new perspective and a new set of friends for your lifetime. But to succeed, do your research, know the rules, and above all be resourceful.

BIBLIOGRAPHY

Armour, Nancy. "NBC Universal pays $7.75 billion for Olympics through 2032." USA Today, 2014. https://www.usatoday.com/story/sports/olympics/2014/05/07/nbc-olympics-broadcast-rights-2032/8805989/

Advertising Drives the Sports Engine

No engine runs without fuel. The revenue generated by advertising and sponsorship is the fuel that drives the live sports industry around the globe. Every professional sport and many amateur sports rely on money from advertisers and sponsors to stage their games and events, pay salaries and taxes, build or lease venues, and do everything else required to maintain and promote an entertainment product that will attract and hold an audience. The media contribute a major portion of that revenue to the sports organizers and leagues in the form of licensing fees for the rights to televise their events. The media in turn must sell advertising and sponsorships that will appear in those live broadcasts and streams to recoup the billions of dollars, euros, or any other currency they spent to purchase the live coverage rights.

It is therefore vitally important for the entire industry that sports competitions draw large media audiences to attract advertisers who will pay dearly to reach their target market of prospective customers. That makes building and sustaining a mass audience through the promotion of sports events and their charismatic stars a critical factor in the equation. Convincing advertisers to buy commercials and sponsorship in sports programming demands accurate audience measurement that can be refined down to every minute in every show segment, specific demographic data as to who is watching, and how much time those people spend viewing each game or event on any and every platform.

The live sports media attract a loyal core audience that is more predictable for advertisers than any other programming category. Anyone who has grown up as a fan of a particular team, or attended a university and followed its sports, will tend to watch when that team is playing. These lifelong loyalties are far stronger and more enduring than any allegiance to a situation comedy, dramatic series, or "reality" show. Advertisers can count on sports fans, which makes targeting them by demographics much more reliable than estimating who will tune in and in what numbers for the premiere of any new entertainment series. Live sports deliver a consistent level of viewership: a sizable percentage of men, specific age ranges, ethnic backgrounds, income and education levels, and legions of fans dedicated to their regional or national favorites.

DOI: 10.4324/9781003165590-10

The unit of measure for media advertising is the cost per thousand or CPM (the "M" is mille, the Roman numeral for a thousand). The price that advertisers are charged to reach 1,000 viewers is multiplied by the number of thousand viewers reached. If a weekly series of games routinely has an audience of 100,000, and the network charges a CPM of $40, an advertiser would pay $4,000 (100 × 40) for one commercial in one game. For digital platforms, the standard is CPC, cost per click. Advertising in sports content is usually priced at a higher CPM or CPC than any other content for two main reasons: 1) the live, unpredictable, and perishable nature of live sports guarantees that well over 90 percent of viewers will watch the games live as they happen. That means people are more likely to see messages in commercial breaks that they can't speed through on fast-forward; and 2) ads for products like beer, tires, and pickup trucks will reach a larger concentration of the men who buy these products in sports programming than in ads running in broad, general interest entertainment shows. The media charges advertisers a premium for the live, concentrated audience of consumers that watch sports.

That is not to say that sports viewers do not do their share of channel-surfing during commercial breaks to check out what else may be other channels or platforms. To deal with that challenge, advertisers each year are putting greater emphasis on sponsorship and branding within the sports events themselves through the use of entitlement, sponsorship, "brought to you by" billboards, product placement, hybrid ads that blend sports content with commercial messaging, and signage which can be actual or virtual. Actual signage can be seen by every spectator in the venue or watching on a television or other digital device. These include the banners, video boards, billboard signs, and logos on uniforms or painted onto playing surfaces. Virtual signage is electronically superimposed on fields, floors, backstops, sideboards, or any other surface that comes into camera range, making it visible only as part of the produced video coverage of a game or event. A sales message that is integrated into sports media content is designed to have a greater impact on potential customers than the purchase of a 30-second commercial that may share time in a three-minute break between action with at least five other advertising messages. Advertisers pay a premium for the increased exposure that sponsorship brings because it adds value and can improve the brand's connection to and recognition by the people in the target market.

Success in sports advertising requires a *functional congruence* between the brand and the sport, team, event, or athlete it chooses to sponsor. The objective is to transfer the attitude and characteristics of the popular sport or admired athlete to the sponsor's brand. A maker of precision watches will connect its advertising with a sport such as golf or tennis where precision is of utmost importance. The prestige and exclusivity of these sports are congruent with the characteristics of well-made, expensive timepieces. Manufacturers of trucks or tires will connect with sports where strength and durability are the most valuable traits. Advertisers whose products are not functionally congruent with the sports or athletes they sponsor run the risk of achieving lower levels of effectiveness in their media campaigns.

When fans make the connection, the advertiser effectively borrows the "emotional capital" of its sports partner. By connecting its brand with the action, achievements, and excitement of a sport or athlete, an advertiser can link its product to the passion felt by fans, creating a value that cannot be measured in sales figures alone. Reaching customers on an emotional level is important because the decisions people make about what they buy tend to be more often driven by emotions than rational thought.

The key for advertisers is brand identity: linking their product names to the favorable attributes of specific sports, teams, events, and athletes that will be admired and remembered for the great performances and the powerful emotions they evoke. Corporations collectively spend billions of dollars each year to achieve this "positive image transfer." The three most obvious means of doing this are 1) paying to attach a corporate name to the venue where a renowned team plays its games, 2) adding a corporate name or logo to the attire that teams or athletes wear during competitions, and 3) buying sponsorship of a team or league's entire season of games or of a recurring video feature within the live network or streaming coverage.

The promise of media exposure that brings national and international brand recognition has sent the price of venue and uniform naming rights into the stratosphere. Scotiabank is headquartered in Toronto, but its marketing strategy extends far beyond the borders of Ontario. The multinational financial and banking services company saw value in identifying itself with the Toronto Raptors of the NBA and the Toronto Maple Leafs of the NHL, elite professional teams that evoke Canadian national pride and play to international audiences. Scotiabank paid a reported US$30 million per year for 20 years to put its name on the building. On Canada Day 2018, what had been the Air Canada Centre since its opening in 1999 became Scotiabank Arena. The next year the Raptors won the NBA Championship and Scotiabank's recognition factor soared.

Media rights agreements and credentialing by teams and leagues require that the sponsored name of every stadium or arena be used whenever the broadcaster refers to the venue verbally, in graphics, or in promotions. This guaranteed media exposure has turned entitlement into a revenue stream for teams, leagues, and venue ownership across the United States and around the world. Of the 30 NBA arenas, 29 had corporate entitlement when this book was published. The only one without a sponsor name was Madison Square Garden, the home of the New York Knicks and Rangers. The Garden has such an esteemed historical standing in New York that any corporation even rumored to be attempting a name change would undoubtedly become the target of such a public uproar that any hoped-for "positive image transfer" would almost certainly become negative.

Corporations that pay to add their names to events such as tennis or golf tournaments, auto races, football bowl games, or other sports championships or trophies are seen by the public as important supporters that help make these entertainment options possible. The positive impact comes in the form of connecting the prestige of a powerful national brand with a community and the increased flow of money into the regional economy and to non-profit charities that are aligned with those sports events.

Sponsors that pay for signage on the hats and shirts worn by the stars of any professional sport, or on the uniforms or kits of selected teams, align themselves directly with the success or failure of those athletes or teams. The ones who are the most successful will be featured most often on national and international telecasts. Those who lose in the first round or fail to make the cut generate little or no positive image transfer. The success and international media exposure of Manchester United in the English Premier League has been attracting kit sponsors since 1982 when Sharp Electronics turned the team's players into living, breathing billboards. It is almost impossible to watch any live Man U game or highlight without seeing an advertising message in every frame of video, which has enticed a series of corporations from Sharp to Aon, AIG, Vodafone, Chevrolet, and now the German-based software maker TeamViewer to spend hundreds of millions of pounds to share the glory of Manchester United and identify their products as belonging on the same elite level as this storied team.

Broadcasters provide a wide array of opportunities for sponsors to achieve the same results by connecting the best qualities found in sport: strength, stamina, endurance, innovation, precision, character, finesse, teamwork, and success with their products and services, corresponding to every positive aspect of sports competition. If a company is on the cutting edge of technology, it can enhance its reputation by buying the sponsorship of innovative new cameras or devices such as computerized line-scoring or analytics applications that clearly demonstrate to viewers the difference between average and exceptional performances. If only the very best drivers are permitted in the "winners' circle," that's where corporations that market themselves as the very best in their fields will want their logo and messaging displayed.

An unanticipated setback for corporations with naming rights or sponsorship agreements was precipitated by the COVID-19 pandemic. Games that were suspended, canceled, or moved to insulated "bubble environments" did not draw crowds to the named arenas or provide live media exposure for their sponsors. The Independent Evaluation Group (IEG) estimated that the value gap between what was promised in sponsorship agreements and what the nearly 20,000 sports and entertainment properties delivered was $10 billion. The signage remained outside and inside venues, on uniforms and hats, or ready to insert into telecasts, but its messaging was not seen by the targeted audiences when the games were not played, and the shows were not produced. To bridge that $10 billion gap, many properties have extended agreements for additional years, offered a variety of make-goods, and in a number of cases they have made refunds. But the long-term impact of the pandemic has been a broad re-evaluation of the sponsorship model by both advertisers and sports properties.

Identification with a sport, team, or athlete can represent a tremendous market advantage for an advertiser when public perceptions are positive. But the unpredictable nature of sport and the imperfections of its stars can quickly erode that advantage if perceptions change from positive to negative. Brands that choose to identify themselves too closely with one athlete endorser or with one sport or team run the risk of having to abandon an entire campaign overnight if adulation turns to revulsion. Athletes who run afoul of the law or reveal character flaws can become instant liabilities.

The seasonal nature of sport is another advantage for advertisers because reaching potential customers when they are ready to buy is far more effective than reaching the very same people when they are not in the market for an advertiser's product or service. Airlines and travel services offering tropical vacation getaways will buy time in hockey or basketball games, as will the makers of snow tires and snow blowers because winter is when the sales of these products peak. By the same token, you will not see advertising for these products in summertime sports like baseball or volleyball, but you will see commercials for cold beer and soft drinks.

Another important factor in measuring the effectiveness of advertising is the *share of voice*. Of all the commercial messages about the products or services in its category, each advertiser needs to know what percentage they command. This carries even more weight in sports because of the limited set of product categories that primarily target men. The brewer of Sam Adams beer, for example, may have selected a specific sport which is watched by a large number of potential consumers, but if competing beers already represent half or more of the advertising in those games, Sam Adams' share of voice would be minimal. Their advertising strategy would probably shift to another sport or event that appeals to the same target audience, but in which their brand would have a greater share of voice.

Measuring the share of voice goes beyond the actual advertising in the programs to the impact that advertising has on social media traffic. Research companies are able to do what is called "listening," the process of tracking every mention of brand names on Facebook, Instagram, Twitter, or any other social network. Brands can gauge the effectiveness of their advertising campaigns by comparing the share of mentions they receive to how often people are mentioning their competitors. It is also possible to determine what percentage of social media or blog posts regarding a product contain positive or negative comments since not every mention of a product or service will be a "rave review."

To achieve maximum effectiveness in advertising, professionals in the field prescribe *integrated packages* that deliver brand messages across multiple platforms. Several research studies show that people have significantly greater recall of the brands and messages they see in television commercials if those messages are reinforced by product placement, entitlement, or signage within sports programs, and by online video, social media, radio, and/or print media advertising. Branding the same sports product or series across all communications platforms increases reach and binds the advertiser even more closely to that sport.

MEASURING THE AUDIENCE

Live sports and live news have become the most valuable properties for broadcasters and every pay TV service including cable television, satellite TV providers like DirecTV or Dish Network, and any multichannel video program distributor (MVPD) for which you pay a monthly fee and get a vast array of channels. The success of subscription video on demand (SVOD) services such as Netflix, Hulu, Amazon Prime Video, Disney+, HBO Max, and Peacock has shifted the allegiances of entertainment viewers away from broadcast and cable networks. Before the pandemic of 2020, Netflix, which had no live sports content, was already serving more subscribers in the United States than the entire cable industry combined. The worldwide total of Netflix subscribers had exceeded 200 million by the beginning of 2021. The changes in everyday work, life, and viewing patterns that came with the pandemic brought with them a surge in SVOD subscriptions. More than 80 percent of American homes had subscribed to at least one streaming service by the time that vaccinations against COVID-19 had become widely available. The rapid expansion of direct-to-consumer streaming services such as Peacock, ESPN+, and Paramount+ that offer a rich mix of sports content has put more pressure on the broadcast and cable networks to retain their exclusive rights to live sports events.

Digital distribution of video entertainment has been progressively putting the squeeze on broadcast and pay TV networks as high-speed broadband internet access has become more common in the United States and in developed countries around the world. The Federal Communications Commission reported that high-speed broadband penetration in the United States had reached 95.6 percent of the American population by the end of 2019. That trend continues to grow as broadband service is extended to more rural areas.

The capability of high-speed broadband to transmit broadcast quality picture and sound has given consumers access to hundreds of digital channels without having to subscribe to cable. The direct result of this technological advance has been the acceleration of "cord-cutting" with millions of cable TV viewers canceling their subscriptions each year. Cable was at its zenith in 2012 with 88 percent of homes in the United States hooked up and paying monthly subscription fees. That had fallen to less than 70 percent in 2021 with no signs of recovery in sight. The total hours per day that the average American adult aged 18 or older now spends consuming video from digital sources has drawn even with the number of hours spent watching traditional television, and the trend is for digital to continue its rise, and for pay TV ratings to slide lower.

Access to technology is one of the primary factors in determining how much media people will watch every day, every week, year by year. The other factors that demographers use in measuring viewing totals and the size of the audience for specific types of programming on each platform are:

- Age
- Gender
- Ethnicity
- Education level
- Income level
- Employment status
- Marital status and family size
- The season or time of the year

Older people tend to spend more time watching television than any other age group. The Nielsen Company reports that an average American aged 65 or older watches more than seven hours of television per day. On the other side of the digital/ age divide, 18–34-year-olds are watching only about an hour and a half of television content each day, but they spend nearly five hours per day connected to digital devices. They were the earliest adopters of streaming and are the least likely to subscribe to any cable or any pay TV service.

Most live sports viewing is done by males, but it varies widely by sport and event. The audience for the Super Bowl has moved from roughly 60 percent male to nearly a 50–50 split in the 21st century. But the audiences for regular season NFL games and sports such as Major League Baseball, the NBA, college football, college basketball, and auto racing tend to be more in the range of 65–70 percent male. More women traditionally watch the Olympics than men by a margin of approximately 55 to 45 percent.

Sports viewers tend to be slightly better educated on average than people who don't watch sports. Their average incomes are higher, they are more likely to have fulltime jobs and be married as opposed to single when compared with the American population as a whole. Regardless of age, gender, or any other demographic distinctions, more people watch more television when the weather is cold and wintry. Media viewing levels are highest in the winter and lowest in the summer, except in years when there are Summer Olympic Games. The pattern has been that in Olympic years overall sports viewing rises. If the Super Bowl were in August instead of February, it would undoubtedly still be the most-watched show of the year, but it is very likely that the total audience would be smaller because of the competition for people's time from vacation activities and outdoor recreation.

The numbers that the Nielsen Company and other audience research organizations gather are used to make decisions that affect the livelihood of thousands of people working on events and shows and at networks, millions of viewers, and the expenditure of billions of dollars. Advertisers spending that amount of money want to know far more than who is watching and how many people in each demographic group are reached by their ads. Manufacturers and service providers need data on who is buying their products and at what time of the year to position their commercial messages accordingly in the shows those people watch, as well as the media they use and the seasons in which their purchase intent is highest. Companies also want to instill a favorable disposition toward their product that will distinguish it from other options in the market. A person who is familiar with a product and sees it in a favorable light is likely to consider that product and then develop an intent to purchase. Advertisers can cultivate greater awareness, favorability, and purchase intent by increasing the reach of their commercial message and the frequency with which it is delivered. The chances that someone who rarely sees or hears a message will become a buyer are very low. The interpretation of ratings data for networks and sponsors is a valuable specialty that can determine how efficiently advertising dollars are being spent and predict future audience trends.

Here are some of the reasons why ratings are so important.

Audience Growth

When networks know which of their programs or series are drawing large audiences and which ones are lagging behind, they can expand the strong franchises and drop the underperformers. By eliminating low-rated programming from its schedule, a network can increase its overall daily and weekly ratings and make room for new shows that may attract more viewers. When networks are fortunate enough to develop ratings winners, they can increase the number and/or length of those shows or create similar programs that will appeal to the same mass audience.

Program Development

Identifying who is watching at what hours makes it possible for networks to design programs and acquire series and events that will be attractive to those demographic segments. If a network has targeted the 18–34-year-old audience, it is more likely to add new mixed martial arts programming than PGA Tour golf tournaments.

Ratings data on how the viewership rises and falls during specific parts of the day can lead to the development of new lead-in shows or shows that can capture a large percentage of the audience that was watching the program preceding it on the network's schedule. It's called the "coattails" or "halo" effect. The goal of every network regardless of its content genre or how it is delivered is to keep you watching for longer periods of time. The longer you watch, the longer you are part of the total audience being measured. Therefore, networks can increase their ratings without adding more viewers if they can entice their current viewers to simply watch for longer periods of time. One of the best ways to achieve that goal is by surrounding successful shows with programs that will appeal to the same large audience.

Compete and Win

Networks that subscribe to ratings services can get information not only on who is watching their programs, but also who is watching the competition. The tracking is available minute by minute, not just for every half-hour or quarter-hour.

With minute-by-minute data, programmers and audience research professionals can accurately identify which segments within a show are drawing the most viewers and which segments fail to retain viewers. Segments that repeatedly cause audience erosion will quickly be dropped in favor of new ones. It is predictable that viewers will tune away when the live action in an event comes to a halt, but it is remarkable how many loyal fans will stay tuned to certain auto racing telecasts even if there is a rain delay. Ratings data can identify what type of reports and interviews cause viewers to keep watching during a pause in action during any sports event, and for how long.

The networks competing against auto racing, pro football, or any live sports event will study the demographic characteristics of the audience and then consider their best options for counterprogramming. The goal is to either appeal to a different demographic or steal viewers away with events or shows that the viewers on competing networks will find more attractive.

Maximize Advertising Revenue

The key to success and survival for any media network or platform that relies upon advertising revenue is to sell the largest number of commercials and sponsorships at the highest possible prices. Ratings data are used to convince advertisers that buying commercial time or entitling a sponsored feature within a popular program's content will be an effective means for that company to increase the sales of its products or services. Advertisers use several factors when deciding which shows they will sponsor, the most important being the size and composition of the audience they can reach with their commercial messages.

The advertiser's goal is to spend efficiently for the greatest effectiveness. The key ratings number they want to see is how many potential customers in their target market they can reach for every $1,000 they spend on commercials or sponsorships in a particular program. If Cadillac or Lexus is targeting men or women who earn more than $100,000 per year, it would be a waste of money for them to buy commercials in programs that are watched by an audience of younger viewers or teenagers with limited buying power. Networks use the details of how many viewers in each demographic category are watching their shows to devise the pitches they will make to each advertising client. For example, series such as Major League Baseball and PGA Tour golf that have older male viewers are attractive to the pharmaceutical makers of erectile dysfunction drugs such as Pfizer and Lily Icos. The CPM for reaching older customers is much more favorable in live baseball or golf events than it would be in sports that have a younger audience or a larger percentage of female viewers.

Track Seasonal Trends

Ratings information that is tracked over a period of several weeks and months, not simply day to day or week to week, can be especially useful as networks design their future programming schedules. Sports leagues and organizers and their live media partners identify the times of the year when interest starts to build for their events and when it wanes. Ratings can be a determining factor when decisions are made to start the season a week earlier or later, expand the post-season playoffs, or move a game or program to a different date.

Assess the Effects of Change

Television networks constantly change show formats, features, and talent in the hope of increasing audience and profits. The feedback they get via the ratings provides an unbiased report card on whether their changes succeeded or failed. If the number of sponsored features a network sells in any sports telecast were to reach the saturation point at which their recurring presence annoyed viewers so much that they started tuning out or watching for shorter periods of time, that network would be forced to cut back on sponsor sales in favor of audience retention.

Any programming change that a network sees as positive, such as a new series, host, or segment, will more than likely be launched with a major promotional campaign. Decisions made by networks as to how many promos will run in what part of the day on which non-TV platforms, and how far in advance of the premiere they need to begin the campaign to reach potential viewers, will have a greater impact if they are based on audience measurement data. When that new show finally hits the air, its ratings will tell the network how effective its promotional campaign was, and it will provide valuable information as to how to improve promotion for the network's next initiative.

THE SUPER BOWL: KING OF THE ADVERTISING JUNGLE

The most prominent event of the year in advertising is the Super Bowl, not just in sports. It provides the largest audience, charges the highest prices for commercials, and generates more revenue than any other event or single entertainment vehicle on the calendar year after year. And the Super Bowl is unique in that it is the only program that millions of people say they watch just to see the commercials. This makes the Super Bowl "king."

If you want your brand to be identified with the biggest game of the year and to be seen as elite in your field, the Super Bowl is where you'll spend your advertising dollars. It is the most-watched American television program every year, a virtual holiday that celebrates so many of the things that Americans hold dear: football, television, socializing with family and friends, and the mass consumption of food and drink. Buying a Super Bowl commercial doesn't simply reach the largest audience in media, it sends an economic signal to the public that your company is one of a select few that is so strong that it can buy advertising in the Super Bowl. That is an important message meant to enhance the status of a brand.

In the decade from 2010 to 2020, the asking price for a single 30-second commercial in the Super Bowl rose 104 percent from $2.7 million to $5.6 million. Inflation in the United States during the same 10 years was only 17.6 percent, according to the federal Consumer Price Index. The price of a Super Bowl commercial more than doubled in the decade, but an advertising message in 2020 of the live telecast actually reached six million fewer television viewers per minute than it did in 2010 when the price was much lower. However, Super Bowl advertisers have benefited from the proliferation of video on the internet giving them added value from the tens of millions of online views that commercials receive on the USA Today Ad Meter® and dozens of other sites that post Super Bowl ads before and after the game.

The total advertising revenue from the game that is collected by the network broadcasting the Super Bowl exceeds $400 million every year. More money is spent advertising in the Super Bowl game itself than is spent on all the commercials in every World Series game combined or on all three games of the NCAA's Final Four men's basketball championship weekend.

The Super Bowl represents the largest mass audience that an advertiser can reach at any one time on American television. Despite the growing competition from subscription video and streaming services, the Super Bowl broadcast on pay TV attracts four times more viewers than any entertainment program on any day of the year. It clearly demonstrates the value and importance of live sports to the broadcast networks and thereby appears to justify the huge increases in media rights fees to which they have committed for the 11 years from 2023 through 2033. CBS, NBC, Fox, and ESPN/ABC have contracts to each pay the NFL over $2 billion per year for the rights to televise regular season games and one Super Bowl each on a four-year rotating schedule. Offsetting that huge price tag with advertising revenue is a challenge for all four networks, but the greater challenge would have been holding onto a mass audience *without* live NFL content. The new rights agreements also speak to the emerging power of digital platforms. Each of the traditional broadcast networks received broader streaming rights as part of their packages, and they are joined for the first time by an SVOD service, Amazon's Prime Video, which is paying $1 billion per year for exclusive rights to *Thursday Night NFL* games.

As long as people are sports fans, loyal to their chosen teams, avidly following the exploits of their favorite stars, and enjoying the drama of competitions that can hold their interest until the final seconds for a single deciding shot or play, advertisers will be fans of sports. On whatever service fans choose to watch these games, whether it be broadcast, streaming, or not yet invented, sponsors will join the migration. They will be there to ensure that their commercial messages are seen and heard by the persons most likely to become their customers. And when fans watch sports heroes wearing sponsored uniforms or golf shirts celebrate victories by lifting a championship trophy that bears the name of a major corporation in an entitled winners' circle or against a backdrop of logos, they are apt to, on some level, connect the qualities responsible for that success with the brands that were with them along the way.

BIBLIOGRAPHY

Campbell, Morgan. "Air Canada Centre to be renamed Scotiabank Arena." *Toronto Star*, 2017. https://www.thestar.com/sports/2017/08/29/air-canada -centre-to-be-renamed-scotiabank-arena.html

IEG. "$10 Billion in sports and entertainment sponsorship value gap will need to be made up." *IEG*, 2020. https://www.sponsorship.com/IEG/files/5a /5ab67489-c528-4ed9-b128-c8550f4a0121.pdf

Leichtman Research Group. "60% of TV Households Have Both Pay-TV and SVOD." Leichtman Research Group, 2020. https://www.leichtmanresearch .com/60-of-tv-households-have-both-pay-tv-and-svod/

Nielsen. "The Nielsen Total Audience Report: March 2021." *Nielsen*, 2020. https://www.nielsen.com/us/en/insights/report/2021/total-audience -advertising-across-todays-media/

Sauter, Michael B. "Super Bowl commercials: Ads cost $5M+ for 30 seconds now." *USA Today*, 2021. https://www.usatoday.com/story/money/2021/02 /06/super-bowl-commercials-cost-for-every-year-game-played/115437118/

US Bureau of Labor Statistics. Consumer Price Index (CPI) database. https:// www.bls.gov/cpi/

The Power Game

The massive audiences that the live sports media deliver and the billions in revenue that they generate combine to make media conglomerates a formidable center of power in the sports industry. One could argue that their power rivals that of the sport organizers: the leagues, teams, conferences, and event owners that create and stage the live competitions which draw millions of fans and command hefty annual rights payments and sponsorships. The other major component in the sports "power game" is the performers, the stars whose charisma and remarkable athletic feats attract legions of loyal followers who watch them in action in stadiums or arenas, as well as on their video screens of choice.

The ultimate power in sports however rests with the public. Strong support and fan allegiance transfer power to the owners and organizers of popular events, to the stars who adults admire and youngsters emulate, and to the media whose profits come from attracting the large audiences that are targeted by advertisers. The sports teams and events with the strongest public support, and the television ratings to match, can charge more for their broadcast rights, sell more advertising and sponsorships, build new arenas and stadiums, and develop new opportunities in new markets. A sport that does not adapt to changes in society or media consumption behaviors is doomed to suffer declines in attendance and viewership, and with them reduced earning potential and power.

Before the rise of televised sport in the middle of the 20th century, before the formation of player unions, before free agency, the internet, or social media, the owners shared power with no one. They made all the rules, arbitrarily set salaries, decided who would play based on factors that included the color of an athlete's skin, and in every way acted as medieval lords with exclusive control over their fiefdoms. The broad distribution of live sports on television indirectly started the erosion of that unchallenged power monopoly. The sports establishment increasingly found itself driven to attract larger and larger television audiences that would bring with them untold new wealth from advertising and sponsorship dollars. The availability of sport to the masses which encompassed a broader cross-section of the public gradually opened the door to the influence of societal and cultural change.

DOI: 10.4324/9781003165590-11

THE POWER OF CONTENT

The organizers, leagues, conferences, and teams that own and control the events and series that generate the largest audiences and revenue have tremendous power. The NFL and its member teams for example, own the content which consists of every game played in the pre-season, regular season, playoffs, and championships including the Super Bowl, plus all the names, marks, and video archives accumulated since the founding of the league. The NFL sets the rules of play, including how many individuals will wear the uniform of each team, and they establish the schedules: who will play whom on what dates and which games will appear on what networks and live media platforms. Every professional league in the United States functions in a similar manner and has the same level of control.

The NCAA is an organizer that owns and controls 90 national championships in men's and women's sports including the wildly popular "March Madness" men's national collegiate basketball tournament. The tournament is so successful that television rights for 14 years of coverage on CBS and Turner Sports sold for $10.8 billion in 2010, and six years later were extended from 2024 until 2032 at an increased price of over $1 billion per year.

The International Olympic Committee (IOC) and FIFA, the Federation Internationale de Football Association, are the two most powerful global organizers of sport. The IOC owns the Olympics, which includes every minute of every contest at the Winter and Summer Games, the name "Olympics," its five rings logo, and every second of footage from every one of its events. FIFA owns the World Cup of soccer for women and men, every qualifying event played to select the field of teams that gathers to compete for the cups every four years, and, of course, all the logos, marks, and archives.

The list of sports organizers includes groups that control just one annual event such as the AELTC's Wimbledon tennis tournament or The Masters golf tournament, which is the property of the Augusta National Golf Club, or annual series of events such as SEC (Southeastern Conference) and ACC (Atlantic Coast Conference) games in every sport that is contested by these conferences and their member colleges. Each organizer decides when and where their events will be held, dramatically affecting local and national economies. Decisions made by the International Olympic Committee or FIFA as to which countries will host the upcoming Olympic Games or World Cup have billion-dollar impacts on those nations.

Organizers also have the power to choose their partners for marketing, sponsorship, stadium and site construction, transportation, supplies and services, and media distribution. No governmental body nor set of laws dictates who they choose to work with: neither the highest bidder for media rights nor the lowest bidder for any contracted service is guaranteed selection. The power to choose is at the sole discretion of the organizer.

Organizers pay close attention to the annual calendar of sports with the goal of capturing the largest live media audiences possible and avoiding time conflicts with other major events that could cut into their viewership. It makes sense for the Augusta National Golf Club to schedule The Masters for the weekend after the NCAA Final Four each year, but it doesn't have to abide by that schedule. The club has the power to choose any weekend it wants regardless of whatever time conflicts that might cause for other sports events. The popularity and power of The Masters would more than likely force any conflicting events to find alternate dates.

The organizers, leagues, and teams that own content also control how their games and events will be televised and covered by the news media. This includes the dates and times their games or matches will be played. Television networks set start times *only* if the organizers sell them the rights to do so. Any league can retain its freedom to play games at any time of day or night it may choose *if* it is also willing to accept less money from the network or platform to whom it is selling the television rights. The network would offer less money if it projected that televising games on an organizer's preferred schedule would not generate a large primetime audience with its corresponding higher advertising revenue. The economic reality is that no league commissioner will risk going back to his or her team owners after negotiating a live media rights contract and tell them, "I could have gotten you another $100 million to share, but I thought retaining the right to set our start times was more important." The next stop for the commissioner delivering that message would be his or her office to start packing.

Rights contracts with the owners of content specify how many games or events will be featured on live media platforms over a set period of years for an agreed-upon figure. These contracts include guidelines for the rights-holding networks that go into excruciating detail:

- Network access to camera positions, sidelines, and locker rooms.
- The list of advertisers approved by the organizer and the maximum number of minutes of advertising time that may be sold per hour of each game or event.
- The sponsorship, logos, and graphics that the media may or may not add to live content.
- The extent of the promotion that the rights-holding network must provide in its programs and on its multiple platforms leading up to each game or event.
- How the two parties will work together on the internet in the development of social media sites, interactive games, and the streaming of any live coverage or highlights videos.
- The number of minutes of highlights per game or event that the television partner is allowed to use on its owned platforms while play is underway or following its conclusion. How long after the event that

highlights can be used before all rights revert to the organizer, and what access is provided, if any, to historical archive footage from past games or events.

- The procedures for negotiating contract extensions or renewals.
- The number of credentials that will be issued to the media partner for event coverage and the number of tickets to be made available free or for purchase for the network to use entertaining clients, executives, or guests.

By approving or denying requests for media credentials, the organizer controls who is allowed to enter its venues for the purpose of reporting on, recording, or photographing competition, conducting interviews with players, coaches, or other participants, or performing any other function controlled by that organizer. An analyst or columnist not employed by the rights-holding networks who the organizer deems to have been unfairly or overly critical can be denied a credential and banned from access to press areas. Denial of a credential does not abridge a person's First Amendment rights in the United States because he or she can still buy a ticket and write about the event. But an organizer is not compelled to admit everyone claiming press status free of charge, allow them to record audio or video of a contest, or grant access to the press box, locker rooms, or news conferences.

The ultimate power for content owners is when a league, conference, team, or organizer also owns one or more of its media distribution platforms. This self-distribution of content, which bypasses all intermediaries to deliver live coverage and promotion with no negative messaging and limited or no criticism is discussed in greater detail in Chapter 6 under the heading "The Disintermediation of Sports Television."

THE POWER OF THE LIVE SPORTS MEDIA

The media and the content owners have a symbiotic relationship. It is mutually beneficial. The live sports media have the power to increase the reach, demand, popularity, and profitability of sports. Sports programming benefits the live media sector of the business because it attracts a loyal core audience of fans to their channels and platforms. They make money by selling commercial time in sports programming to advertisers who have targeted those fans as their potential customers, and by charging monthly fees to the multichannel video program distributors (MVPDs) or other distributors who want sports fans to subscribe to their programming packages. The power of the live sports media is directly tied to the number of viewers each medium can reach. Changes in how the public consumes sports will always shift power from networks with declining viewership to services whose audiences are increasing.

The sports events that each network presents also play a role in defining their media brands. One of the signature events of CBS Sports is The

Masters golf tournament which it has televised every year since 1956. NBC has branded itself as the Olympic Network in the United States by virtue of its being the TV home for every Summer and Winter Olympic Games since the year 2000. The successful launch of the Fox network relied in no small measure on tying its brand to the NFL Sunday package that it obtained in 1993 by outbidding CBS.

On the other side of this symbiotic partnership, the teams, leagues, and organizers benefit because the live sports media introduce their teams and stars to new generations of fans, which expands their drawing power and increases value. The rights payments made by media networks to content owners represent the lifeblood of sport, collectively pumping billions of dollars into their operations each year. Signing a television rights deal also guarantees sports organizers, leagues, and teams broad distribution of their marketing and promotional messages, which helps build a fan base and sell tickets.

When more than one network bids for the rights to an event or season of games, the advantage goes to the content owner. Competition invariably increases the amount of money offered in rights bids. When the NFL was negotiating its American live media rights deals for 2023 through 2033, Amazon's Prime streaming service joined the bidding and acquired exclusive rights to the Thursday Night package of weekly regular season games for $1 billion per year. When the rights agreements were announced in the spring of 2021, Prime had nearly 150 million subscribers in the United States, each paying $119 per year for the service. That put annual revenue in the United States alone at over $17 billion, making the $1 billion commitment to the NFL seem quite affordable.

Prime's entry immediately made the streaming service a force to be reckoned with in sports, and it helped inflate the prices for the broadcast networks. The $1 billion contracts that CBS and NBC had for 2014–2022 doubled to $2 billion. Fox had been paying the NFL $1.65 billion each year for their Sunday games and the Thursday Night package that Prime is taking over. But despite getting fewer games over the course of the new 11-year deal, the Fox annual rights fee went up to $2.2 billion. The Walt Disney Company renewed ESPN's *Monday Night Football* package, secured one out of every four Super Bowls for the company's ABC network, and expanded its streaming and year-round highlights rights for $2.7 billion per year, an increase of $800 million per year over the previous contract. All of these rights fees increased despite the fact that the average audience for live NFL games declined by 11.5 percent from the 2014 season to 2020, and the viewership for the Super Bowl hit its zenith of 114.5 million viewers per minute back in 2015.

The NFL's ability to double the price for a product reaching fewer people is testimony to the weakened position of the broadcast and pay TV networks that have been dramatically impacted by changes in audience behavior and preferences. Back at the end of the year 2011, when the networks concluded their negotiations with the NFL for the 2014–22 seasons, cable television was at its peak, delivering broadcast and cable networks to over 100 million American homes. Ten years later, more than 30 million people had abandoned cable, and young people who never subscribed to cable were almost exclusively streaming all their video entertainment. Dissatisfaction with the high monthly cost of cable and the expanded availability of subscription video on demand (SVOD) services via high-speed broadband prompted the stampede to "cut the cord" and move to streaming.

Broadcast and cable networks have not only lost viewers they have also lost their edge as the preferred destinations for entertainment programming. The streaming services such as Netflix, Disney+, HBO Max, and Prime are increasingly the place where Americans go for children's and family entertainment, dramas, and comedies. The strongest "tentpole" content remaining for broadcast and cable is live news and sports. The retention of proven draws like live NFL games has never been more important for the survival of the pay TV business. The choice is either commit billions of dollars to sports rights fees or fold up the tent and go home.

Competition for sports programming will continue to intensify as more streaming services enter the fray. Buoyed by their rapid growth rates which accelerated during the COVID-19 pandemic when in-home entertainment was virtually the only entertainment available, several streaming services saw sports as a means to quickly establish identity and credibility just as Fox had done with its first NFL deal in the 1990s. At its launch in early 2021, Paramount Plus announced plans to stream over 1,000 sports events each year including NFL games from co-owned CBS and UEFA Champions League and Europa League soccer games. NBC's discontinuation of NBCSN cable network moved hundreds of hours of sports to its Peacock streaming service.

This migration of video consumers to streaming has tipped the balance of power in favor of those organizers and owners who control the content that is in the greatest demand. Their power is not affected by *how* fans receive those games and events. The only threat to sports content owners is if fewer people identify as fans, and in turning away from sports, that reduces the demand for live games and events.

Synergy

The power of media conglomerates is directly related to the number of networks and platforms each one controls. Their aggregate power is greater than the sum of their individual parts because of synergy: the cooperation among all co-owned platforms to cross-promote their products. The Walt Disney Company is obviously the center of the sports synergy universe with ESPN, ESPN2, ESPN+, ESPNU, ESPNews, ESPN deportes, ESPN Radio, ESPN.com, and ABC Sports, plus the SEC, ACC, and Longhorn Networks all promoting each other's content for the purpose of reaching the largest number of potential customers wherever and however sports is viewed, listened to, read about, or discussed.

ESPN has expanded this power to encompass the ownership of events that are valuable content for its many media properties and an additional source of sponsorship and advertising revenue. ESPN owns and operates the Summer and Winter X Games, the ESPY Awards, and a portfolio of 35 collegiate events that includes football bowl games and college basketball tournaments. The network pays no rights fees for any of this owned content, which amounts to approximately 500 hours of programming per year.

Consider the synergistic forces that NBC Universal can marshal to deliver the largest possible audience to a Super Bowl or the opening game of its *Sunday Night Football* series: the *Today Show* live from the site of the game along with correspondents from *NBC Nightly News*, CNBC, MSNBC, E!, The Weather Channel, *Access Hollywood*, Telemundo, and any of its eight regional sports networks or the 235 local television stations affiliated with or owned by NBC. The Comcast NBC Universal conglomerate also owns the Peacock streaming service, the Golf Channel, the Olympic Channel, USA Network, Bravo, SyFy, Oxygen, plus the Universal movie studio and its resorts. The lists of multiplatform media assets owned by News Corp./ Fox, Time Warner Discovery, and Viacom/CBS are just as impressive.

Whenever one of these conglomerates identifies a priority, such as increasing the ratings for a series or special event, it has the power to reach millions of people across all demographics through a variety of delivery systems to ensure that each potential viewer gets the message on multiple occasions and in several different forms. That power of synergy is precisely what leagues and organizers want from their media partners so it can be applied to enhance the value of their games and events.

THE POWER OF THE PERFORMERS

The live sports media have the power to create stars by showcasing the remarkable success and memorable performances of individuals and teams to millions of fans, including close-ups of jubilant celebrations and smiling faces. Stars who become regional or national celebrities in this manner have the power to draw paying customers to attend sports events or watch the live coverage. Star status can bring endorsement contracts worth more than their annual salaries to athletes like LeBron James, Serena Williams, Lionel Messi, or Conor McGregor, with whom the public makes lasting emotional connections. The value of endorsements and the power of these athletes within their respective sports is multiplied geometrically when their stories are told and their legends are built by the live sports media.

The achievement of national and international star status tends to be more straightforward for performers in individual sports such as golf, tennis, mixed martial arts, and boxing. Team sports may get larger audiences, but athletes in individual sports don't share the spotlight with any teammates when they win championships, and they alone decide where and when they will compete. That gives them tremendous power over organizers of events whose success at the gate and in live telecasts is heavily dependent upon having recognizable stars in their competitions. The impact they have on television ratings and therefore on the value of the television rights is significant, which gives individual performers more power with the media as well.

Tiger Woods has been the biggest name in golf since he won his first Masters championship as a 21-year-old in 1997 by a 12-stroke margin over his nearest competitor. Whenever he was in contention to win, the ratings for golf telecasts were at their strongest. When he wasn't on the leaderboard for the final round, the drop-off in viewership was precipitous. Compare the audience for the final round when Woods won The Masters in 2019 to the final round in 2021 when Hideki Matsuyama won, and Woods was out of action recovering from injuries suffered in an auto accident. An average of 15.4 million viewers per minute were glued to their sets in 2019, but only 9.45 million were watching in 2021. That's a 38 percent decline. The Masters will undoubtedly continue to be the most-watched golf tournament each year in the United States, but it's a lot less watched when Tiger Woods isn't among the leaders.

Events that rely on star power are subject to much wider fluctuations in attendance, TV ratings, the value of rights, advertising, and sponsorship deals than the leagues and team sports that have built up fan loyalty over generations. The power that stars in individual sports have to affect the bottom line for organizers and the media can translate into steep appearance fees, bonuses, and special considerations in addition to the income they receive for wearing branded apparel and endorsing products while they compete in any televised event.

Social media has radically altered the power dynamic for athletes, especially those who play in team sports. Superstars like Cristiano Ronaldo, whose social media following exceeds 500 million, can directly connect with far more fans than the teams or leagues they play for. When Ronaldo transferred from Real Madrid to Juventus in 2018, his vast social following came with him, adding value to Juventus and its sponsors. When he signed with Manchester United in 2021 his new team inherited Ronaldo's vast power to connect. In the United States, LeBron James has far more social media followers than any team for which he played or the NBA. That gives him a unique, independent, and powerful platform upon which to share his observations and beliefs in ways that did not exist for athletes in past generations.

Athletes were at the forefront of the social justice initiatives in sport that followed the death of a Black man, George Floyd, at the hands of police in Minneapolis in May 2020. Players in the NBA, more than 70 percent of whom are African American, could have called a boycott for the remainder of the season in protest. But that would have removed them from the national stage and seriously undermined their ability to take a public stand. Instead, the games continued with the support of the NBA, and ending systemic racism and "Black Lives Matter" became part of the league's messaging. Players in the NBA and in virtually every other sport made their fans and their sport leadership aware of just how serious they judged the problem to be and how committed they were to serve as powerful catalysts for change.

Their individual and collective ability to directly deliver their calls for equality and societal change to millions of loyal fans created a groundswell of support that included their teams and leagues in what became a powerful movement. Four years earlier when San Francisco 49ers quarterback Colin Kaepernick tried to raise awareness about police violence against persons of color, the NFL did not listen or encourage its players to speak out. In a short span of time, the power of the performers in sport had strengthened dramatically.

Free Agency Changed the Sports Power Equation

The power that athletes have today would have been unimaginable to players, team owners, fans, and reporters who were part of organized sport from its origins until the late 20th century. From the 1880s into the 1970s, every professional baseball player's contract included a "reserve clause," which allowed teams to arbitrarily renew any contract at a salary determined by the team. This left players virtually powerless, undervalued in the marketplace, and bound to their teams for life.

Major League Baseball also enjoyed an anti-trust exemption as a result of the US Supreme Court's Federal Baseball Club of Baltimore vs. National League of Professional Baseball Clubs decision in 1922. The Federal League was being organized as a rival to the National and American Leagues, but its ability to sign players away from their National League or American League teams was restricted by the reserve clauses in their contracts. The Federal League claimed that the two established leagues were violating antitrust laws, but the Supreme Court disagreed. Justice Oliver Wendell Holmes stated that baseball was not subject to antitrust regulation and that "the charges against the defendants (the NL and AL owners) were not an interference with commerce among the states."

This 1922 ruling was upheld in 1972 when Curt Flood, an outfielder for the St. Louis Cardinals, sued baseball in an attempt to void his trade to the Philadelphia Phillies. Flood argued that after his contract with the Cardinals had expired, he should have the option to sign with any other club that may seek his services. The Supreme Court ruled against Flood calling baseball "an exception and an anomaly," and making it clear that the anti-trust exemption could only be overturned by an act of Congress.

Curt Flood did not win free agency for baseball players, but three years later a combination of factors nullified the reserve clause and ushered in a new era of power for the performers in American team sports. The Major League Baseball Players Association (MLBPA) negotiated its first collective bargaining agreement with MLB in 1968. When players and owners failed to reach an agreement on a new contract before the start of the 1972 season, the MLBPA organized the first strike in American baseball history. The dispute had focused on player pension issues and was settled after 86 scheduled games were missed in the first two weeks of April. When a new collective bargaining agreement was reached effective in 1973, it included a clause that provided for binding arbitration in cases where players and owners could not agree on levels of compensation. The reserve clause remained in effect.

Two years later in 1975, a pitcher for the Los Angeles Dodgers, Andy Messersmith, who did not accept the team's new salary offer, played out his contract and sought bids from other teams for his services. When not one team made him an offer, Messersmith filed a grievance and invoked the arbitration clause. The arbitrator found in Messersmith's favor, saying that teams could only renew an existing contract for one year after it had expired, not for every year of a player's career. Playing out that one option year would legally free players to seek better offers from other teams. That is precisely what Curt Flood had envisioned and fought in vain to achieve.

Free agency gave each player more control over his career and diminished the power of owners, forcing them to pay fair market value or face losing their stars. In 1975, when Andy Messersmith filed his complaint, the average major league baseball player was earning $44,676. Ten years later that average had increased eight-fold to $371,157, conclusive evidence that before free agency owners had not been paying players what they were truly worth.

NFL players were also subject to a reserve clause system from the founding of the league in 1920 until 1947. That's when a one-year option was established allowing teams to hold onto players for one year after their contracts expired. Then the player would be free to negotiate with any other team. A series of modifications were made over the next 45 years until the "White Agreement" in 1993 settled a federal antitrust suit brought by Reggie White and four other players. The agreement gave NFL players unrestricted free agency in exchange for accepting a salary cap that would be imposed by the league. Modifications since have given players more freedom to make their own career decisions.

Every work stoppage in professional sports has been a struggle to tip the balance of power between the team owners and leagues that own the content, and the performers without whom there would be no product for fans to watch in person or on any device. Each side wants more control over its percentage of revenues, work rules, schedules, and a host of lesser but not inconsequential issues. Resolution is usually achieved when it becomes apparent that when games aren't played, like the World Series that was lost to a player strike in 1994 or the entire 2004–05 National Hockey League season, the media rights money that fuels professional sport disappears.

THE POWER OF SPORTS AGENTS

The subject of sports agents may very well deserve its own chapter or an entire book. Their presence has added leverage and expertise to the power of the athletes they represent, forcing leagues and organizers to negotiate terms that would otherwise be unilaterally enforced. In the era of free agency, player agents can affect the fortunes of professional franchises on and off the field by facilitating the movement of one or more stars from one team to another.

The most powerful agents are those who represent a group of stars in one sport. An agent whose client list accounts for a significant percentage of the active players in a sport becomes a force in that sport with influence far greater than an agent who has only a few clients. He or she can set standards for what will or will not be included in contracts and have an effect on the relative pay scales for comparable performers. Powerful agents have contributed behind the scenes to the settlement of labor disagreements by building consensus among their player groups. Their vested interest in solving disputes is obvious: when players aren't being paid, agents don't get their commissions. An agent such as David Falk who in the 1990s represented more than 50 of the NBA's 348 active players including Michael Jordan, Patrick Ewing, James Worthy, Alonzo Mourning, and John Stockton has the power to attract new advertisers to a sport through his clients and expand the influence of the sport by marketing its stars outside the game.

As player unions have negotiated collective bargaining agreements with leagues that include fixed rookie salary levels and pay scales for players based upon their years of service, it has become harder for agents to differentiate themselves except for their ability to generate endorsement income. Agreements with set compensation ladders and provisions that share a specific percentage of league revenues with players have given those leagues and their teams greater control over annual budgets and diminished the overall power of agents in the industry.

The father of modern sports representation was undoubtedly Mark McCormack, who founded the International Management Group (IMG) in 1960. As a college golfer at William and Mary in the early 1950s, McCormack met Arnold Palmer who was on the Wake Forest golf team. McCormack went on to Yale Law School and then joined a law firm in Cleveland. Palmer became the most charismatic golfer on the PGA Tour. In 1960, McCormack reached out to his old friend with a pitch that he could make more money for Palmer through endorsements and appearances in one year than the golfer could earn winning golf tournaments. The two men sealed the deal with a handshake. One year later, having seen his success with Palmer, golf's two other top players of the era, Jack Nicklaus and Gary Player, also signed with IMG. It was just the beginning of what would become the world's largest athlete representation firm.

Mark McCormack's greatest contribution was his vision of how integrating multiple aspects of the sports business could maximize profits and power.

- He started with representing individual athletes, then created or bought events in which they could compete or perform.
- IMG sold sponsorships to these events and did all the marketing, brand management, and licensing. The company extended these services to organizers and leagues around the world including the All England Lawn Tennis Club, the English Premier League, the PGA, LPGA, the US Golf Association, the US Tennis Association, and through its IMG College division, to the NCAA and more than 200 universities.
- IMG's subsidiary, Trans World International (TWI) became the world's largest independent producer of sports television by packaging the live coverage and edited shows for events owned by IMG as well as non-owned events.
- In many cases, IMG represented the network television commentators who would be in the booths for the live coverage of IMG-owned events.
- And to keep fresh young talent flowing into the IMG pipeline, the company established a worldwide network of IMG Academies to train promising athletes, many of whom were destined to become new stars and IMG clients.

Under Mark McCormack, IMG proved that it was possible to amass power in the industry by assuming a role in virtually every aspect of sport management at which a commission or fee could be earned. That structure gave IMG the power to affect change and create synergies for clients and partners that would not be possible if it had not been simultaneously a content owner, media producer and distributor, agent, marketing, branding and licensing representative, and a network of sports training academies. McCormack died in 2003, and IMG was acquired by Endeavor Holdings in 2013 for $2.2 billion.

Having power and the proper exercise of power are two very different things. In an industry that is so susceptible to changes in public behavior and consumption patterns, and that can be dramatically transformed by the introduction of new technologies, every move must be measured against its impact on fans. Any application of power to increase revenue that might result in the exclusion or alienation of an audience segment could have long-term negative effects on the fan base and levels of viewership. Sports that experience audience declines suffer a corresponding reduction in their power and in their ability to generate income for teams, players, and events. No power over content, rules, access, distribution, assets, or capital has value unless it includes the capacity to attract, engage and maintain public support.

BIBLIOGRAPHY

Falk, David. *Interviewed by the Author*, 2021.

Federal Baseball Club of Baltimore, Inc. v. National League of Professional Baseball Clubs, https://supreme.justia.com/cases/federal/us/259/200/

Justia US Law. *White v. National Football League*, 836 F, supp. 1458 (D. Minn, 1993). https://law.justia.com/cases/federal/district-courts/FSupp/836/1458/1949361/

Justia US Supreme Court. *Federal Baseball Club v. National League*, 259 U.S. 200, 1922.

Lewis, Jon. "Masters Sunday up big, but not back to normal." *Sports Media Watch*, 2021. https://www.sportsmediawatch.com/2021/04/masters-ratings-up-cbs-still-lower-than-normal/

Lewis, Jon. "Tiger win huge for morning, low for masters." *Sports Media Watch*, 2019. https://www.sportsmediawatch.com/2019/04/masters-ratings-tiger-morning-cbs/

NCAA. "What is the NCAA?" *NCAA*. https://www.ncaa.org/about/resources/media-center/ncaa-101/what-ncaa

NFL Media Research. "The History of NFL Free Agency." New England Patriots, 2021. https://www.patriots.com/news/the-history-of-nfl-free-agency

Shaiken, Bill. "A look at how Major League Baseball salaries have grown more than 20,000% the last 50 years." *Los Angeles Times*, 2016. https://www.latimes.com/sports/mlb/la-sp-mlb-salaries-chart-20160329-story.html

Sherman, Alex & Young, Jabari. "NFL finalizes new 11-year media rights deal, Amazon gets exclusive Thursday Night rights." *CNBC*, 2021. https://www.cnbc.com/2021/03/18/nfl-media-rights-deal-2023-2033-amazon-gets-exclusive-thursday-night.html

Spangler, Todd. "Amazon prime tops 200 million members, Jeff Bezos says." *Variety*, 2021. https://variety.com/2021/digital/news/amazon-prime-200-million-jeff-bezos-1234952188/

Political Influence in Sports Television

If there were a sports utopia, most fans would want it to be a place of joyful camaraderie and a festival of thrilling spectacle. All games would be contests of skill and will, matching the best athletes and teams in competitions that would, with each renewal, reach new heights and create ever more amazing moments to cheer as they happen and highlights to enjoy long afterward. In a sports utopia, politics and government would play no role whatsoever. But no such place exists.

SPORTS AND POLITICAL SYMBOLISM

Games and matches are more than just competitions; they are events that play a role in the construction and representation of local, regional, and national identities. The quest for victory and the unwillingness to settle for anything less are paramount in sports and politics. Winning tells neighbors and challengers alike that your city, region, or nation is stronger or better than theirs. The victorious set the highest standards, work the hardest to reach their goals, endure every struggle, and overcome all obstacles to prevail. For much of the world and millions of Americans, gridiron football symbolizes the United States. Success in football and in global power struggles is the product of superior strength, teamwork, and the ability to impose your will by every means available. The symbolism of baseball as America's original "national pastime" is intertwined with the values upon which the country was founded, where boys and girls played on the village square or in open fields, and regardless of an individual's humble beginnings, working hard and striving to excel would reap the rewards of success.

A nation's values however can be called into question and its identity tarnished if part of that success is discovered to have been achieved through illegal or unethical means. Baseball fans in 1998 filled stadiums to watch Mark McGwire of the St. Louis Cardinals and Sammy Sosa of the Chicago Cubs obliterate the single season home run record. And television ratings for regular season games during the home run chase were the highest in more than a decade. McGwire ended the season with 70 homers and Sosa had 66, both surpassing the record of 61 that had been set by the New York Yankees' Roger Maris in 1961. Only three years after the McGwire–Sosa

DOI: 10.4324/9781003165590-12

barrage, Barry Bonds grabbed the national spotlight in 2001 when he hit 73 home runs for the San Francisco Giants. The success of these three players raised questions in the minds of many critical observers as to whether their astounding output could have been fueled by more than superior strength and conditioning.

Among those asking questions were elected representatives who took their roles as protectors of the public and the national reputation seriously. Spurred by accusations and suspicions that performance-enhancing drugs were being widely used by major league baseball players, a subcommittee of the US Senate Commerce, Science and Transportation Committee held a hearing in June 2002. The Commissioner of Baseball, Bud Selig, and Donald Fehr, the executive director of the Major League Baseball Players Association, were called to testify before the televised session. They received a tongue-lashing from the committee chair, Senator John McCain, who said:

> We're here today because the sport is about to become a fraud in the minds of the American people... The status quo is not acceptable. And we will have to act in some way unless the major league players union acts in the affirmative and rapid fashion.

Less than three months later, the players and owners announced a new collective bargaining agreement that included a joint drug-testing program for the first time since October 1985.

Millions of people consuming more and more sports via the expanding electronic media have given governmental leaders a stronger political base upon which to stand. The US House of Representatives Committee on Oversight and Government Reform has frequently used its status as a public watchdog to raise awareness and in so doing, prod major sports organizations to either make changes in their self-regulation or face more onerous government intervention on behalf of the public. In 2005, after Jose Canseco's book *Juiced* claimed that many major league players were using steroids, the committee began hearings on Capitol Hill. Canseco had become a national sports celebrity as the star power-hitter and base-stealer for the Oakland Athletics. He was named the Most Valuable Player in the American League in 1988 and won two World Series titles in his career that ended in 2001.

During the televised hearings, former Baltimore Orioles slugger Rafael Palmeiro waved his finger at the Congressional panel as he stridently denied using any drugs that would have helped him hit 569 home runs in his career. Mark McGwire was asked under oath about use by him or his teammates of androstenedione, which had been a legal supplement when he was playing. McGwire's evasive response was that he was not there "to talk about the past." The representatives made it clear that their concern for the future compelled them to ask questions about what happened in the past. They maintained that American youngsters' lives and health could be endangered if they chose to follow the examples of and make the same choices about the use of performance-enhancing substances as the highly successful players they watched hitting home runs on television.

The Committee on Oversight picked up the mantel again in 2008 with televised hearings that followed the December 2007 release of findings from an investigation by former Senator George Mitchell that was conducted at the direction of the Commissioner of Baseball. The Mitchell Report concluded that, "For more than a decade there has been widespread illegal use of anabolic steroids and other performance enhancing substances by players in Major League Baseball, in violation of federal law and baseball policy." The Mitchell Report accused 86 major league players of using illegal substances, the most notable among them being Roger Clemens, who had won 354 games and seven Cy Young Awards as the best pitcher in the American League over the course of his 24 seasons in the major leagues. Clemens' testimony was contradicted by his former trainer Brian McNamee, who told the Congressional panel that he had administered banned substances to Clemens with the pitcher's knowledge and approval.

Neither of these sets of televised hearings by the Committee on Oversight resulted in the passage of federal legislation to impose governmental jurisdiction over the testing of athletes for any substances, but Major League Baseball and its players' union did take the threat seriously and made changes. In the years since these Congressional investigations focused the nation's attention on activities that Mark McGwire "didn't want to talk about," the testing of players has expanded to now include blood tests for human growth hormone (HGH) and documentation by the World Anti-Doping Agency. The penalties for violation of the stricter anti-drug policies are also more onerous, including a lifetime ban from the sport.

The power of symbolism is important to political leaders as is their ability to reach a vast media audience of potential voters. President William Howard Taft started a tradition that has connected politics and sports since 1910: he threw out the ceremonial "first pitch" of the baseball season to Walter Johnson of the Washington Senators as the team prepared to play the Philadelphia Athletics at a small wooden ballpark in the nation's capital called American League Baseball Park II. From their seat in the stands, Taft and successive presidents presented a smiling, positive image of themselves as men of the people who enjoyed taking in a game just as much as the average guy. The symbolism changed in the 1980s when Ronald Reagan became the first president to step out of the stands and onto the field to make the "first pitch" from the mound. This change of stage transformed the portrayal of the president from dignified observer sitting with the people he represents to a man of action, standing shoulder to shoulder with elite athletes on ground where only they and a select few are permitted to set foot. Sitting in the stands was fine for newspaper photos but pitching from the mound made better television.

The first pitch or attendance at any major sporting event is symbolic and largely devoid of any political message beyond that of a leader openly sharing his or her love for the sports that a nation holds dear. However, any gathering with thousands of spectators in the audience and millions watching on television can be used as a political forum by individuals or groups who seek to increase awareness and invite public support for their causes and allegiances. The greater the support, the more political power can be generated.

"THE STAR-SPANGLED BANNER" AS A POLITICAL TOUCHSTONE

Every country's national anthem is an emotional rallying call for its citizens to come together and express their collective nationalistic pride. The common expectation is that everyone will show respect when the anthem is played, remove their hats, and if not join in to sing the words, at a minimum, stand tall and share allegiance to their country with fellow citizens. But what if not everyone shares that pride and they do not sing or stand? If television cameras are there to record the scene the result can be a national outcry. When San Francisco 49ers' quarterback Colin Kaepernick chose to sit during the anthem at a pre-season game on August 26, 2016, live cameras were there, and his silent protest was noticed (Figure 12.1). After the game, Kaepernick told reporters that,

■ **Figure 12.1** San Francisco quarterback Colin Kaepernick (7) with Eli Harold (58) and Eric Reid (35) kneeling during the national anthem before a game against the Los Angeles Rams in December 2016. (Photo by Michael Zagaris/San Francisco 49ers/Getty Images)

"Ultimately it's to bring awareness and make people realize what's going on in this country. There are a lot of things going on that are unjust, people aren't being held accountable for, and that's something that needs to change." Kaepernick had become a celebrated star when he led San Francisco to Super Bowl XLVII, which was seen on television by more than 108 million people in February 2013. He said he was moved by the deaths of unarmed Black citizens at the hands of police in several communities across the United States for which no charges were ever filed or arrests made.

Kaepernick continued his protest into the 2016 regular season, his last with the 49ers, but instead of sitting he chose to kneel during the playing of "The Star-Spangled Banner." And every time he did, the television cameras were there to document his act of non-conformity. Kaepernick said he changed to a kneeling posture to show more respect during the anthem but also as a sign of grieving or sadness in the way that a veteran would take a knee after losing one of his compatriots. The San Francisco team issued this statement in response:

> The national anthem is and always will be a special part of the pre-game ceremony… it is an opportunity to honor our country and reflect on the great liberties we are afforded as its citizens. In respecting such American principles as freedom of religion and freedom of expression, we recognize the right of an individual to choose to participate, or not, in our celebration of the national anthem.

The playing of "The Star-Spangled Banner" as part of the ceremonies at American sporting events began at the first game of the 1918 World Series between the Boston Red Sox and the Chicago Cubs on September 5, 1918, at Comiskey Field in Chicago. The Great War was raging in Europe and US forces had already suffered more than 100,000 casualties. The Spanish Flu epidemic was claiming as many or more lives away from the theater of hostilities. And the day before the game a terrorist bomb had been detonated outside the Federal Courthouse Building in Chicago killing four people and injuring 30.

Two weeks earlier a jury in that courthouse had found 101 members of the International Workers of the World (IWW), a socialist labor organization founded in Chicago in 1905 that opposed America's entry into the war, guilty of violating the Espionage Act for interfering with the war effort and "disloyal speech." The presiding judge was Kenesaw Mountain Landis who would become the first Commissioner of Baseball in 1920. He was in his sixth-floor courtroom when the bomb went off but was not injured. Authorities in Chicago immediately suspected that members of the IWW (less than affectionately nicknamed the "Wobblies") were to blame for the bombing, but no one was ever convicted in the case.

The Cubs ownership decided to honor those who had lost their lives in the bombing and in the war across the sea by having a military band play "The Star-Spangled Banner" during the seventh inning stretch of the World Series opener. When the song began to play, Boston's third baseman Fred Thomas, who was on furlough from the US Navy, snapped to attention and saluted. *The New York Times* reported the next day on the scene at Comiskey Park, which the Cubs had rented for the games because it had a larger seating capacity than Wrigley Field: "the onlookers exploded into thunderous applause and rent the air with a cheer that marked the highest point of the day's enthusiasm." The Cubs repeated the ceremony between halves of the seventh inning for games two and three, which were also played in Chicago.

When the Series moved to Boston for the next three games, the Red Sox elected to play the song before the game when the team would be introducing wounded US veterans who had returned from the war in Europe and were admitted free to the game at Fenway Park. It should be noted that "The Star-Spangled Banner" was not officially adopted as the national anthem until 1931, but the World Series of 1918 forever connected the song with sporting events played in the United States.

Colin Kaepernick's protest flew in the face of this century-old tradition, but he was not the first professional athlete to do so. Twenty years earlier, in March of 1996, a star guard for the Denver Nuggets of the NBA, Mahmoud Abdul-Rauf, refused to stand for the anthem citing his personal and religious beliefs. He negotiated a compromise with the NBA and agreed that whenever the anthem was played, he would stand and pray with his head bowed and his hands open as if he were reading from a holy book. Abdul-Rauf's choice did not spark a national debate in the way that Kaepernick's did because unlike NFL games, the national anthem was almost never part of NBA game telecasts. It was usually played in arenas *before* the live coverage began. And the Denver Nuggets were rarely featured on nationwide broadcasts.

Kaepernick's attempt to raise awareness and bring about change would not have garnered huge national headlines had President Donald J. Trump not "dropped the gauntlet" at a rally on September 17, 2017. Kaepernick had left the San Francisco 49ers and had not been signed by any other NFL team. But other players had carried his kneeling demonstration forward into the new season. Trump told his supporters in Alabama:

> You know what's hurting the game? When people like yourselves turn on television, and you see those people taking the knee when they are playing our great national anthem. The only thing you could do better is if you see it, even if it's one player, leave the stadium, I guarantee things will stop. Things will stop. Just pick up and leave. Pick up and leave. Not the same game anymore, anyway.

Trump's admonition for NFL owners was, "when somebody disrespects our flag, to say, 'Get that son of a bitch off the field right now. Out. He's fired. He's fired!'"

Commissioner Roger Goodell responded promptly with a statement that defended the league and its players and the choices they made.

> The NFL and our players are at our best when we help create a sense of unity in our country and our culture. There is no better example than the amazing response from our clubs and players to the terrible natural disasters we've experienced over the last month.

Goodell was referring to the league's fundraising and relief efforts that were still underway after Hurricane Harvey left 68 people dead and caused $120 billion damage in Texas at the end of August in 2017. He called the President's comments "divisive" saying that they demonstrated, "an unfortunate lack of respect for the NFL, our great game and all of our players, and a failure to understand the overwhelming force for good our clubs and players represent in our communities."

The following weekend NFL players on every sideline linked arms with each other and in many cases kneeled with their team owners in a sign of solidarity that was witnessed by millions of viewers on TV. Dr. Richard Lapchick, the director of The Institute for Diversity and Ethics in Sports, called that Sunday, September 24, 2017, "the most important sports day since Ali decided not to fight in Vietnam."

The Event as a Political Stage

Less than three years later, professional and amateur athletes alike came together with even greater strength following the death of George Floyd at the hands of Minneapolis police in May of 2020, and later that summer when another Black man, Jacob Blake, was shot and seriously injured by police in Kenosha, Wisconsin. Blake's shooting on August 23, 2020, triggered player protests and boycotts of several scheduled games and matches for the ensuing several days. Athletes wanted their voices and opinions heard, and leagues that had previously been resistant to political expression provided them with a national platform and millions of dollars in aid for social programs. When play resumed, messages of "Black Lives Matter" and "Racial Equality," and calls for justice to memorialize victims of police shootings, were inscribed on courts and playing fields, on uniforms and helmets across America and the world. Mike Tirico described how the movement changed the way broadcasters cover live sports.

> I think broadcasters have much more of an awareness to properly rep-resent athletes, to listen to athletes' voices about their stories and share them. Sometimes the audience might not want to hear it, but I think you

need to have the background, and more and more of these athletes want to be seen as more than jerseys with numbers. They want to be seen as the people who are wearing those jerseys with the numbers on their back. I think we have a new-found responsibility to make sure that we tell all of those stories not just the sanitized ones.

The players had won the support of their colleges, conferences, leagues, and players associations, and their message was broadcast in public service announcements that aired in live event coverage across multiple networks. This powerful coalition also mounted voter registration drives to ensure that as many voices as possible would be heard in the US presidential election of 2020 that pitted former Vice President Joseph Biden against the incumbent President Donald Trump. The advocacy for systemic change that came to the forefront in 2020 made the point that in sport, there was more at stake than who scored the most points, and that sporting events of mass public interest were an effective stage upon which forceful political statements could be made.

The world was watching on October 16, 1968, when American sprinters Tommie Smith and John Carlos used the Olympic medal stand in Mexico City to make a statement about racial repression in the United States. In the months leading up to the Olympics, the United States was in turmoil. Dr. Martin Luther King, Jr. and Robert F. Kennedy had both been assassinated. Riots in American cities had led to death, destruction, recriminations, and heightened racial tension. A sociologist at San Jose State University in California, Dr. Harry Edwards, established the Olympic Project for Human Rights and attempted to organize a boycott of the games by African American athletes.

The boycott did not come together, but Smith and Carlos felt compelled to make a silent statement in Mexico City to show their solidarity with Blacks who they saw as the victims of oppression back home. Tommie Smith won the 200 meter race in what at the time was a new world record of 19.83 seconds, and John Carlos finished third. Both men had trained at San Jose State where Dr. Edwards was based.

When they walked into the stadium to receive their medals, Smith and Carlos shed their shoes to portray the poverty that African Americans had endured. Smith wore a black scarf and Carlos a beaded necklace that they later explained represented their Black pride and memorialized "those individuals that were lynched, or killed, and that no one said a prayer for, that were hung and tarred. It was for those thrown off the side of the boats in the Middle Passage."

When "The Star-Spangled Banner" began to play, Americans watching on the ABC network and a television audience of millions more around the globe saw Smith and Carlos with their medals around their necks and Olympic Project for Human Rights badges on their chests. Each bowed his

■ **Figure 12.2** American sprinters Tommie Smith and John Carlos raised gloved fists at the 1968 Olympic Games in Mexico City as a symbolic protest against racism in the United States. Smith and Carlos were subsequently suspended from the US team and sent home. (Photo credit Bettman Archive/Getty Images)

head and raised a black-gloved fist (Figure 12.2). "We are Black and we are proud of being Black," said Carlos after the medal ceremony. "Black America will understand what we did tonight."

The International Olympic Committee did not understand, reacting sternly and immediately to what it saw as an inappropriate insertion of domestic political issues into the Games. The IOC president Avery Brundage said, "If these boys are serious, they're making a very bad mistake. If they're not serious and are using the Olympic Games for publicity purposes, we don't like it." Smith and Carlos were immediately evicted from the Olympic village, sent home, and banned from all future international competition. They each suffered economically and personally for decades, but they were eventually saluted by a growing segment of the American population for what heavyweight boxing champion Muhammad Ali later called "the most courageous act of the 20th century."

A tragic attempt to use the international sports stage for political coercion was made by terrorists at the 1972 Summer Olympics in Munich. Germany had not hosted an Olympics since the Berlin games in 1936, and the goal in hosting what were called "the Games of Peace and Joy" was to show how the nation had changed since the end of the Third Reich and World War II. Those hopes were dashed in the pre-dawn hours of September 5, 1972, when eight Palestinian terrorists from the "Black September" movement invaded the Olympic village, killed two members of the Israeli team, and took nine others hostage. The terrorists demanded the release of 234 Palestinians and other prisoners in Israeli jails as well as freedom for the two German founders of the violent Baader-Meinhof group, Andrea Baader and Ulrike Meinhof.

Americans watched in horrified disbelief as Jim McKay anchored ABC's coverage. The 18-hour standoff ended in a failed rescue attempt by West German authorities at the Furstenfelbruck NATO airbase, where the terrorists and their hostages had been flown by helicopter. A firefight erupted that left all nine remaining hostages dead along with five of the eight terrorists and one German policeman. Three other terrorists were wounded and captured alive. Upon receiving official word of the tragedy, McKay turned to the camera in ABC's Munich studio and said in utter sadness, "When I was a kid, my father used to say our greatest hopes and our worst fears are seldom realized. Our worst fears have been realized tonight... they're gone, they're all gone."

The Munich massacre forever changed international athletic events and their television coverage, pushing the security of participants and spectators to the forefront. The selection of host nations is now viewed through a geopolitical lens to identify any potential targeting by factions who might seize the opportunity to state their ideologies and demands to a worldwide television audience. The screening, credentialing, and access for media to venues and athletes was also tightened to prevent infiltration by elements that might seek cover for their extremist motives by masquerading as members of the press. The Black September terrorists who had slipped into the Olympic Village in Munich were disguised as trash collectors.

The Event as a Political Statement

Every international sporting event held before 1994 that excluded the Republic of South Africa can be interpreted as a political statement in opposition to that nation's apartheid policy that separated the races into a hierarchy with whites at the top and everyone else at the bottom. In 1994, South Africa held its first democratic elections open to all races. Following the election of Nelson Mandela as president, teams and athletes from South Africa were once again welcomed at international competitions.

Mandela himself used a sporting event as a political statement when the Rugby World Cup was to be played in South Africa in 1995. It was the first major international event awarded to the republic since Mandela's 1994 election and the revocation of apartheid as national policy. Racial violence that for months followed the elections had South Africa teetering on the brink of a racial civil war, but Mandela saw sport as a bridge that could be used to unite his nation. In office only one month, he invited the captain of the Springboks, the all-white national rugby team, to meet with him. He asked the Springboks to serve as "ambassadors of peace" to both the white minority and Black majority populations. To white South Africans, the Springboks were a symbol of their pride and identity. For the Black population, the Springboks were a hated symbol of apartheid. Mandela then personally asked all South Africans to join with him to support the team that would represent the entire nation in the upcoming Rugby World Cup.

As the tournament got underway, the South African team put together a string of victories that brought people out into the streets, not to fight but to cheer and celebrate. On the day of the championship final between the Springboks and New Zealand, President Mandela walked out onto the field to shake the players' hands. He was wearing a green Springbok jersey, and the mostly white crowd broke into a cheer of, "Nel-son, Nel-son," which stunned the Black South Africans watching on televisions around the republic and a worldwide TV audience estimated at 2.5 billion. In the most improbable and poetic of endings, the Springboks defeated the Kiwis 15–12 and saluted their supporters, all the citizens of South Africa, and their president. There was no civil war. Racial violence did not instantly disappear, but the war that was feared did not break out.

Money Makes Sports Political

When government intervention can determine who benefits from the billions of dollars spent on sports and by the sports media each year, legislators and judges can become far more important players than any all-star performer or a coach who wins championships year after year. The judicial decision that has had perhaps the greatest effect on the availability of sports content to American television viewers was handed down by the US Supreme Court in 1984 in a case brought by the Universities of Oklahoma and Georgia, representing the College Football Association (CFA), against the National Collegiate Athletic Association, the NCAA. Beginning in 1951, and continuing through a succession of contracts with NBC, CBS, and ABC, the NCAA had tightly controlled how many college football games could be televised per weekend and per season. The original fear shared by the NCAA and its member universities was that games on TV would diminish the number of fans attending in person. Therefore, the 1951 contract limited NBC to a total of 12 Saturday afternoon telecasts during the college football season, and no university could be featured in more than one game.

Restrictions were loosened over the years as the popularity of college football on American television raised the sport's profile and its in-person attendance. But in 1981, the NCAA contract with ABC still limited the appearances of any team to no more than six over the course of two consecutive seasons. The newly formed College Football Association (CFA), which represented 63 NCAA Division I universities with major football programs, signed a separate deal with NBC that year that would dramatically increase television exposure, and with it the rights fees, for its members. In response, the NCAA announced in September of 1981 that it would take disciplinary action against any CFA member school that complied with the NBC contract.

That is when Oklahoma, Georgia, and their fellow CFA universities filed a complaint in Federal District Court charging that the NCAA had been violating the Sherman Antitrust Act by placing anti-competitive limitations on how many games could be sold to television networks, and the price that universities could charge for their rights fees. The case, *NCAA v. Board of Regents of the University of Oklahoma (468 US 85)*, went all the way to the US Supreme Court which in 1984 ruled in favor of the CFA. That opened the floodgates allowing hundreds of games to be televised on various platforms each year and for the universities participating to be compensated at the highest rates the market would bear. In his majority decision, Justice John Paul Stevens wrote "the finding that many more games would be televised in a free market than under the NCAA plan is a compelling demonstration that the plan's controls do not serve any legitimate precompetitive purpose." The judicial branch of government gave more fans more games and made college football a bigger sport with geometrically more revenue than the NCAA on its own may have ever achieved.

A ruling by the US Supreme Court 34 years later is having the same kind of impact on sports industry revenues. In 2018, the court overturned a law that had been enacted in 1992 to protect amateur and professional sports from the influence of gambling. For generations, gambling was anathema to organized sports, the surest route to corruption as evidenced by the 1919 "Black Sox" scandal in which members of the Chicago White Sox were paid to lose the World Series so that gamblers could win big by betting on the underdog Cincinnati Reds. Players or officials caught betting on a variety of sports from college basketball in the United States to international tennis have been disgraced, banned from competition, and in the celebrated case of baseball's career hits leader Pete Rose, prevented for life from recognition by the Baseball Hall of Fame.

Beginning in 1993, the Professional and Amateur Sports Protection Act (PASPA) had made it illegal in 46 of the 50 states for any governmental entity "to operate, sponsor, advertise, promote, license, or authorize a lottery, sweepstakes, or other betting, gambling, or wagering scheme" that was based directly or indirectly on any sports competition involving amateur or professional athletes. It was not effective in all 50 states because established sports books in Nevada and sport-based state lotteries in Delaware, Montana, and Oregon were grandfathered in and allowed to continue.

In a case brought by the state of New Jersey that sought to allow sports gambling at its casinos and racetracks, the Supreme Court ruled that PASPA was unconstitutional because it took away the sovereignty of individual states to make their own decisions. Writing for the majority, Justice Samuel Alito Jr. said, "It is as if federal officers were installed in state legislative chambers and were armed with the authority to stop legislators from voting on any offending proposals."

As of 2021, sports betting had been legalized in 32 states and the District of Columbia. The motivation for states is to tap a new source of revenue by taxing activity that previously existed but had been dominated by illegal gambling organizations. For the sports media, the new revenue source comes in the form of advertising from and partnerships with betting services such as FanDuel, Caesars, and Draft Kings, new video features and television programs that provide gambling information on upcoming games to an avid audience, and in a new crop of live media viewers.

Sports bettors are predominantly male, half are in the 18–34 age bracket that is coveted by advertisers, and close to half report earnings of at least $75,000 per year. Surveys by the American Gaming Association indicate that bettors are very likely to watch games that they have money on, stay tuned longer, and are more likely to watch pre-game and analysis shows. Two of the primary objectives of sports media networks are increased fan engagement and more time spent viewing or using dedicated websites. Sports betting authorized by the US Supreme Court and legalized by state legislatures has the potential to help the networks achieve both objectives.

THE FEDERAL COMMUNICATIONS COMMISSION

Before there was sports television there was an FCC. The agency was established by The Communications Act of 1934 to regulate interstate and international communications in the 50 states, the District of Columbia, and US possessions. At the time, those communications included just radio and telegraph, but advancements in technology broadened the scope of the FCC's regulation to encompass television, satellite, cable, wireless, and broadband.

The airwaves that are used for the transmission of broadcast and data signals are designated as a public resource in the United States that, just like the air we breathe, cannot be owned by any individual or organization, corporate or otherwise. The spectrum of airwaves has no borders that would allow for local, regional, or state regulation, so it fell to the federal government to make the decisions as to how those frequencies would be used, by whom, and for what purposes. The fact that today there are media communicating exclusively via the internet, fiber optic or coaxial cables, or other systems, which do not use public airwaves, has not excluded them from governmental regulation.

The areas of FCC oversight that relate most directly to the live sports media are:

- Media ownership
- Public access to television programming
- "Must-carry" and retransmission consent regulations

Media Ownership

The number of frequencies available for broadcasting is not unlimited, so the FCC early on instituted a licensing application procedure by which it approves the allocation of space on the broadcast spectrum to only those companies or individuals who meet or exceed a set of federal standards. Broadcast licenses are never granted in perpetuity, but rather they are reviewed every five years, or more frequently if judged necessary by the FCC, to ensure that all standards are being met.

As the regulator of communications for a democratic nation, the FCC has from its beginning included as an important part of its mission a guarantee to the public that no one corporation, no matter how powerful, could ever control all the messages that any American receives via television, satellite, cable, wireless, broadband, or any future medium yet to be invented. The FCC's stated goal is to protect the public interest by fostering competition, localism, and diversity. It enforces a set of media ownership rules and restrictions that it reviews and adjusts every four years to ensure that there will be a multitude of "independent voices" accessible to all Americans.

The current rules prohibit any merger among the top four broadcast networks in the United States: ABC, CBS, NBC, and Fox. There are no limits on the number of television stations that any one company can own, however, collectively, no media owner is permitted to control stations that would reach a market universe larger than 39 percent of the total US population. For example, if one corporation owned television stations in New York City, Chicago, and Los Angeles, its total market universe would be approximately 10 percent of all the TV homes in the United States. It could buy more stations, but only until its universe as a group hit 39 percent. (The 39 percent figure was a compromise in 2003 when the FCC had approved a change in the ownership limit from 35 to 45 percent of the population. Congress voted to keep the limit at 35 percent. A compromise brokered after a threatened veto by then-President George W. Bush set 39 percent of the population as the ownership ceiling.)

There is a provision called the "UHF discount" that does allow a corporation to exceed the 39 percent of population ceiling. Television stations that operate on channels 14 or above on UHF (ultra high frequency) are attributed only half the number of TV households in their designated market area (DMA), as opposed to 100 percent of the number of households attributed to stations on Channel 13 or below, which are the VHF (very high frequency) channels. To television consumers, VHF and UHF have grown virtually indistinguishable because the majority of American homes don't receive television signals via over-the-air antennas. But the rules put in place to favor UHF stations, which were traditionally less dominant in their communities, make it possible for media ownership groups to reach more than 39 percent of the population if their portfolio includes one or more UHF properties.

In 2017, the FCC eliminated its rule that had previously prohibited common ownership of a full-power broadcast station and a daily newspaper in the same relevant "area of dominant influence" (ADI). At the same time, the Commission also eliminated the radio-television cross-ownership rule, which had restricted the common ownership of broadcast radio and television stations located in the same market. These two rules, the newspaper-broadcast cross-ownership and radio-television cross-ownership rules, were eliminated due in part to the growth in the number and variety of sources of entertainment, news, and information in the modern media marketplace.

The impact of these regulations on sports television is that there will always be competition for broadcast rights. Local teams and events will have equal opportunities for coverage even if they are not owned by or in partnership with a major media company, and when controversies arise, a multitude of reports and opinions will share the airwaves.

Public Access to Television Programming

The Federal Communications Commission "is committed to fostering a strong and independent broadcast media that provides Americans with multiple and diverse sources of news, public affairs and entertainment programming," said former FCC Chairman Julius Genachowski. Access to live sports coverage is a major part of that "entertainment programming." That is why it is highly unlikely that a widely consumed event such as the Super Bowl will ever move to a cable channel or digital distributor exclusively: anyone who didn't subscribe to that service would be denied access to the event. That would not be tolerated by either the FCC or the senators and representatives with constituents who do not to subscribe to pay TV services.

Must-carry and Retransmission Consent

The FCC first adopted "must-carry" rules in 1972 responding to the fears of local television station owners that they would lose audience and advertising dollars if people could get entertainment, news, and sports from a cable running directly into their homes as an alternative to local over-the-air signals.

Federal courts found the must-carry rules to be a restriction of the First Amendment right of free speech following challenges in the 1980s by several cable operators and by Turner Broadcasting. Congress stepped in and passed the Communications Act of 1992 that required cable companies to carry local commercial and public stations, but allowed them to drop redundant signals if, for example, there were two stations within a 50-mile radius that both carried the same network's programming. Two years later, the FCC gave stations a choice of maintaining their must-carry status with the local cable systems or be carried under a new regulation that required the cable operator to obtain "retransmission consent." The retransmission consent rules gave strong local network affiliates and independent stations increased power to negotiate their terms of carriage, including channel preference, with cable or online subscription video services.

The price charged by networks for retransmission or by any platform for monthly subscriptions becomes a public relations battle any time these contracts come up for renewal. These disputes are almost always timed to coincide with major sporting events at the beginning of long-anticipated seasons or championships. The networks and the distribution platforms can both send subscribers dire warnings that they won't be able to watch their favorite sports unless the other side adjusts its price in time. These campaigns have sent a signal heard loud and clear to cable subscribers that as their subscriptions grew more expensive, they also appeared to become less reliable. This would become just one more factor in the "cord-cutting" epidemic of the past decade as consumers searched for new, cheaper video delivery systems to replace their cable subscriptions.

GOVERNMENT REGULATION AND OVERSIGHT

The level of governmental interest and intervention in the live sports media has grown in direct proportion to the industry's growth in audience and income, as would be the case with any expanding sector of the economy. A major milestone was the Sports Broadcasting Act of 1961 that was discussed in detail in Chapter 4. It allowed leagues of individually owned teams in multiple states to act as single entities in negotiating broadcast rights with television networks, without fear of being found in violation of any federal anti-trust statutes.

As cable television reached a majority of American homes in the late 1980s and early 1990s, and live sports coverage began to migrate to ESPN, TBS, and other networks that were not available free over-the-air, legislation was proposed by a number of representatives on Capitol Hill to limit "pay-per-view siphoning from free TV." In an effort to protect broadcast stations, the FCC had adopted rules in 1975 to restrict the programming that cable or subscription TV services could offer, but these "anti-siphoning" regulations were struck down as invalid, arbitrary, and capricious in 1978 by the US Circuit Court of Appeals in the case of *HBO v. FCC.*

That ruling did not however halt the efforts by some representatives to win Congressional approval of laws that would impose restrictions on cable sports programming. None succeeded. The cable industry was able to demonstrate that despite the thousands of hours of sports that were being shown exclusively on cable stations, the volume of sports programming and the choices available on the free, over-the-air broadcast networks had increased, not declined.

Government scrutiny will be a fact of life in sport as long as events attract millions of viewers, and the annual economic impact is measured in the billions. There can be no other reasonable expectation when celebrity athletes command multimillion-dollar contracts, compete at risk of injury to themselves and others, and are emulated by young people across the world. Nor is it likely that politicians will miss any opportunity to increase the public awareness of issues they deem important to the public welfare, and which also may enhance their political stature.

The ideal clung to for generations by the International Olympic Committee and nostalgic sports fans that politics should play no role whatsoever in sport is unrealistic. It may have been possible in the era before television when sports were neither a stage nor an economic powerhouse, but not now. The innocence may be long gone, but the symbolism of sport remains in its celebration of games and athletes that represent what nations value most: high standards, the pursuit of excellence, determination in the face of obstacles, and the ability to rally teammates and far-flung followers.

BIBLIOGRAPHY

American Gaming Association. "Americans' 2019 NFL Betting Plans." 2019. https://www.americangaming.org/resources/americans-2019-nfl-betting-plans/

American Gaming Association. "Interactive Map: Sports Betting in the U.S.." 2021. https://www.americangaming.org/research/state-gaming-map/

Araton, Harvey. "From the N.B.A., a Cautionary Tale on National Anthem Protests." *The New York Times*, 2017. https://www.nytimes.com/2017/11/06/sports/basketball/anthem-nba-abdul-rauf-kaepernick.html

Cornell Law School and Legal Information Institute. "Murphy v. National Collegiate Athletic Assn." 2018. https://www.law.cornell.edu/supremecourt/text/16-476

Cyphers, Luke and Trex, Ethan. "From the Archives: History of the National Anthem in Sports." *ESPN*, 2020. https://www.espn.com/espn/story/_/id/6957582/from-archives-history-national-anthem-sports

Federal Communications Commission. "The Public and Broadcasting." 2019. https://www.fcc.gov/media/radio/public-and-broadcasting

FindLaw. "U.S. Supreme Court." *NCAA v. Board of Regents of the University of Oklahoma* (468 U.S. 85), 1984. Findlaw.com. https://caselaw.findlaw.com/us-supreme-court/468/85.html

Goodell, Roger. "Statement from NFL Commissioner Roger Goodell." *NFL Communications*, 2017. https://nflcommunications.com/Pages/Statement-From-NFL-Commissioner-Roger-Goodell.aspx

Haden, Jeff. "Colin Kaepernick Had Every Right to Sit During the National Anthem (Even Though I Wouldn't Have)." Inc., 2016. https://www.inc.com/jeff-haden/colin-kaepernick-has-every-right-to-sit-during-the-national-anthem-even-though-i.html

Jenkins, Aric. "Read President Trump's NFL Speech on National Anthem Protests." *Time*, 2017. https://time.com/4954684/donald-trump-nfl-speech-anthem-protests/

Justia US Law. "U.S. Court of Appeals and D.C. Circuit." *Home Box Office, Inc., et al., Petitioners, v. Federal Communications Commission and United States of America*, 587 F.2d 1248, 1978. https://law.justia.com/cases /federal/appellate-courts/F2/587/1248/37737/

Macur, Juliet. "Was It a One-Day Revolt in the N.F.L., or Something More?." *The New York Times*, 2017. https://www.nytimes.com/2017/09/25/sports/ football/trump-nfl-anthem.html

McManus, Sean and Guthrie, Marisa. "My Dad, Me and the Munich Massacre." *The Hollywood Reporter*, 2012. https://www.hollywoodreporter.com/tv/tv -news/my-dad-me-munich-massacre-352894/

Mitchell, George J. "Report to the Commissioner of Baseball of an Independent Investigation Into the Illegal Use of Steroids and Other Performance Enhancing Substances by Players in Major League Baseball." December 13, 2007. http://files.mlb.com/mitchrpt.pdf

Moore, Kenny. "A Courageous Stand." *Sports Illustrated*, 1991. https://vault .si.com/vault/1991/08/05/the-1968-olympics-a-courageous-stand-first-of-a -two-part-series-in-68-olympians-tommie-smith-and-john-carlos-raised -their-fists-for-racial-justice

Thomson, Ian. "A Big Day Dawns for Rugby – And for South Africa." *The New York Times*, 1995 https://www.nytimes.com/1995/05/25/sports/IHT-a -big-day-dawns-for-rugby-and-for-south-africa.html

Tirico, Mike. *Interviewed by the Author*, 2020.

U.S. Senate Subcommittee on Consumer Affairs, Foreign Commerce and Tourism. "Hearing on Steroid Use in Professional Baseball and Anti-Doping Issues in Amateur Sports." Govinfo.gov, 2002. https://www.govinfo.gov/ content/pkg/CHRG-107shrg94608/html/CHRG-107shrg94608.htm

Social and Cultural Impact of Sports Media

The sports media pass social values and ethics lessons from generation to generation in the form of dramatic narratives that recount stories of success and failure. They provide us with a mirror that reflects our social and political values and hierarchy, as well as a means of escape into a world of intense rituals, charismatic leaders, magical performances, and victories.

Sport has been a precursor of social change in the United States as in the case of the NFL and Major League Baseball which were both integrated in the 1940s, but public schools weren't compelled to integrate nationwide until the 1954 *Brown v. Board of Education* ruling by the US Supreme Court. Our exposure to sport via the mass media affects our perceptions of the world around us, our attitudes regarding gender and race, what we value, and the choices we make.

THE PORTRAYAL OF WOMEN IN LIVE SPORTS MEDIA

Televised sport has played an important role in changing the dominant ideas about gender in American society. Our cultural understanding of femininity has been radically altered by images of women with athletic skill, muscles, and endurance. In the United States up until the last few decades of the 20th century, the individual sports that required grace, glamour, and self-sacrifice such as figure skating, tennis, golf, or gymnastics were seen as most suitable for women. Sports that demanded strength, stamina, and speed, any team sport involving contact, or any sport such as auto racing that came with a degree of risk were traditionally the domain of males only.

For example, the version of basketball that was designed specifically for women by Senda Berenson at Smith College less than a year after James Naismith published his original rules of the game in 1891 divided the court into three sections to limit the amount of running and exertion required of female players. In 1938, the three sections were reduced to two, with six players per team, three each were restricted to one half of the court

DOI: 10.4324/9781003165590-13

only. Each team had three fulltime offensive players at one end and three fulltime defenders at the opposite end of the floor who were never allowed to shoot or score. Only three dribbles were permitted per possession and "snatching or batting the ball away from a player" was a violation. Basketball for women was meant to be a form of exercise that promoted socialization and cooperation, not strenuous competition. Full court, five-on-five women's basketball was not officially sanctioned until 1971, but the less strenuous six-on-six version was widely played until 1993 at high schools in a few Midwestern states, most notably Iowa.

By the end of the 20th century, women had experimented with and adapted to virtually every sport. The competition they relished coupled with the strength and endurance they built represented a form of female empowerment to a society that for generations had accepted male domination as the natural order. To many men and women alike, the new reality threatened their preconceived notions of what the ideal woman or mother should be. A female athlete with muscles did not fit what had been the cultural template, nor did a woman who dared challenge a man on the field of play.

One of the true pioneers of gender equity did just that in 1973, and because of Billie Jean King barriers began to fall and previously unimagined opportunities opened for women in sports and society. Her tennis match against former Wimbledon champion Bobby Riggs called *The Battle of the Sexes* aired live from the Houston Astrodome in primetime on ABC television on September 23, 1973.

Riggs had won Wimbledon in 1939, but by 1973, he was a 55-year-old hustler hoping to get publicity and make a few bucks challenging women professionals of the era. He goaded them with "male chauvinist pig" rhetoric about how a woman's place was in the home "barefoot and pregnant" and how no woman athlete could beat a skilled man regardless of his age. Riggs' favorite T-shirt bore the acronym "WORMS" for a fictitious "World Organization for the Retention of Male Supremacy." Margaret Court took the bait and played Riggs on Mothers' Day in 1973. The Australian star was 25 years younger than her opponent and had won 17 grand slam singles titles, including all four majors in 1970, but she lost 6–2, 6–1 to Riggs in just 57 minutes in a match from San Diego that aired on CBS.

Billie Jean King had resisted Riggs' taunts, but when she saw that Margaret Court had lost, she resolved to play him so that her campaign for gender equity including equal prize money for women players on the tennis tour would not suffer a setback. King was 29 and had won the Wimbledon singles and doubles titles in 1973. In her career, Billie Jean King won a total of 39 grand slam singles and doubles tournaments, but no victory would have a more momentous impact than *The Battle of the Sexes*.

King was carried onto the Astrodome court on a gold litter carried by four muscular men dressed as Roman slaves. She appeared to be smiling at the absurdity of it all. Riggs, wearing a satin "Sugar Daddy" jacket from his hastily signed candy sponsor, was wheeled out to the court on a rickshaw pulled by scantily attired models he called "Bobby's Bosom Buddies." Howard Cosell, ABC's provocative commentator from *Monday Night Football* and virtually every Muhammad Ali boxing match, added his dramatic observations to heighten the sense of theater.

Before a worldwide television audience estimated at 50 million, Billie Jean King out-hustled Bobby Riggs, winning 6–4, 6–3, 6–3, and in so doing "she convinced skeptics that a female athlete can survive pressure-filled situations and that men are as susceptible to nerves as women," wrote Neil Amdur of *The New York Times*. Martina Navratilova later said of King, "She was a crusader fighting a battle for all of us. She was carrying the flag; it was alright to be a jock." Life Magazine named Billie Jean King one of the "100 Most Important Americans of the 20th Century."

Billie Jean King helped change how young women thought about themselves and how men thought about women. The role of sportscaster, which had been monopolized by men, was also beginning to change. Donna de Varona had been seen nationally reporting on *ABC's Wide World of Sports* and the network's Olympic telecasts, but when Phyllis George debuted in 1975 as the co-host of *The NFL Today* on CBS alongside Brent Musburger and Irv Cross, the male-only domination of major team sports commentary in the United States started to crumble.

Phyllis George had toured the country as Miss America 1971, impressing media executives with her personality, poise, and intelligence during television guest appearances. She brought far more than a pretty face to her interviews, feature stories, and on-set reports for CBS. Phyllis George added character and depth to storylines, often getting athletes to open up and reveal their personal sides because of her engaging style. Girls who loved sports but who were never going to achieve the international athletic success of Billie Jean King now had role models in George and de Varona, whose visibility on television made them important trailblazers in the process of redefining women in American culture.

THE IMPACT OF TELEVISION SPORTS ON RACIAL ATTITUDES

When the dramatic series *I Spy* premiered on NBC in the fall of 1965, Bill Cosby became the first Black person to have a starring role in a weekly American television program. Up to that point, the only minority stars that Americans saw on TV with any regularity were professional athletes such as Willie Mays of the San Francisco Giants, Bill Russell of the Boston Celtics, or heavyweight boxing champion Muhammad Ali. Their representation in the media helped to broaden and improve the understanding of diversity and race in the United States.

Americans who grew up in the 1950s, as television penetration was exploding from less than 10 percent of homes at the beginning of the decade to nearly nine out of 10 homes by 1960, came of age recognizing that people of different races played for the same teams. In 1946, the unwritten color ban that had been a "gentlemen's agreement" among NFL owners since 1933 was broken when the Cleveland Rams moved to Los Angeles. Three days after the league approved the move, the Los Angeles Memorial Coliseum Commission met on January 15, 1946, to consider the Rams' request for a lease. At that hearing, Halley Harding, a columnist for the *Los Angeles Tribune*, a weekly Black newspaper, told the nine commissioners that tax dollars from Los Angeles residents of all colors had built the Coliseum. Therefore, he contended that permitting a league which barred Blacks to use the publicly owned Coliseum would be nothing less than a retreat from democracy. Harding also said it was strange that Kenny Washington, one of the best collegiate players of 1939, had never been offered a tryout by any NFL team. The Rams' general manager Chile Walsh responded by saying there was no NFL rule, written or unwritten, barring Blacks from playing. But he did make this offer, "We will take any player of ability we can get. Kenny Washington is welcome to try out for our team anytime he likes." Two months later, the Rams signed Washington who along with fellow UCLA star Woody Strode, reintegrated NFL football in the fall of 1946.

The following spring Jackie Robinson broke Major League Baseball's color barrier that had excluded players of color since 1889. Robinson helped lead the Brooklyn Dodgers to the National League pennant in 1947 and into the first televised World Series against the New York Yankees. His presence in professional baseball attracted more Black fans to ballparks and to watch games on television. These breakthroughs were part of the societal shift that gained momentum following World War II, during which Black soldiers had proven their valor and dedication as citizens of the United States. Midway through Jackie Robinson's second season with the Dodgers, President Harry S. Truman repudiated 170 years of officially sanctioned segregation in the American military by signing Executive Order 9981. It stated that "there shall be equality of treatment and opportunity for all persons in the armed forces without regard to race, color, religion, or national origin."

The NBA's first Black players made their debuts in 1950: Earl Lloyd for the Washington Capitols followed by Chuck Cooper with the Celtics and Nat Clifton with the New York Knicks. The presence of these men on major teams and in the media coverage of their games by no means implied that professional sport was a space devoid of racial discrimination, but it did begin to build a sense among those who saw them play in person and on television that players from diverse backgrounds would be selected based on merit and that their contributions to team success were valuable. The fan bases for teams and sports have expanded to include more minorities in the decades since these pioneers made their mark. These increasingly diverse crowds and television audiences collectively cheering for victories and championships helped bring people of all colors together.

Minorities Assume Leadership Positions

The opportunities for minorities in the major American sports however were limited for decades to the role of "performer." African Americans and Hispanics had made their way onto playing fields and into arenas, but their absence from any leadership positions such as coach, manager, captain, or quarterback reinforced a racial hierarchy that had always put whites in positions of authority. At its core racism is about domination, one group exerting its control over others. As long as leadership positions were for "whites only," sport in America would never be a true meritocracy. These exclusionary practices were reaffirmed every time a television camera showed a white quarterback calling signals or cut to the sidelines or dugout to show only white managers and coaches directing their players.

The athletic skill of minority players in the NFL had become increasingly evident in the years following the integration of the league in 1946, but there was an insidious perception among many white fans in America that men of color did not possess the combination of intellect and leadership required to be a quarterback. In 1953, the Chicago Bears had just two African Americans on their roster; one was a rookie quarterback from Michigan State named Willie Thrower. On October 18, 1953, he entered the Bears' game against the San Francisco 49ers in relief of starter George Blanda. He threw eight passes and completed three before Blanda returned. Willie Thrower was the first Black quarterback to play in the NFL since the league's color barrier had fallen, but his name is largely forgotten because those eight passes were the only ones he was ever allowed to throw in his professional career, and his appearance was not seen by a nationwide television audience.

The first Black quarterback to start a game in professional football was Marlin Briscoe who took the opening snap for the Denver Broncos in the fourth game of the 1968 season vs. the Cincinnati Bengals. He faltered in the first half and was replaced by Steve Tensi. The first African American to start a full season at quarterback for an NFL team was Joe Gilliam, Jr. who led the Pittsburgh Steelers for the first six games of the 1974 season. He too struggled and was replaced as the starter in the seventh game that year by Terry Bradshaw, who went on to win four Super Bowls with the Steelers and was elected to the Pro Football Hall of Fame. The stumbles made by these early pioneers gave those who still believed in the old racial hierarchy what they could claim as justification for their prejudice. The process of burying the myth that Blacks could not succeed at quarterback gained momentum when Doug Williams led Washington to victory and was named the Most Valuable Player of Super Bowl XXII before a television audience of more than 81 million people in January of 1988.

The responsibilities and decision-making skills required to lead a team on the field are not insignificant, but they pale in comparison to those of a coach or manager. Bill Russell was the cornerstone for the Boston Celtics during the team's run of nine NBA championships in the 10 years from 1957 to 1966. He was named the Celtics' player-coach for the 1966–67 season, succeeding the legendary Red Auerbach who was retiring. Russell thus became the first African American to coach a team in any of the major American sports. He served as player-coach for three years and stepped aside after having led Boston to 11 NBA titles in his 13 seasons. Russell was named the NBA's Most Valuable Player five times and is a member of the Basketball Hall of Fame.

Major League Baseball's first Black manager was perennial all-star Frank Robinson who took the helm with the Cleveland Indians in 1975, just as his Hall of Fame playing career was coming to an end. In the NFL, the first minority head coach was Hispanic. Tom Flores was promoted from assistant coach to head coach of the Oakland Raiders in 1979, and he proceeded to lead the silver and black to championships in Super Bowls XV and XVIII. When Flores retired in 1988, he was succeeded by Art Shell making Shell the league's first Black head coach.

As diversity spread from the player level to management, the identity of minorities in sport and throughout society underwent a reconstruction as Americans watched on television. A milestone came quietly in early 2007 when the coaches of both teams in Super Bowl XLI were both African American: Tony Dungy of the Indianapolis Colts and Lovie Smith of the Chicago Bears. These two men at the pinnacle of their sport were the leaders of men from many different ethnic backgrounds. They were the bosses, making decisions that would determine how millions of dollars would be spent and how the careers of hundreds of players would turn out. And at the conclusion of that 2006 regular season, 60 years after the NFL had begun to reintegrate, Dungy and Smith would be judged by the majority of fans based on the quality of their work and their won-loss records, not the color of their skin.

The following year Barack Obama became the first man of color elected to the most powerful post in the world, President of the United States. His election can in no way be attributed to Super Bowl XLI, but the success of Tony Dungy and Lovie Smith as leaders of powerful organizations was witnessed by nearly 100 million Americans who watched the game. Directing their teams from the sidelines, these two head coaches represented one more very public piece of evidence that men of color could shoulder the responsibilities of leadership and prevail. It spoke to how dramatically public opinion about race in America had changed in the decades since Black men had been excluded from even playing professional football.

Muhammad Ali "Shook Up the World"

No one in the history of sport since the advent of television challenged racism more boldly than Muhammad Ali. Born Cassius Clay in Louisville, Kentucky in 1942, he won a gold medal as the Olympic light heavyweight champion at the Rome games in 1960. He was 18 years old. In 1964 at age 22, he won the world heavyweight championship by knocking out Sonny Liston at Miami Beach, then proclaimed to the world that he "must be the greatest." Shortly after the fight, Ali made another announcement: he had joined the Nation of Islam and was changing his name, first to Cassius X, then to Muhammad Ali. "I know where I'm going," he said, "and I know the truth and I don't have to be what you want me to be. I'm free to be what I want."

Ali was stripped of his title in 1967 after he refused induction into the US military on the grounds that he was a conscientious objector whose religion forbade taking up arms against others. Ali won his case against the US Justice Department three years later when the US Supreme Court found in his favor, but those were three years in which he was unable to pursue his livelihood and compete in the ring. He regained the world heavyweight title in 1974 by defeating then-champion George Foreman in "The Rumble in the Jungle" in Kinshasa, Zaire, which is now known as the Democratic Republic of the Congo.

Muhammad Ali's arrival on the sports scene was a watershed event. His impact on the sports media was immense because he was never afraid to speak, he looked confidently into the camera, and he was controversial and quotable, never subservient. Ali dashed any semblance of racial hierarchy. He held his own and traded barbs over the course of several interviews with ABC's Howard Cosell, a man who had many more years of education than Ali, but no greater command of the language nor understanding of the world around him (Figure 13.1). Muhammad

■ **Figure 13.1** Muhammad Ali with Howard Cosell of ABC Sports during an interview on December 15, 1970, in New York, NY. (Photo by Santi Visalli/Getty Images)

Ali would not be dominated; his words and actions transmitted into homes across the country and around the world shook those who had complacently perpetuated the two-tier society that put whites on the top and everyone else beneath. Ali retired from boxing in 1981 having won the heavyweight championship three separate times. He died in 2016 at age 74.

If sport is indeed going to completely shed the inequities of the past, there is still catching up to be done. Calling the plays on the field and calling the shots from the sideline or bench are one beachhead. Calling the games on television is quite another. The representation of minorities in the announce booth and in television studios lags far behind their numbers on the field or court. Every year, the University of Central Florida's Institute for Diversity and Ethics in Sports does a "Race and Gender Report Card" for each of the major sports in the United States. Its annual surveys have shown that while at least 70 percent of the players in the NBA are African American, less than 20 percent of the radio and television talent covering the games are Black. The same discrepancy between the ethnicity of players and those who report or broadcast their games persists across all sports.

The argument is not necessarily that achieving racial equity requires that the ratio of minority broadcasters to players in any sport should be one-to-one. A case could be made for the desirability of a one-to-one ethnic ratio not between players and sportscasters, but instead between the make-up of each sport's fan base and the sportscasters who serve those fans. Using that premise, if more than 50 percent of all NBA viewers are non-white, then the same percentage of minority NBA broadcasters would be equitable. The argument is about the end of racial discrimination and the accurate portrayal of minorities and women as equal partners in society, capable of achievement to the fullest extent of their talents and deserving of the opportunity to reach their goals.

SOCIAL AND CULTURAL EFFECTS

Sport is a vibrant part of the social and cultural fabric of almost every nation around the world. The media have woven the stories and values of sport into the context of life in the United States and wherever the exploits of athletic champions are embraced. The attributes and personalities of successful teams and stars factor into the identity of nations and individual citizens as well. Consider your friends and fellow sports fans, or simply look in the mirror, to see the evidence of how the mass distribution of sports in the United States and around the world has affected what people wear, the food and drink we consume, the words and phrases we use in daily speech, how we spend our time, who we spend it with, and how we perceive people from other races or cultures.

Social Interaction

Loyalties to teams and connections with star players develop early in youngsters who follow or play sports, fostering social interaction within peer groups, across generations, and across gender and ethnic bounds. Sport brings together athletes and fans of every color, background, nationality, and orientation. Interacting with fellow fans and cheering for athletes who look different or speak different languages can help us figure out how we fit into social structures. There is comfort in gathering at games or in front of television screens with individuals who share the same team devotion, celebrate the same heroes and victories, share sorrow in defeat, and optimistically anticipate the next game or the next season.

What We Say

If you did not watch televised sports, would you speak a different language? To answer that question, think about how often you may use words or phrases from sports as metaphors or shorthand to make your listener quickly understand your point. When it is time to "step up to the plate" do you "take your best shot" and "go for the gold?" Did you "knock it out of the park" and "hit a home run," or are you "behind the eight ball," or worse, "down for the count." If you are a "heavy hitter" will you "go one on one" then "hit full stride" and "reach the goal line?" Was it a "slam dunk," "touch-and-go," or a "sticky wicket?" Did you "make a pit stop" then have to "pass the baton?" Are you a "Monday morning quarterback" or are you "out in left field?" You don't want to "drop the ball," "jump the gun," or "strike out" then go into "extra innings." These and dozens of other terms heard while watching live sports have become a prevalent and expressive part of our common discourse.

What We Do

The sports that people watch on whatever video screen is available can directly affect the pursuits they choose for the hours when they are not watching and for years to come. The events and stars that children see on television can influence the decisions they make about what sports they will pursue, which in countless instances are decisions that will determine their lifelong friends and affect the course of their lives. To prove this hypothesis, one need only check the rising enrollment figures at local gymnastics schools after every Summer Olympics is televised.

The hours each week that upwards of 60 million fantasy sports aficionados in North America spend drafting and trading players, managing their teams, and gleaning websites for research is time they would spend doing other things if it were not for sports on television. It is possible to play fantasy exclusively online using statistics, analysis, and projections, but scouting players and tracking their performances in live games is a large part of the appeal. Research done for the Fantasy Sports and Gaming Association projects that 19 percent of Americans over the age of 18 play at least one fantasy sport. Fantasy football is the runaway favorite with 78 percent of all players owning at least one team. Fantasy baseball is a distant second with just under 40 percent participation. The research done by Ipsos Public Affairs includes demographic profiles showing that fantasy players are more likely to be college-educated than not and are also more likely to be employed fulltime than the average person.

What We Wear

It is difficult for most people alive today to remember a time when sports apparel and footwear were worn only by athletes and did not constitute such a large percentage of a sports fan's wardrobe or closet. Look back at photographs or films of sporting events from the 1940s, 1950s, or 1960s and focus on the crowds. In the summer, they wore shirts and blouses, many men wore ties and felt hats, and in the winter, you saw overcoats and jackets, none with team logos. They did not wear the team jerseys and caps proudly proclaiming team loyalty that fill the stands at games in the 21st century. The transition from fans who dressed like average people to fans who dressed like their favorite athletes, or in the colors of their favorite teams, is concurrent with the expansion of the live sports media in the years since 1970.

Michael Jordan's role in the growth of Nike presents an excellent example of how sports on television and the marketing of sports celebrities has changed how Americans identify themselves through their choice of clothing. In fiscal 1984, the year that Nike signed an endorsement deal with Jordan as he was leaving the University of North Carolina, the company had total revenues of $919,806,000. Jordan led the NBA in scoring in his first season with the Chicago Bulls and again in the 1986–87 season. Nike sales went over the $1 billion mark for the first time in 1986, and another crucial milestone came in 1987. That year, ESPN's cable penetration pushed past 50 percent of all American homes, putting Michael Jordan's amazing highlights in front of a growing national audience every night on *SportsCenter*. Jordan won the first of his five NBA Most Valuable Player awards at the conclusion of the 1987–88 season just as Nike introduced its "Just Do It" advertising campaign. The company's sales hit $1.7 billion in fiscal 1989, an increase of more than 70 percent in the five years since they had signed Michael Jordan.

By 2003, the year in which Jordan played his last NBA game as a member of the Washington Wizards, Nike's annual revenue had reached $10.7 billion, which translates to millions of Americans wearing Nike sneakers and athletic gear, "just doing it" dressed like their favorite professional athlete. If the NBA's exposure on television had remained limited to one or two games per weekend on the broadcast networks, and video from every one of his games was not featured nationally on a nightly basis, it is safe to assume that Jordan's impact on consumer behavior and Nike's sales would have been geometrically smaller.

What We Consume

The impact that Michael Jordan had on behavior went beyond what Americans put on their feet and on their backs, to what they put in their stomachs. Gatorade signed Michael Jordan as its brand spokesman in 1991 and launched its "Be Like Mike" advertising campaign. He led the Bulls to their first NBA Championship that season, winning awards as the NBA regular season and finals Most Valuable Player, and Gatorade sales increased faster than the rest of the soft drink industry. The product got plenty of television airtime with its bright orange coolers and green cups visible on the sidelines at basketball and football games. Gatorade was what the viewing public saw the best athletes drink to keep themselves hydrated, so it became a more popular choice among active young people and adults who had the same kind of thirst that they could satisfy with a beverage offering the same beneficial effects. The pattern repeats itself over and over with products from energy bars to golf clubs and baseball caps. Each of us makes a social statement about ourselves through the products we use and wear, and for millions, the decision to buy is made to follow the lead of the star athletes we see on our screens of choice.

The passion for sports and its proliferation in the live sports media affect millions of people's lives, their personal decisions, and their preferences. The mass electronic dissemination of sports content has helped society change by providing a platform upon which racial hierarchies and gender stereotypes could be challenged and overthrown, where personal initiative, skill, and determination could overcome obstacles, even racial discrimination. The recognition that people of color were deserving of and capable of success in sports leadership positions, and their ascension to those jobs in increasing numbers, has been a major step forward in the drive for racial equality that began with the integration of player rosters in the 1940s and 1950s.

This is not to say that sport has become race-neutral or that racism and stereotyping do not still exist, nor that more work is not needed to reach equitable participation at all levels. In fact, the multitude of African Americans seen succeeding in professional basketball and football games has created a false stereotype for many minority youths who perceive sports as providing a vast opportunity for their personal upward mobility, when in reality the number of jobs as a "pro athlete" is infinitesimal compared with the workforce as a whole.

Media coverage of sports has helped people understand social issues, allowing them to construct collective and individual identities that reflect the growth of diversity and the higher standards for performance and competition that are its direct result. The live sports media magnify reality, and at their best, expose inequities and accelerate societal and cultural change.

BIBLIOGRAPHY

Amdur, Neil. "Take That, Gents!" *The New York Times*, 1973. http://archive .nytimes.com/www.nytimes.com/packages/html/sports/year_in_sports/09 .20.html?scp=1&sq=ted%2520ray&st=cse

Fantasy Sports & Gaming Association. "Industry Demographics" *FSGA*. https://thefsga.org/industry-demographics/

Fay, Martha, John Neary, Sue Allison, Ann Bayer, and Tony Chiu "The 100 Most Important Americans of the 20th Century Life." *Life Magazine*, 1990. Edited by Mary Youatt Steinbauer.

Fenno, Nathan. "How the Media Helped Overturn the NFL's Unwritten Ban on Black Players." *Los Angeles Times*, 2017. https://www.latimes.com/ sports/sportsnow/la-sp-kenny-washington-rams-20170128-story.html

Lapchick, and E. Richard. "2020 Racial and Gender Report Card." The Institute for Diversity and Ethics in Sport, DeVos Sport Business Management Program, College of Business Administration, University of Central Florida, 2021. https://43530132-36e9-4f52-811a-182c7a91933b .filesusr.com/ugd/138a69_bee975e956ad45949456eae2afdc74a2.pdf

Lipsyte, Robert. "Clay Discusses His Future, Liston and Black Muslims." *The New York Times*, 1964. https://archive.nytimes.com/www.nytimes.com/ books/98/10/25/specials/ali-future.html

National Archives Foundation. *Executive Order 9981: Ending Segregation in the Armed Forces*. https://www.archivesfoundation.org/documents/ executive-order-9981-ending-segregation-armed-forces/

Nike, Inc. *Annual Report*. Beaverton: Nike, Inc, 1986. https://s1.q4cdn.com /806093406/files/doc_financials/1986/Annual_Report_86.pdf

TheFSGA.org. https://thefsga.org/industry-demographics/

Coming Up Next

The COVID-19 pandemic took a devastating toll on human life, resources, and industry around the globe, disrupting habits, behaviors, routines, and the sports world more dramatically than any event since World War II. The return to more normal lives with less fear and no social distancing, with people returning to their places of work and school, is helping the sports industry and the live sports media, but it will not be enough to bring about a full recovery. Conditions and expectations for the live sports media have been irreversibly transformed from what existed before the worldwide crisis. Perspectives have been altered, priorities and preferences have changed, past practices are being reinvented, and forces undermining the sports industry that were at work before the pandemic have gained new momentum.

THE NEW REALITY

Sports viewership had begun trending downward before the pandemic, but now what is perhaps more worrisome for the industry and the live sports media is that fewer people are identifying themselves as avid fans. In 2019, almost 30 percent of Americans polled identified themselves as "avid" sports fans. One year later, only 27 percent described themselves as "avid," which is the lowest percentage on record. Subtracting three percentage points from 30 percent represents a dramatic 10 percent reduction in avid fan avidity in just one year. Will the love of sports that these people once felt be rekindled? Can the ranks of avid fans be replaced by a new generation? The outlook is not promising when you consider how the most important factors that go into instilling young fans with a love for sport were disrupted during the pandemic. These include connecting with friends or parents who are avid fans, active participation in sports, having a favorite player, and reading about sports.

The broadcast networks and cable exclusive national and regional sports networks (RSNs) have been the home of live sports coverage for the past 40 years or more, but the size of their audience is slipping. The trend that has taken hold and continues to accelerate is that people under the age of 55 are spending less time each year watching traditional television, an equal or greater amount of time on their digital devices, and they are far

DOI: 10.4324/9781003165590-14

more likely to sign up for new streaming video services than retain their cable subscriptions. Many of the streaming video offerings like Netflix currently do not include sports content, so children growing up in homes that have abandoned pay TV have less opportunity to get interested in a sport or find themselves a favorite player.

For years, the number one complaint about cable and satellite multichannel video program distributors (MVPDs) has been the price of subscribing. Most people only watch a small number of channels regularly, so they understandably balk at paying $100 or more per month for a bundle of networks that they do not watch. The MVPDs are saddled with the payments they make to every one of those networks, starting with ESPN at over $9 per month per home per month and on down to much lower fees for networks that attract smaller audiences. Plus, the MVPDs as a whole pay more than $10 billion per year to the broadcast networks for "retransmission consent," which allows them to carry ABC, NBC, CBS, and Fox. The cable industry's failure to meaningfully respond over the years to the persistent clamor for "a la carte" pricing that would have allowed subscribers to select and pay for only their favorite channels is a major factor at the root of the current cord-cutting epidemic.

Competitors responding to the public discontent have arrived in two distinct and powerful manifestations. The first came in the form of services like YouTube TV, Hulu, and SlingTV that provide smaller, lower-priced lineups of channels via high-speed broadband. Their resemblance to traditional cable offerings has given them the designation as "virtual multichannel video program distributors," or vMVPDs. The second attractive option that is stealing viewers away from cable and satellite TV is the direct-to-consumer (DTC) apps offered by individual networks. They are the true embodiment of "a la carte" programming. For a monthly fee, you can select only the channels that appeal to you and put the expensive cable bundle in your rear-view mirror forever.

The migration of sports to streaming began in earnest in 2018 with the introduction of ESPN+, and now the stampede that will forever reshape the live sports media is on. ESPN president and Disney Media Networks co-chair Jimmy Pitaro described their focus as "cross-platform." "If our fans want to consume ESPN through traditional means like cable or satellite, we deliver. And if they want to consume digitally, through an app or website, or even on social platforms, we deliver there as well." In its first three years, the ESPN+ subscriber base had grown to more than 12 million, while at the same time, the number of cable television subscribers continued to decline by several million each year. And the new Walt Disney Company rights contract with the NFL for the 2023–33 seasons allows ESPN to stream all the live games that the network produces for television. The lesson is that when the audience moves, it is essential for the media and sports to move with them. ESPN+ was joined by more direct-to-consumer services during the COVID-19 pandemic. NBC's Peacock, Paramount Plus from ViacomCBS, and HBO Max all included sports content in their video menus.

The most common questions you probably heard during the pandemic were, "Have you had COVID? Did you get vaccinated? Which vaccine did you get?" And "what are you streaming?" The ability for individuals to personalize their viewing experiences by making on-demand and direct-to-consumer choices is a primary reason for the increased popularity of streaming. By the end of 2020, 80 percent of American homes had subscribed to at least one streaming service, and so many had abandoned cable television that its penetration rate in the United States had fallen to less than 70 percent.

The shift to streaming will reshape the live sports media business at an ever-increasing pace in the coming decade. The clearest indicator that the sports streaming stampede is unstoppable came in the spring of 2021 when it was announced that Amazon Prime would become the exclusive distributor of the NFL's Thursday night package of live professional football games beginning with the 2022 season. These games had previously been available on the NFL Network cable channel and the Fox television network. The annual $1 billion rights fee to stream the live games on Prime is clear evidence of the value that Amazon has placed on 1) connecting its name with the pre-eminent sports brand in America, and 2) reaching the average of 14 million viewers per minute who watched the Thursday NFL games in 2020. Amazon can surround its coverage of live football with customized sales offerings for consumers to buy sports premiums and other products and promote the myriad of entertainment offerings that are on Prime.

- A fixture on American cable television for more than 30 years has been live coverage of local professional sports teams on regional sports networks. But that too is changing as NBC Universal and the Sinclair Broadcast Group have begun the process of moving their combined 26 regional sports networks to streaming services. Access to live sports and news has been the most important component in the consumer retention of cable and broadcast television. Survey data show that more viewers now consider subscription video on demand offerings as more important to them for the non-live content they want, dramas, comedies, family, and children's programming.

This new reality will force the traditional broadcast and cable networks to put an even greater emphasis on live content, filling their schedules with expanded sports and news programming that they can simulcast on their direct-to-consumer digital apps.

We will likely see many cable systems radically alter their business models in the years to come, moving away from the MVPD role of providing multiple networks in programming bundles to become strictly broadband internet providers. In that scenario, the value of entertainment and sports channels would be as promotional incentives to attract new broadband customers. The higher profit margin for broadband than for the carriage of assorted networks is a compelling factor in this equation. And direct broadcast satellite (DBS) services such as DirecTV and Dish Network have been losing subscribers at such an alarming rate that they are pivoting to a streaming-centric model of programming delivery.

THE CLUTTERED SPORTS LANDSCAPE

The introduction of new sports streaming options and expanded live coverage by broadcast and sport-specific networks to attract and hold viewers will add opportunities in the marketplace for production personnel, performers, and advertisers. But it will also add clutter to the video landscape that is already filled with over 400,000 hours of sports programming per year. More sports spread thin across more networks and apps will splinter the sports audience into thinner and thinner slices. Lower ratings however cannot support the higher rights fees that the sports media conglomerates have committed to the most popular leagues for live events. "I think the premium properties will become more premium and continue to command escalating fees for the most part," said Burke Magnus, ESPN president of programming and original content. He expects that a lot of live sports events and series that previously were either in the middle or lower end or in slow-growth mode will "feel a little bit of compression." Magnus added that, "the more you're forced to escalate fees on that premium cut of properties, the more everything else gets squeezed in a declining environment."

If the bulk of resources is to be concentrated on a select group of premium sports, it is almost inevitable that the sports "in the middle" will need to wean themselves off revenue from rights fees and configure new barter or revenue-sharing agreements with networks to retain the live media exposure that is vital for them to stay connected with their fan bases. Finding ways to cut through the clutter and stay relevant becomes even more difficult. "Wherever you go there's more clutter, there's more competition, there is more of everything," said Sandy Montag, whose Montag Group develops programming and represents media talent. "You have to figure out a way to cut through the clutter, to make a difference, and if you're selling something make sure that whatever you're selling or putting on air is better than what's on the next channel."

STORYTELLING AND MESSAGING

One of the keys to improving live sports coverage is to tell better stories to increase viewer interest and add meaning to the outcome of games. A major consequence of the pandemic, however, has been a dramatic expansion of remote productions where very few production personnel and often no reporters or commentators are traveling to the sites of the live events that they televise. "I think because the financial impact is so significant, that part of the business is here to stay," said NBC's Mike Tirico. And to tell better stories and keep standards high he said, "we're just going to as individuals have to do a better job of fostering teamwork, camaraderie, and communication."

Calling games from home or a remote studio makes the job more difficult, and no matter how much effort producers and commentators put into remote productions, if they are not at the event, the quality of the telecast will always be diminished. "You cannot be excellent when you're not there," said Tirico.

Regardless of where the productions are done, live sports telecasts in the United States will integrate more gambling storylines in each successive year as more states legalize sports betting. Professional leagues, sport organizers, and the networks that televise their events are all banking on expanded gambling to strengthen audience ratings. The United States is playing "catch up" to several countries where sports gambling operations have been thriving for years. Sports enthusiasts in Australia, the UK, Mexico, China, New Zealand, South Africa, the Philippines, Peru, Nigeria, Ghana, Russia, and a handful of other nations have long been able to buy a stake in the outcome of a broad range of competitions.

Leagues are partnering with gambling sites and casinos, and networks are producing more gambling content because no matter the sport, betting increases viewer engagement. It can, however, put the integrity of games or matches and the credibility of their results in jeopardy. The history of sport is littered with stories of athletes conspiring with gamblers to influence the score by missing a few serves or dropping a ball, or of referees calling an extra foul or two. The leagues that have partnered with gambling operations have all pledged to redouble their security and intelligence gathering efforts, but if just one illegal scheme eludes their oversight, the stories of scandal that ensue will not benefit television ratings or game attendance figures.

How sports and the live sports media deal with the racial and social justice issues that became dominant stories in 2020 will also have an impact on viewership and audiences going forward. Fans who supported the athletes' stand for justice, equality, and an end to racism were encouraged by the new freedom of expression and remained loyal viewers. But others who sought refuge in sports from the distressing news of the day tuned out. Performers in every entertainment genre have personal political and social points of view, but in non-live, scripted programs they cannot turn to the camera and voice their opinions. In live, unscripted events like sports, however, participants do have the opportunity to share their views, even if it is only in the addition of a word or a name to their uniforms or helmets. They can also share their opinions in live and recorded interviews across all the media that cover sports.

To bring back fans who have tuned out, leagues and teams will have to find a way to balance their efforts for social change with the entertainment value of their events. As one league executive told me:

> It's important for players to deliver messages and make us aware of things that need to change. But when the first pitch is thrown in a baseball game, the puck is dropped, or the jump ball happens, a lot of people just want to watch the game and forget about this crazy world.

NEXT UP

When asked what lies ahead for the live sports media, my answer is always, "Anything you can imagine can happen. The means to make it happen may already exist, and if it doesn't, it soon will." As the rate of technological progress continues to accelerate, creative and industrious people will always put new tools to work in a myriad of ways, only a few of which the inventors may have foreseen. In the 1920s when Philo Farnsworth conceived of the world's first all-electronic television, he could never have predicted the power and reach of national and international networks that offer the widest variety of live and recorded programming to billions of people around the world. The developers of the internet and high-speed broadband surely did not imagine the extent to which their creations would spawn new digital networks and provide platforms for hundreds of original entertainment options, award-winning creative content, and live sports coverage. When technology opens a door, people with imagination will always step through.

Technological Innovations in Live Sports

Innovative technologies that provide new ways to observe and analyze the action of live sports, and thereby engage viewers, can improve the viewing experience by making what we see more interesting and meaningful.

Augmented Reality

Sports producers have only scratched the surface of what augmented reality (AR) can do to provide viewers with an immersive experience such as creating 3D graphics that enhance the live play and replays for better in-depth analysis. AR gives the television audience unique views that they could not see if they were at the stadium or arena, and by synthesizing millions of data points, it can improve a fan's understanding of what's at work within each game.

Virtual Reality

Virtual reality applications can attract younger viewers and add to everyone's enjoyment of live sports regardless of their age. Apps such as Intel's True VR® will see greater use as more stadiums and arenas are equipped with arrays of high-definition cameras that capture volumetric video of every moving object in three dimensions. The massive amount of video is processed at the speed of light and transmitted to broadcast, digital, and mobile platforms delivering remarkable views and 360-degree replays that cannot be captured by traditional cameras.

Advancements in Camera and TV Technology

Live television since its inception has seen a never-ending succession of new, improved cameras that take the industry to never-before-achieved levels of clarity and definition, only to be replaced in short order by the next generation of cameras that deliver even more realistic pictures to the latest technologically advanced video screens. The newest innovation is a family of cameras that have a very short depth of field that serves to focus a viewer's attention on a single player in the goal, on the field, or in the batter's box by defocusing the background. The result is a cinematic live picture quality that compares to the exaggerated reality style of many video games.

BT Sport in Europe got rave reviews in 2020 when it introduced 8K cameras in its Champions League games, and CBS achieved the same effect with the SONY Venice® full-frame digital cameras that it used in Super Bowl LV a few months later. Broader use of this camera technology in the future will add interest and appeal to live sports coverage and undoubtedly lead the way for the next generations of cameras that can do even more.

Innovations in television screen technology also have the potential to increase the viewership of live sports. When HD TVs were introduced, the people who bought them reported spending more time watching sports because the wider screen and better resolution brought them closer to the action. The high dynamic range (HDR) televisions that hit the market in 2016 could have the same effect. HDR boosts the contrast and brightness and provides a wider range of color detail, all of which enhances the sports viewing experience.

Inside the Game and Each Player

Every advance in information communication technology (ICT) and miniaturization makes it possible to place sensors inside pucks or balls, on uniforms, equipment, on goals, or on any surface in a sports venue. They detect speeds, angles, any number of forces, and real-time data about respiration rates and heartbeats that analysts can use to explain the subtle differences between success and failure. Each new reading has the potential to become a new storyline that will add interest and depth to live sports. Leagues and sport sanctioning bodies that want their events to appeal to new audiences can be expected in the future to approve more sensors in more places, and television technical crews will quickly find new ways to connect and display the data they generate.

Increased Sponsor Integration

The economic losses suffered by sports and their media partners during the pandemic downturn created a less-restrictive climate for the integration of sponsored messages into live game content. Virtual imagery that inserts sponsor logos onto the turf of a soccer field, the floor of a basketball court, or the back of a pitcher's mound have all helped generate additional advertising revenue. So has the more liberal use of sponsorship identification on American sports uniforms and equipment, which had already become a mainstay in international team sports. We should also expect to see far more hybrid advertising that incorporates a sponsored sales message into the context of the live sports events themselves, blurring the lines between event coverage and commercial content. While watching an NFL game on Prime Video, it is not beyond the realm of possibility that fans will be able to click on a jersey, a hat, or a ball and instantly buy that item from Amazon as they continue to watch the action.

One word of caution. As networks aggressively seek to recoup their pandemic-induced loss of revenue, sales departments and producers need to beware of overstepping the threshold of annoyance at which the over-saturation of sponsored elements becomes an irritant for viewers. Too much sales content within televised sport detracts from the original purpose of properly documenting the event for the fan.

More Competition

In the first two decades of the 21st century, eSports and mixed martial arts competitions captured significant segments of the sports-viewing audience. The older traditional sports were hurt by the pandemic, but the conditions that forced millions of young people across the globe to isolate at home and avoid groups at school or sports venues where they would have normally been at play were a boon for eSports. The *League of Legends* world championships in 2020 peaked at 45.95 million concurrent viewers, reaching a total of 300 million global online viewers. The number of concurrent viewers for this event was higher than the average per-minute viewership of any American sporting event for the entire year except for one, the Super Bowl.

UFC bouts on ESPN platforms and those available as pay-per-view events bucked the trend of sports ratings declines during the pandemic, positioning mixed martial arts for strong growth in the years to come. In prior generations, the predominantly younger UFC and eSports audiences would likely have been tuned in to the sports that now find themselves struggling in the increasingly splintered live media landscape.

Organizers of new leagues and event series are surveying the changing landscape and developing partnerships with networks and digital platforms that will guarantee them the mass exposure needed to build loyal followings. The new contenders, sure to be joined by many more in years to come include the Premier Lacrosse League and Major League Rugby on NBC channels, the Spring League of Football, and the return of the USFL on Fox, Athletes Unlimited volleyball, softball and women's lacrosse on the CBS Sports Network and Fox Sports, and SRX short track auto racing on CBS. The most successful new ventures will be those that not only partner with sports media distribution networks but also sign agreements with charter sponsors to underwrite their costs and promote the new events to their millions of customers.

Shorter Is Better

One of the challenges facing the live sports media is how to hold viewers once they tune in. People have a hard time sitting still for sports contests that may take three hours or more because the pace of their lives has quickened, and each year their time and attention are diverted by more and more media platforms. "We just don't have the patience to sit through three hours of anything, even an NFL football game," said Montag. That is part of the reason why the Montag Group joined with three-time NASCAR champion Tony Stewart and former crew chief Ray Evernham to launch SRX Racing in 2021. The "SRX" stands for Superstar Racing Experience, and it debuted on CBS with a national entitlement sponsor. It is auto racing designed for the fan with a short attention span. A field of racing legends including Stewart, Helio Castroneves, Michael Waltrip, Bill Elliott, and Tony Kanaan competes in two 15-minute timed heats and a 100-lap short track feature event in each show.

With highlights on ESPN's *SportsCenter* averaging less than a minute each and videos on social media that run 15 seconds or less getting millions of plays, our collective patience to get to the "big finish" has fallen to new lows. It is not uncommon for a teenager to say, "I don't watch regular season games. I just catch the highlights on my phone." In the long run, this viewing trend is going to force leagues and the sports media to find new ways to monetize the value of highlights. The NBA launched Top Shot® online in 2020 as a marketplace where fans can buy and trade great video "Moments" as non-fungible tokens (NFTs). The revenue generating potential of the NFT market surely signals what lies ahead for more leagues and their media partners. If the value of short clips approaches that of full live games, expect to see more proprietary agreements that will restrict the use of highlights to only the rights holding broadcast licensees.

More Games or Less?

The 2021 season was the NFL's first with a 17-game schedule, which pushes the Super Bowl one week deeper into February, increasing the overlap of this "fall" sport with those that play winter seasons like hockey and basketball. The rescheduling forced upon leagues during the pandemic gave them pause to consider whether there might be wisdom in adjusting the customary start and end dates of their seasons. The overriding objective however is to recoup as much revenue as possible in the coming years. That requires plenty of games, extended playoffs, and championship series, all delivered live to multiple digital platforms and packed with as much advertising and sponsorship as possible.

Watch for the next NFL agreement with the NFL Players Association to bump the season up to 18 games. On that schedule, the Super Bowl would land on Presidents' Day weekend every year, giving millions of fans the Monday after the game off from work and granting Super Bowl Sunday virtually the same three-day weekend status currently reserved for official holidays in the United States.

In the long run though, considering the shorter attention spans of viewers and their migration to alternative competitions, the addition of more games to already crowded sports schedules may not be the right move. No one game can have much compelling interest or importance if it is just one of 162 regular season Major League Baseball games or one of the 82 games played in both the NBA and NHL seasons. The fewer games per season, the more consequential is the result of each one and the greater the chance it will attract a larger audience. If the ratings levels for sports do not return to their pre-pandemic levels, legendary agent David Falk said, "It will force the leagues to look at how to make each game more important and how to make the fan experience better." But fewer games will not satisfy the networks' appetite for the live content they require to keep attracting the audiences and advertisers they need to offset their billion-dollar rights payments.

Sport Without Borders

Supersonic aircraft now in development are on schedule to be in the air by the year 2029, which will make global sports leagues and true "World" championships possible. NASA has partnered with Lockheed Martin to build the X-59 QueSST with a cruising speed of Mach 1.4 (which is 925 mph or 1,488 km/h) at an altitude of 55,000 feet (16,764 meters). Boom Technology of Denver is working with Rolls Royce to build the Overture passenger jet. At Mach 2.2 (1,450 mph or 2,335 km/h), it will cut the flying time from New York to London almost in half, down to three hours 30 minutes. The first 15 Overture jets were ordered by United Airlines in 2021. With all business class cabins accommodating approximately 80 passengers each, these new planes will be the perfect size to fly teams to games across oceans as easily as they currently fly from coast to coast.

Supersonic jetliners in the air could hasten the establishment of an American sports franchise in the UK. The NFL's International Series in London began in 2007, and every game was an instant sell-out. With the five to six-hour time difference, live primetime games played in London, or any other major European city would be early afternoon games in the Eastern and Central US time zones. Day games played in the eastern half of the United States featuring a European club could be seen in primetime back in their home country. Considering the international appeal of hockey and the number of European players in the National Hockey League, the same scenario is eminently feasible for the NHL.

The NBA's Basketball Africa League, which completed its first season in 2021, could be a foreshadowing of the future for all major sports. International tournaments involving the best teams from affiliated leagues around the world, all traveling at supersonic speeds, would create events of global interest, attracting huge audiences and huge media rights fees to match. The massive followings for basketball and baseball in Asia could foster more permanent connections with Major League Baseball and the NBA there. Supersonic flight times from San Francisco to Tokyo are projected to be six hours 30 minutes, and flights back to the West Coast would be even quicker. The time difference between Asia and the United States, however, would mean that live coverage of afternoon games in China or Japan would show up on American screens in the middle of the night. But primetime games in Asia could become regular morning attractions in the Americas.

NEW OPTIMISM

In the years ahead, sport can play a major role in the revival of the human spirit. Gathering with friends and family at arenas or in front of television screens is a perfect antidote for the isolation and social distancing that the world has endured. Throughout history, sport has had the power to connect people of all races, classes, orientations, generations, and national origins across borders, oceans, and every divide. The stories delivered to millions by the live sports media entertain and unite people in the celebration of inspiring achievements by remarkable individuals and teams that embody the values we all hold in high regard: courage, determination, the never-ending quest for excellence, and the dedication to working together and caring for others. The greater the level of optimism that these shared stories instill, the stronger will be the return of sports in the years beyond the pandemic. Sports, traditional, emerging, or yet to be invented, delivered to us on every available platform in dramatic new forms and formats have the potential to attract new fans, add value to our lives, and bring us all closer together.

BIBLIOGRAPHY

Boom Technology. "Overture, The Fastest and Most Sustainable Supersonic Airliner." 2021. https://boomsupersonic.com/overture

Falk, David. *Interviewed by the Author*, 2021.

Fantasy Sports & Gaming Association. "Industry Demographics." *FSGA*. https://thefsga.org/industry-demographics/

Hirsch, Lauren. "United Is Gearing Up for Supersonic Flights." *The New York Times*, June 4, 2021.

Kao, Victor. "Retransmission Fees Give Lift to TV Broadcast Revenue as Advertising Declines." *The Real Economy Blog*, 2019. https://realeconomy.rsmus.com/retransmission-fees-give-lift-to-tv-broadcast-revenue-as-advertising-declines/

Lockheed Martin. "Silencing the Sonic Boom." Lockheed Martin, 2021. https://www.lockheedmartin.com/en-us/products/quesst.html

LoL eSports. "Worlds 2020 By the Numbers." 2020. https://lolesports.com/article/worlds-2020-by-the-numbers/bltb346b99544910228

LRW. *Plan to Cut the Cord*. LRW study, Q1 2020.

Magnus, Burke. *Interviewed by the Author*, 2021.

Montag, Sandy. *Interviewed by the Author*, 2021.

Nielsen Sports Polls. *1995–2019 and 4Q19 P12+*. *Nielsen Media Research*, 2020.

Palmeri, Christopher. "NFL Signs $105 Billion TV Deal, with Amazon Taking Thursdays." *Bloomberg.com*, 2021. https://www.bloomberg.com/news/articles/2021-03-18/nfl-signs-historic-tv-deal-with-amazon-taking-thursday-rights

Pitaro, Jimmy. *Interview Notes Provided to the Author*, 2021.

Tirico, Mike. *Interviewed by the Author*, 2021.

Index